Educational Goals, Attitudes, And Behaviors

Educational Goals, Attitudes and Behaviors

A Comparative Study of High School Seniors

85819

Dale Tillery
Ted Kildegaard

Center for Research
and Development in
Higher Education

University of California, Berkeley

Ballinger Publishing Company ● Cambridge, Mass.
A Subsidiary of J.B. Lippincott Company

International Standard Book Number: 0—88410—151—1

Library of Congress Catalog Card Number: 73-9573

Printed in the United States of America

Library of Congress Cataloging in Publication Data

Tillery, Dale.
    Educational goals, attitudes, and behaviors.

    Bibliography: p.
    1. High school seniors. 2. Student aspirations. 3. College attendance.
    4. Vocational interests. I. Kildegaard, Ted, joint author. II. Title.
LB2350.T55   373.1'8   73—9573
ISBN 0—88410—151—1

Table of Contents

List of Charts

List of Tables

Acknowledgments

This is one of a series of publications from the SCOPE Project which was begun in 1965 under joint sponsorship of the College Entrance Examination Board and the Center for Research and Development in Higher Education. Other manuscripts in preparation, like this and earlier reports, will be part of a growing body of research by the SCOPE staff and other researchers across the country using SCOPE data. To the students, school and college personnel, and advisory committees who made this important source of information possible, we express our deep appreciation.

Special thanks go to Charles Gehrke and his staff, especially Diana Fackenthal and George Myland, for organizing the data base generally, and processing the complex analyses of this study specifically. The authors gratefully acknowledge the special contributions made to this publication by Carol Omelich, Alice Sund, and Gary Nickelson. Final preparation of the manuscript was done with great skill under pressure by Claire Alameda and Sarah Walker. All of these were members of the SCOPE staff.

Essential contributions were made to the conceptualization and design of this study by Barbara Sherman and Denis Donovan, who were associate directors of SCOPE. In thanking them, we also recognize the useful consultation of Professors Leonard Marascuilo and Charles Woodson, and of Fred Dagenais, who is himself doing research using SCOPE data.

Sam Kendrick and his staff in the New York office of the College Entrance Examination Board have provided essential criticism and suggestions. The thoughtful support of the SCOPE Project by officers of the College Entrance Examination Board and its regional offices has been important from the inception of SCOPE in 1966. Our appreciation is given to each of them.

Chapter One

The Educational Goal Projections of High School Seniors

INTRODUCTION

What students say about the education they seek after high school becomes the locus and perhaps the maelstrom of school and home relationships. A declaration of educational aspiration brings both peer and adult intervention to the decision-making processes. In reasonably predictable ways such declarations set into motion complex guidance activities and reactions from family, school people, and friends. There are mounting pressures during the adolescent years to take a stand on what to do after high school. What students say about these issues is reinforced, rejected, ridiculed, or compromised by the significant others in their lives.

For some students there is a high congruence between what they say they want to do and what others want for them. In fact, there is a very high congruence between what students say about their own educational goals and what they perceive as their parents' aspirations for them (Tillery, 1973). But for others, lack of agreement among what their teachers, parents, and friends think right for them may exceed their own internal ambivalence. More importantly, many students, particularly those in doubt about what to do and how to go about making decisions, do not know what key people in their lives expect of them in regard to educational and career choices (SCOPE Working Papers, 1971).

Subtle as well as tangible rewards may flow from home, school, and friends when one boy, for example, says he expects to graduate from an elite university. But for another boy a similar declaration may bring a flood of test scores to show that he ought to lower his sights and warnings from his father that he will have to make it on his own financially. However, this same boy's stock may well go up in the eyes of his girl friend. Furthermore, similar aspirations may have quite different implications and outcomes for a girl than for a boy with similar backgrounds and attributes, or for equally similar students living in different parts of the country.

A student's declaration of his hopes for the future is part of his persona—changeable, yes, but remarkably persistent over time for most students. Nevertheless, declarations of educational aspirations can be considered only half-truths. To be sure, most students who say they do not plan to attend college do not; and most who say they do actually enter college after graduation. Moreover, there are strong positive relationships between levels of aspiration (for example, how long a student expects to stay in school) and the incidence of college going, as well as the type of college attended (Tillery, 1973). But the relationships are by no means perfect. This is true, in part, because high school students have only partial knowledge of their own motives and aptitudes, have limited consumer information about the world of higher education, and possess faulty maps to guide them from school to college or other suitable environments.

The gaps between the educational aspirations of youth and their outcomes are particularly disturbing in view of declared national educational policies which seek to insure that inequities of past generations are not passed on to future ones. Nevertheless, rising expectations spotlight the stubborn barriers to postsecondary education. In the last quarter of the twentieth century such barriers are subtle and insidious, and they are associated with personal characteristics such as sex, race, and social class (Cross, 1971). They are also very likely associated with interpersonal conflicts at home, in school, and with friends.

The near-universal aspirations for college among high school seniors, when weighed against the bare majority of youth now entering college, suggest a future of mounting demands for educational opportunities but inadequate resources to satisfy them. How are legislators and educational planners to interpret reports which consistently show that 80 percent or more of high school seniors say they plan to continue their education after high school? What new programs and guidance services are school people to develop when faced with evidence that nearly as high ratios of students *entering* high school declare postsecondary educational aspirations as do their seniors? Do we discredit such goal declarations as being unrealistic because we have years of evidence to show how many college aspirants fall by the wayside? Predictions of who will and who will not achieve fulfillment of their aspirations have been rather good, but it is also likely that they have been self-fulfilling.

There is no virtue in assuming that all young people should attend college in order to achieve success and happiness, nor is it valid to assume that all would do so if barriers to equal educational opportunity were removed. There is both virtue and validity, however, in providing educational experiences which fit the remarkable diversity of human talents, interest, and aspirations in this nation, and in seeing that all students have opportunities to explore educational, career, and life-style alternatives while still in high school.

It is in the service of such goals that the SCOPE Project was undertaken in 1965. The present report, as one project of this longitudinal study of high school students in four diverse states, is concerned with the differential educational aspirations of young men and women shortly before leaving high school. As manifestations of motives to behave in certain ways, such declarations can be best understood in relationship to other personal characteristics and behaviors.

This, then is a cross-sectional study (although some of the variables are retrospective) of the relationships of the personal attributes and behaviors of high school seniors to their educational aspirations. In order to make the myriad of variables manageable, a number of conceptual areas of interests were identified. Obviously it would be expected that academic achievement and attitudes toward education would be related to students' educational goal projections, and there is interest in determining the nature of such relationships. Knowing such things as differential personality characteristics or differences in the kinds of problems experienced by students aspiring to different levels of postsecondary education would be useful information for thinking about ways of meeting students' needs. Certainly it would be useful in educational planning, particularly at the high school level, but also at the college level, to know about ways in which students with differing educational goal projections perceive potential obstacles to the completion of a college education. How might behaviors directed toward the implementation of goals, such as information gathering about post-high school alternatives or certain decisions concerning post-high school activities, be related to students' educational aspirations? These kinds of concerns represent the substantive structuring of a wide range of personal characteristics and behaviors for study in this investigation. In all, eight content areas were delineated and studied with respect to the educational aspirations of high school seniors. Many of the variables involved have known relationships to educational outcomes in the years following high school. A few, such as high school grade point average, have known relationships to the educational aspirations of secondary students. Literature reviews and certain relevant theoretical contexts for these substantive areas will be presented in subsequent chapters.

Before briefly presenting the rationale for using analytical controls for state of residence, sex, level of father's occupation (SES), and race, it seems important to examine conceptually the SCOPE measure of educational goal projection within the context of related research.

EDUCATIONAL ASPIRATIONS AND EXPECTATIONS

Studies of projections which students make about their future education or careers have been influenced by two concepts; namely, aspirations and expectations. However, there has been little agreement as to the definition of these concepts or their measurement, and it has been observed that some studies have failed to distinguish between the two (Brookover, Erickson, and Joiner, 1967; Weiss, 1961). Since the primary criterion or independent variable of this study is derived from students' statements of intent or desire with respect to continued schooling, it is necessary to examine this conceptual issue in some detail.

Rehberg (1967) sets forth a clear distinction between an aspiration as an ideal, with no constraints on financial, intellectual, or other resources, and an expectation as the realistic level of occupational or educational orientation, which accommodates restraints on resources. Similar definitions are advanced by Brookover et al. (1967). In their work, a plan is seen as a person's perception of what he will be doing or will have accomplished at some future date ("I expect to graduate from high school" or "I expect to go on to college"). Aspirations are defined as wishes or desires ("I would like to graduate from high school" or "I would like to go to college"). Other studies incorporating a similar distinction between aspirations and expectations include Bailey (1966); Kuvlesky (1970); Lever and Kuvlesky, 1970; and Shill (1968).

In an experiment, Weiss (1961) examined dimensions underlying different types of goal projections. He used ten items which were varyingly reflective of hope or desire, intention, expectation, or a feeling of success. These goal projections were elicited with respect to a specific task with which the subjects had been given previous experience. A factor analysis yielded two factors. The first factor, which had high loadings on goal projections involving an estimate of future performance (expectation) or an estimate of the level of achievement necessary to produce a feeling of success, was interpreted to be a judgmental or expectational dimension. The second factor had high loadings on items dealing with desires and aims. It was interpreted as a motivational or aspirational dimension. These two factors were correlated, sharing about 35 percent common variance. Weiss also found that goal discrepancies (absolute difference between goal projection and actual performance on the task) were larger for goal projection items which elicited desires or hopes than for items calling for an estimate of performance or an expectation. Other studies show that aspirations in general are higher than expectations (e.g., Shill, 1968).

It seems clear that aspirations and expectations do indeed represent two separate though related dimensions. One dimension, expectations, involves reality considerations and judgments or estimates of future performance. The other dimension is more affective, and elicites desires or wishes concerning future performance. In the following discussion, some empirically established differential relationships between aspirations and expectations, on one hand, and grade point average (gpa), socioeconomic status (SES), and educational outcome, on the other hand, will be explored. This discussion will further establish the differences between aspirations and expectations and will aid in determining how the SCOPE educational goal projection variable should be interpreted.

Brookover et al. (1967), in a longitudinal study following male students from the eighth through the eleventh grades, studied the relationships of educational aspirations and educational plans to gpa and SES. It was found that educational aspirations and educational plans are both related to SES and to gpa. At each of the four grade levels, the relationship of gpa and of SES to educational plans was greater than their relationship to aspirations. The Kendall-Tau rank order correlations of educational plans with gpa over the four years were: .38, .32, .31, and .30. The corresponding correlations of aspirations with gpa were: .35, .22, .25, and .23. Thus, while the relationships of educational aspirations and educational plans to gpa are about the same in the eighth grade, in later years educational plans maintain a stronger relationship to school achievement. When statistical control for the effect of educational aspirations (partial correlation) was applied, the correlations of educational plans with gpa were reduced to .20, .26, .19, and .23 for each of the four years of the study. However, when the effect of educational plans was statistically held constant, the remaining relationships between educational aspirations and gpa were essentially zero. Thus the aspiration-gpa relationship contains a large contribution from the educational plans variable. In other words, within levels of the educational plans variable, there is essentially no relationship between educational aspirations and gpa. However, within levels of the educational aspiration variable, there is still a discernible relationship between educational plans and gpa. This is consistent with the interpretation of educational plans as the more realistic indicator.

Very similar relationships were obtained when relating educational aspirations and educational plans to SES. Educational plans were more highly related to SES than educational aspirations and removing the variation of educational plans reduced the aspiration-SES relationship to essentially zero. Statistically controlling for aspirations reduced the educational plans-SES correlations of .29, .26, .30, and .23 to .17, .12, .29, and .18. The educational desires of students and their expectations are clearly not the same thing, and students' educational plans are more likely to be associated with both their academic achievement and SES (Brookover et al., 1967).

Rehberg (1967) studied the relationships of educational aspirations, educational expectations, occupational aspirations, and occupational aspirations, and occupational expectations to SES. Data indicated that the proportion of adolescents expressing aspirations to high occupational or educational goals and the proportion expressing expectations for high occupational or educational goals both vary positively with social status. The relationships between aspirations and SES and between expectations and SES are quite similar, but stronger in the case of expectations. In general, subjects' expectations were lower than their aspirations, especially for lower SES subjects. Similar results have been obtained by other researchers (Himmelweit, Halsey, and Oppenheim, 1952; Holloway and Berreman, 1959; Stephenson, 1957). It has been consistently found that expectations are more highly related to SES than aspirations and that aspirations are generally higher than expectations. In some studies, there has been a negligible relationship between aspirations and SES. On the whole, there is a tendency for subjects to choose as their fantasy job a job of higher social prestige than the one they expect to take up (Himmelweit et al., 1952). The discrepancy between aspirations and expectations is greater for lower class persons. This again supports the interpretation of expectations as involving more reality considerations.

Bailey (1966) obtained data from high school seniors and followed them to determine whether or not they were in college the following year. About one-third of the total sample (almost 1,800 students) went to college after high school. Ninety-nine percent of those in college had expressed college aspirations as high school seniors and 96 percent had expected to go to college. However, among the noncollege subjects, 75 percent had college aspirations as high school seniors, but only 50 percent had college expectations. In addition, among a selected set of variables, educational expectation was the best single predictor of college going when academic ability was controlled. Educational expectation was also an important variable in predicting college persistence based on a second year follow-up. It can be concluded that educational expectation is more predictive of educational outcome than is educational aspiration.

In studies making a distinction between aspirations and expectations, the distinction between reality considerations as opposed to desires is usually incorporated in the measurement. Educational aspirations have been measured with items such as:

> "If you were free to go as far as you wanted to go in school, how far would you like to go?" (Brookover et al., 1967).
> "If you were free to go as far as you wanted in school, how far would you like to go?" (Bailey, 1966).
> "SUPPOSING you had the necessary abilities, grades, money, etc., how far would you *really* LIKE TO go in school?" (Rehberg, 1967) [author's emphasis].

Some examples of the measurement of educational expectations are:

> "Sometimes what we would like to do isn't the same as what we would expect to do. How far in school do you expect you will really go?" (Brookover et al., 1967).
> "Sometimes what we would like to do isn't the same as what we expect to do. How far do you expect you really will go?" (Bailey, 1966).
> "CONSIDERING your abilities, grades, financial resources, etc., how far do you *actually* EXPECT TO go in school?" (Rehberg, 1967) [author's emphasis].

The 1969 SCOPE high school senior questionnaire included two items eliciting projections of educational goals. One of these is most closely identified as an expectation: "Do you think you actually will go to college after high school?" While this item does not explicitly elicit reality considerations as in the expectational items above, it is worded strongly enough to elicit expectations rather than aspirations. On the other hand, the item which was used as a criterion variable in the present study reads: "How long do you expect to stay in school?" In the light of the literature which has been reviewed, this item now seems somewhat ambiguous. It is worded as an expectation but does not expressly elicit either desires per se (aspiration) or the consideration of realistic possibilities (expectation).

Unfortunately not all of the appropriate comparisons can be made in an effort to determine whether or not these two items act like aspirations and expectations in the way they are related to other variables. However, some indications are available. Among the male SCOPE seniors, 83 percent, in response to the item "How long do you expect to stay in school?" (item A), indicated some amount of schooling after high school. In contrast, only 66 percent responded yes to the item "Do you think you will actually go to college after high school?" (item B). Further, among those males of high ability (upper third of the ability distribution) who in response to item A had indicated four or more years of education beyond high school and who did in fact go to college the next year, 92 percent had reported yes to item B. But of those of high ability who indicated four or more years in response to item A but were not in college the next year, 86 percent had responded yes to item B. Of male seniors of low measured ability who responded four or more years to item A and were in college the following year, 81 percent had responded yes to item B; and of the low ability males responding four or more years beyond high school to item A but were not in college the year after high school, only 64 percent had said yes to item B. If item A is seen as an aspiration measure and item B is seen as an expectation measure, then these data are consistent with the findings that aspirations generally are higher than expectations and that expectations are more highly related to outcomes than aspirations.

In the present study, item A, which constituted the primary criterion variable in the analyses, was defined as a measure of aspirations. On a common-sense basis, it is assumed that the SCOPE measure of educational aspiration represents some combination of aspirations and expectations. The psychological set of seniors in response to the question "How long do you expect to stay in school?" may have ranged from high idealism to rigorous reality testing.

RATIONALE FOR SEPARATE ANALYSES BY STATE

In order to determine whether the educational aspirations of SCOPE seniors from each of the project states would be related in similar ways to sets of variables believed to be associated with educational decision making, separate multivariate analyses of variance were run for male and female subsamples from each of the four states. Although it was anticipated that the correlates of postsecondary educational aspirations would be essentially similar across states, some state differences were expected.

Certain state differences in demographic characteristics as well as cultural and educational traditions were compelling factors in the original multistate design of the SCOPE Project and for the decision to run separate analyses for the present study. To be sure, no cause and effect relationships have been established between these state differences and certain diversity in the annual SCOPE profiles of student characteristics from grade nine in 1966 through grade twelve in 1969. Similarly, the state differences which will be noted in this study only suggest promising leads for further study since the differentiating factors which seem to accrue from state of residence will not have been isolated nor controlled.

Demographic Differences

In selecting the four project states in 1965, attention was given to comparative demographic data from the 1960 U.S. Census of Population. Among these were indexes of residential stability which showed California to be the least stable state:

	Cal.	*Ill.*	*Mass.*	*N.C.*
Percentage of population moving since last census	24.5	12.8	12.2	15.0
Percentage of population residing in state of birth	43.7	71.6	80.4	84.2

Indexes of rural distribution of population show general state differences, with North Carolina being most atypical. Other SCOPE data show that the size of school and the scope of educational program are associated with urban-rural location:

	Cal.	*Ill.*	*Mass.*	*N.C.*
Percentage of population in rural nonfarm areas	11.5	13.7	15.7	42.7
Percentage of population in rural farm areas	2.1	5.6	0.7	17.7

Economic differences which would likely affect resources for and family attitudes toward postsecondary education are most marked for North Carolina, although differences among the other states are noteworthy:

	Cal.	*Ill.*	*Mass.*	*N.C.*
Percentage of population in white collar jobs	47.3	42.3	44.1	30.5
Median family income	$6726.	$6566.	$6272.	$3956.

Among the factors involved in the original selection of states were those which indicated differing student representation and modes of participation in education. Massachusetts and California, as our studies have subsequently shown, have higher ratios of their populations participating in postsecondary education than do North Carolina and Illinois. Furthermore, nearly one-quarter of the Illinois and Massachusetts elementary students attend private schools while the other two states have much stronger commitments to public education.

	Cal.	*Ill.*	*Mass.*	*N.C.*
Percentage of population ages 14-17 in school	89.7	87.5	87.5	82.8
Median school age 25 and over population	12.1	10.5	11.6	8.9
Percentage of elementary children in private schools	10.7	24.8	22.0	1.4

Finally, the racial make-up of the states vary, with North Carolina having the largest nonwhite population:

	Cal.	*Ill.*	*Mass.*	*N.C.*
Percentage of population which is nonwhite	8.0	10.6	2.4	25.3

State Plans for Higher Education

In spite of differing traditions of public and private education and of commitments to free-access higher education, all four project states have developed master plans for the extension of educational opportunities beyond high school. Certain similarities and differences are noted in the following brief description of the state plans and practices.

California. The 1960 Master Plan for Higher Education in California provided for improved coordination among the three systems of public higher education and the private institutions and for a more rational program of facilities development. Under this plan, California continues to have the highest rate of college attendance in the nation. It is estimated that three out of four high school graduates attend college. Willingham points out that 86 of the states' 187 colleges in 1968 were free-access institutions, which he defines roughly as a college which "admits at least one-third of its freshmen from the bottom half of their high school class and which charges no more than $400 in annual tuition and fees" (Willingham, 1970, p. 15). In fact, these colleges are open door community colleges which do not charge tuition. It is Willingham's conclusion that 60 percent of California's population is within commuting distance of such free-access colleges. This estimate is considerably lower than the state's own estimates. Very few students leave the state for initial college attendance. The SCOPE 1966 followup of high school graduates showed 5 percent out-of-state attenders, which is consistent with other reports (Tillery 1973).

Illinois. This state has long been recognized for its diversity of educational opportunities beyond high school. However, since establishing a Board of Higher Education in 1961 and the adoption of master plans for higher education in 1964 and 1966, it has become one of the bellweather states in regards to educational opportunity. Although a high percentage of Illinois high school graduates continue to go out of state for first admissions (23 percent in 1966), 56 percent of the state's population lives within commuting distance of a free-access college. Willingham (1970) determined that in 1968, 71 of the state's 125 colleges could be so defined. Almost half of all first-time students enroll in the fast-going system of junior colleges. Although these colleges meet the Willingham criterion of free access, they do charge tuition to cover about one-third the cost of instruction. It should also be noted that Illinois has one of the most generous financial aid programs for college students among the states.

Massachusetts. This state was chosen because it was considered to be a prototype Northeastern state, urbanized, high per capita income, and a stronghold of private higher education. The state continues to have a heavy out-migration of first-year college students, although a 1963 study shows that this is more than offset in numbers by in-migration of college students—out-migration 23 percent, in-migration 35 percent (Rice and Mason, 1965). It is expected that the expansion of the University of Massachusetts and the recent development of junior colleges will have some effect on out-migration of students.

In addition to 75 private colleges, Willingham reports 15 senior and 15 junior public colleges. It is his estimate that 13 of the state's 105 colleges are free-access institutions, and that 52 percent of the Massachusetts population live within commuting distance of such colleges. Massachusetts differs most markedly with California "when it comes to the financial and educational commitment required to attract large numbers of students to local comprehensive education beyond high school" (Willingham, 1970, p. 103).

North Carolina. This "border state," like the other three SCOPE states, is recognized as a regional leader in providing opportunities for post-secondary education. It shares a number of characteristics of other Southern states, however, which are quite different from the other project states. The relatively low per capita income, the high proportion of blacks in the population, the structure of the labor force, and the holding power of the secondary schools are among the most noteworthy differences.

Since 1955 all institutions of higher education are coordinated by the Board of Higher Education. Under such leadership, there has been considerable expansion of postsecondary educational opportunity, particularly at the two-year college level. Twenty-four of the 26 public two-year colleges have been opened in the past decade. Willingham notes that 29 of the 92 colleges in North Carolina (47 private and 45 public) are free-access colleges. "Two-thirds of the population in North Carolina live within commuting distance of a free-access college. This is one of the largest proportions among all states in the country. Furthermore, these colleges are well placed in relationship to population centers" (Willingham, 1970, p. 140). This high availability undoubtedly accounts for the retention by the state of 90 percent of its first-time college students. However almost one-third of its first-time undergraduates are from other states (Tillery, 1973).

In summary it should be noted that state differences in relationship of educational aspirations and other student characteristics are not a primary focus of the present study. Pronounced differences in the data resulting from separate state analyses are pointed out and modest efforts have been made to interpret these differences.

RATIONALE FOR SEPARATE ANALYSIS BY SEX

The educational histories of women are so markedly different from those of men (as are the expectations for schools and colleges to accommodate such difference) that all SCOPE studies, like most contemporary research, have looked at findings separately or comparatively for the two sexes. Sex differences are particularly strong in the variables used for this study. SCOPE's annual profiles of selected student characteristics from grade nine through grade twelve show the nature and strength of these differences (Tillery et al., 1966a, 1966b, 1967). Current manuscripts in preparation will give particular attention to the differential educational histories of boys and girls.

Among the most relevant findings of these studies, which confirm findings in the great body of educational research, are the following:

1. Girls as a group mature earlier than do boys, and such group differences are reflected in measures of learning skills, attitudes toward and achievement in school.
2. Whereas the verbal test scores for girls as a group remain superior to those of boys, their numerical scores drop relative to boys during the course of the school years.
3. The interest patterns (occupational, career styles, use of free time) of the two sexes differ greatly during the school and college years.
4. Whereas the educational aspirations of girls (even when controlled for ability and social class) decrease from grade nine to grade twelve, those for boys remain relatively constant.
5. The postsecondary outcomes of the two sexes are very different. Although the incidence of first-time college attendance is now essentially similar nationally, the patterns of institutional choice, majors selected, and degree plans are not. Fewer girls enter elite universities than do boys, showing preference instead for liberal arts and state teacher colleges. More boys than girls attend public two-year colleges although there are state differences in these ratios of attendance. And finally, girls remain underrepresented in science and high professional majors, and overrepresented in elementary teaching and semiprofessional majors.
6. Boys and girls differ in the style and content of decision making.

Among the recent publications which give special attention to the differential educational experiences of the two sexes are *Equality of Educational Opportunity* (Coleman et al., 1966), *The New Student in Higher Education* (Cross, 1971), and *Distribution and Differentiation of Youth* (Tillery, 1973). In brief, there were compelling arguments for analysing all data separately by sex in order to be able to look at differential relationships of educational aspirations to the variables in question for the two sexes. Some attention was given to major sex differences on selected variables themselves.

RATIONALE FOR CONTROLLING LEVELS OF SES

Since 1965 the SCOPE staff has considered concepts and methods of assessing levels of social stratification of the families of students being studied. Traditional

Table 1-1. Percentage of 1966 Scope Seniors Attending College from Homes of Differing Occupational Levels

Father's Occupation	Percentage of SCOPE Seniors in College
Very High Level:	
Professional (High)	.82
Elected Officials	.72
Managers–Executives	.71
Professional (Low)	.70
High Level:	
Artists and Entertainers	.63
Salesmen	.63
Business Owners	.61
Technicians	.60
Office Workers	.60
Moderate Level:	
Skilled Craftsmen	.46
Farm Owner	.46
Service Worker	.45
Low Level:	
Machine Operator	.35
Workman	.33

Source: Tillery, D. *Distribution and Differentiation of Youth*, to be published by Ballinger Publishing Company, Cambridge.

measures based on family income seemed unsatisfactory, not only because of the questionable validity of student reporting of family income, but because of changing reward structures for occupations in post-World War II America. Equally questionable were assumptions about life-styles associated with various occupational groups in earlier research. For SCOPE purposes generally and for the present study specifically it seemed appropriate to estimate the socioeconomic strata (SES) of SCOPE students on the basis of reported occupations of fathers or guardians as classified in Table 1-1. The criterion of classification is the "productivity" of first-time college students from each of the occupational groups.

These data, taken from a recent SCOPE publication, show that the comparative percentages of college-goers from the composite four-state sample of 1966, high school seniors by type of father's occupation varies from .82 for high professional families to .33 for families of workmen (Tillery, 1973, p. 89).

The relationship between education and occupation has long been a central issue in social research. The stereotype about this relationship "has been that professional men have been to college, other white collar people have been to high school, while manual workers, by and large, have not gone beyond grade school" (Trow, 1967, p. 25). As late as 1950, this stereotype was largely confirmed by United States census data. Although there has continued to be an upswing in participation in higher education by children of middle and lower occupational groups, the upward curve in college enrollments is not as egalitarian as it might appear (Tillery, 1973; Cross, 1971).

These and other studies confirm 1959 findings which led to the conclusion that college attendance was more closely related to father's occupation than to student's ability level (Medsker and Trent, 1965).

Equal opportunity in initial access is only part of the problem of education and social class. Students from different family backgrounds not only enter higher education in different ratio, they also distribute themselves differently across types of colleges and universities, and have different persistence rates (Tillery, 1973; Cross, 1971; Trent and Medsker, 1968). Perhaps one of the most compelling conclusions from recent research is in *Equality of Educational Opportunity*; namely, that social class background of pupils bears a greater relationship to learning than do other factors associated with schools such as student-teacher ratios and learning resources (Coleman et al., 1966).

As will be pointed out in Chapter 2, SES is used as an independent or control variable in the present study as a means of determining how it influences, if at all, the *relationships* between educational aspiration of seniors and sets of dependent variables which are considered to be attributes and behaviors associated with decisions to attend college.

RATIONALE FOR CONTROLLING FOR RACE

The civil rights movement has and is having profound implications for higher education. The demands for equality of opportunity are "clearly to redress injustice and to distribute privilege, power, and dignity in a more socially equitable manner" (Willingham, 1970, p. 3). Since higher education is widely regarded as the most important route to social opportunity there are new concerns not only for equality of access to college, but for new programs, faculty, and services; and for more appropriate preparation and guidance of all students during the school years.

The geographic availability of low cost, or what Willingham calls "free-access" colleges to students from minority groups would appear to be a crucial factor in college-going patterns for such youths. More importantly for this study, proximity of free-access colleges should have implications for school guidance and the shaping of educational aspirations during the school years. Nationwide black and Spanish-speaking populations have somewhat higher percentages within commuting distances of such colleges than do whites. In any case, less than half of any of the population groups live in such proximity and there are important regional and urban-rural differences (Willingham, 1970).

Other factors, then, would appear to be involved in making race one of the major barriers to higher education. Among 1969 SCOPE seniors, when classified by ethnic group, 61 percent of the Caucasians and only 40 percent of non-Caucasians entered some form of postsecondary education in the fall following their graduation from high school. In *Beyond the Open Door*, Cross looked at these data and concluded that:

> Even at the *same* job levels, young people belonging to ethnic minority groups are less likely to continue formal education. Among minority youth whose fathers have managed to make it into the professions against great odds, the rate of college attendance is not as high as for white students; 75 percent of the children of white professionals continued their education, compared with 58 percent for the children of black professionals [Cross, 1971, p. 115].

In spite of barriers or handicaps there is ample evidence that most minority students and their parents have a great desire for education. As reported in the U.S. Bureau of Census data, 67 percent of the non-Caucasians were considering college ("maybe" or "definitely") in 1965 as compared with 60 percent of the Caucasians (Froomkin, 1969). Although at the high levels of ability there seems to be little differences in the aspirations of the two ethnic groups, non-Caucasians of such ability are less likely actually to enroll in college than are their Caucasian peers (Knoell, 1970).

By the time many minority youth reach the age of the students which make up the subjects of this study, the multiple disadvantages of their past opportunities for learning are apparent. The history of these cumulative disadvantages have nowhere been stated more clearly than in *Equality of Educational Opportunity*.

> For most minority groups, then, and most particularly the Negro, schools provide no opportunity at all for them to overcome this initial deficiency; in fact, they fall further behind the white majority in the development of several skills which are critical to making a living and participating fully in modern society. Whatever may be the combination of nonschool factors—poverty, community attitudes, low educational level of parents—which put minority children at a disadvantage in verbal and nonverbal skills when they enter the first grade, the fact is the schools have not overcome it [Coleman et al., 1966, p. 20].

It seems obvious that those attributes and behaviors which are being used in the present study will have been influenced by the dramatically different school and home environments and experiences documented in the Coleman Report. It is possible, however, that Caucasian or non-Caucasian designation will not consistently affect the relationship between level of education and sets of variables which describe certain attributes and behaviors of SCOPE seniors. In effect, controlling for race or ethnic origin as dichotomously defined may show that these relationships are similar for both groups.

Our variable, race, is not properly so defined since it brings together under the classification of non-Caucasian several racial and other ethnic groups. Ideally, this type of research calls for more precise and detailed classification of ethnic background. However, the complex design of the analysis, as described in Chapter 2, made such classification unmanageable if not technically infeasible. In the SCOPE data files from which subsamples were drawn for this investigation, 29,003 seniors had identified themselves in ways listed in Table 1-2.

There is no assumption that the distribution in Table 1-2 is representative of a national sample of high school seniors. There were, of course, state differences in these data which have been accounted for in the decision to replicate each analysis in this study by state of origin as discussed in Chapter 2. The disadvantage in merging the several ethnic identities under the classification non-Caucasian is self-apparent. Table 1-3 will clearly show differences in the several groups on the major independent variable of this study—educational aspiration. Nevertheless, the ratios involved and the opportunity to include these students who consider themselves ethnically mixed (in addition to the problem of complexity of design) dictated the decision to dichotomize the groups.

A very disciplined study of changes in attitudes and values of adolescents from different cultural groups during the high school years is being done by Fred Dagenais using SCOPE data. He will contrast ten ethnic groups, controlling for sex and SES, on measures of and values for his subjects as of the ninth grade and again as of grade twelve (1969).

Table 1-2. Ethnic Self-Descriptions of 1969 Scope High School Seniors (Four-State Composite)

Ethnic Self-Description	Male	Female	Total
Afro-American	954	776	1730
American Indian	555	633	1188
Caucasian	9,170	10,528	10,698
Chinese	87	71	158
Japanese	85	42	127
Other Oriental	167	139	306
Mexican American	193	160	353
Negro	526	783	1,309
Spanish American	118	138	256
Mixed	961	1,197	2,158
No Response	956	764	1,720
TOTAL	13,772	15,231	29,003

Table 1-3. Educational Aspirations of 1969 Scope High School Seniors by Ethnic Self-Descriptions (Four State Composite by Sex)

Ethnic Self-Description	Educational Aspiration											
	H.S. Grad. Only %		Limited College %		4-Year Grad. %		Post-Grad. %		No Response %		Total %	
	M	F	M	F	M	F	M	F	M	F	M	F
Afro-American	28.3	20.7	31.1	40.1	26.3	28.2	13.3	10.6	1.0	.4	100	100
American Indian	38.0	40.0	33.8	41.2	20.7	13.9	7.0	4.4	.5	.5	100	100
Caucasian	13.4	19.1	22.4	28.7	39.2	41.4	24.5	10.5	.5	.3	100	100
Chinese	13.8	22.5	19.5	22.5	29.9	36.6	34.5	15.5	2.3	2.9	100	100
Japanese	16.5	21.4	14.1	28.6	35.3	35.7	28.2	14.3	5.9	.0	100	100
Other Oriental	32.3	41.8	41.3	31.1	16.8	20.1	8.4	4.3	1.2	.7	100	100
Mexican American	20.2	25.0	37.8	43.8	27.0	19.4	15.0	10.6	.0	1.2	100	100
Negro	25.1	22.0	39.7	47.8	24.0	21.3	10.1	8.9	1.1	.0	100	100
Spanish American	28.8	34.1	31.4	39.9	29.7	18.1	9.3	7.2	.8	.7	100	100
Mixed	26.1	31.6	29.9	34.1	30.5	25.5	12.4	8.2	1.1	.6	100	100
No Response	10.6	13.2	10.4	12.4	6.7	8.4	4.5	3.0	67.9	63.0	100	100
Total	17.5	21.7	25.3	31.6	35.5	36.4	21.0	9.9	.7	.4	100	100

Chapter Two

Design of Study

In broad terms this study has as its purpose the investigation of the relationship between a large number of attributes and behaviors and the educational aspirations of high school seniors. This is an attempt to understand the concommitants of students' educational goal projections and ways in which students may therefore be better served in their high school experience.

SAMPLING

The subjects in this study were part of the SCOPE five-year longitudinal study of high school students. More than 45,000 students were originally sampled in four states, California, Illinois, Massachusetts, and North Carolina, when they were high school freshmen in 1966. Nearly all of the data for the present report, a cross-sectional study of high school seniors, was obtained from the SCOPE 1969 high school senior questionnaire. There were approximately 29,000 respondents to this questionnaire, representing an attrition, for purposes of this report, of about one-third. The subjects to be used in this study were further restricted by several conditions: (1) that data (questionnaire returns) be available for all four of the high school years (this was to facilitate possible use of the same subject pool in longitudinal studies), (2) that students maintained the same state of residence, and (3) that data be available on each of the independent variables of this study. After application of these restrictions, the remaining subject pool numbered 22,891. Subjects used in the present study were drawn from this pool.

STATE-SEX GROUPS

A statistical procedure was used which makes possible inferences from a relatively small sample to a population. Therefore small subsamples were drawn from each of the four project states. Since it was deemed desirable to look at the sexes separately, two subsamples, one of females and one of males, were drawn from each of the four states. Each of these subsamples consisted of about 320 subjects. Thus, eight state-sex groups were used for separate but parallel analyses.

DEPENDENT VARIABLES

A large number of items were selected from the SCOPE 1969 twelfth grade questionnaire and grouped into content areas believed to be related to the style and substance of decision making about postsecondary plans and aspirations. In all, eight content areas were used in the study. The groups of variables in each of the eight areas will subsequently be referred to as *variable sets*. In discussing the findings from the study, the variable sets have been combined into six sections, each of which constitutes a chapter of this book. Briefly stated these chapters present the findings and implications from the investigation of how the following attributes and behaviors of SCOPE seniors discriminate among those who aspire to differing amounts of formal education after leaving high school:

1. Selected attitudes toward school and measured academic behavior and school achievement
2. Selected personal propensities and values
3. Information-gathering behaviors about future work and education
4. Selected problems and conflicts during the school years
5. Perceived barriers to continued education
6. Key decisions about postsecondary life.

Where necessary, items were recoded so that all variables would consist of a scale ordered on some dimension; that is, for any variable, a score of two can be considered to designate more of something than a score of one, and so on. No variable was used for which the nonresponse rate was more than about 14 percent, and in most cases the nonresponse was less than 10 percent. Mean values for each variable were used for subjects who did not respond. The eight variable sets and a complete description of all of the variables as finally recoded for use in the study is provided in Appendix A.

INDEPENDENT VARIABLES

In order to partially control for the factors of race and socioeconomic level of family while examining the attributes and characteristics of high school seniors who declared various educational aspirations, a three-way classification of students was employed. With respect to race, students were dichotomously grouped as Caucasian or non-Caucasian. There were four classifications of socioeconomic level of family (SES) which have been designated as follows: (1) low, (2) low-mid, (3) mid-high, and (4) high. A more detailed description of the derivation of this SES variable was provided in Chapter 1.

The educational aspiration groups were based on how long students, near the end of high school, said they aspired to continue their education. The four groups were comprised of seniors who: (1) did not expect to go to college, (2) said they expected to go to business or vocational schools, or to junior colleges, (3) said they expected to graduate from a four-year college, and (4) said they expected to continue college after graduation. For brevity, these four aspiration groups are referred to subsequently as *No College, Limited College, Four-Year*, and *Postgraduate* aspirants. Students' educational aspirations were elicited by the question: "How long do you expect to stay in school?"

With two race, four SES, and four educational aspiration groupings, there were 32 possible cross-classifications. Chart 2-1 shows this cross-classification design. For each of the eight state-sex combinations, subsamples were

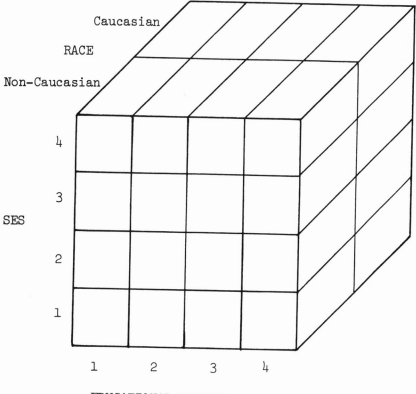

EDUCATIONAL EXPECTATIONS

Chart 2-1. Graphic Representation of a Thirty-Two Cell Cross-Classification Design for Analyses

drawn such that there would be, with rare exception, 10 students in each of the 32 cells.

THE MULTIVARIATE ANALYSIS OF VARIANCE

Each of the eight variable sets was analyzed for each of the eight state-sex groups. For example, the analysis of the variable set "Attitudes Toward School, Academic Behavior, and Achievement" was replicated eight times, for California females, California males, Illinois females, Illinois males, Massachusetts females, Massachusetts males, North Carolina females, and North Carolina males. On one hand, this replication of the analyses of the variable sets provides something of a check on the generality of the conclusions beyond that provided by the statistical inference procedures themselves; on the other hand it allows some assessment of the extent to which the characteristics and experiences of students with particular educational aspirations may depend upon state of residence or upon sex. The balancing of these two sides of the coin, in formulating conclusions and implications, is often a subjective process and was done with great caution.

The analysis employed was a three-way multivariate analysis of variance and discriminant analysis. In essence, the multivariate analysis of variance procedure, as applied to the 32-cell, three-way cross-classification design, allows an examination of the following questions:

1. Are there ways in which groups of students with different educational aspirations are different from each other with respect to each variable set defined as a conceptual entity? In other words, can it be concluded that students with differing educational aspirations have different attributes and characteristics as measured by the variable set involved in the analysis?
2. Do the SES groups have different attributes and characteristics as measured by the variable set?
3. Do the two race groups have different traits as measured by the variable set being analyzed?
4. When looking at the ways in which educational aspiration groups may differ in traits measured by a variable set, is such a difference influenced by race? In other words, does the answer to question one, above, depend on whether students are Caucasian or non-Caucasian?
5. Similarly, are differences among educational aspirations groups influenced by SES?
6. Again in a similar way, do differences among SES groups (question two) depend on whether students are Caucasian or non-Caucasian? Questions four, five, and six are defined as "interactions." Question four, for example, may be referred to as the interaction of educational aspirations and race.

All of the above questions can be posed with respect to each variable set taken as a whole. They are the broadest or most general questions which provide a point of entry to any given analysis. When concluding that the answer to any of these questions is yes (for example, that high school seniors with different educational aspirations do in fact have different characteristics as measured by the variable set), then it is possible to examine the individual variables within the set to arrive at conclusions about which particular variables that make up each set characterize the ways in which the groups are different from each other.

Although attention will not be given to all of the above questions for each variable set, emphasis will center on questions one, four, and five, since the primary purposes of this study are to determine whether high school seniors grouped according to their educational aspirations differ from one another in terms of the variable sets; how these differences can be described by individual variables in each set; and the ways in which these differences may or may not depend on race and SES. In other words, the essential focus of this book is on understanding how certain values, decision-making behaviors, academic behaviors, problems, and relationships may differ for seniors who anticipate different levels of education beyond high school. The presence of the SES and race classifications in the design allows the determination of ways in which these relationships may be influenced by family characteristics associated with socioeconomic stratification and Caucasian or non-Caucasian identification.

In reporting the results of the multivariate analyses of variance, several kinds of displays will be employed. Often the charts are graphs of the mean values of the educational aspiration groups on individual variables. In many instances, all eight state-sex groups have been shown in such charts, with the female and male groups shown separately. However, where two or more state-sex groups of the same sex have similar profiles across the educational aspiration groups on a particular variable, these data were averaged together and graphed on the chart as a composite. In effect the educational aspiration group means shown on the charts, when composites are used, are based on more cases, providing better estimates of the relationship being described than any of the single state-sex profiles.

There are several cautions to be observed in interpreting the graphs of means. None of the variables have been standardized, since this would have confused both state-sex comparisons and comparisons with reference to the original score dimensions. There are instances when desired comparisons among several variables are therefore difficult. However, the range of standard deviations obtained from the several state-sex groups has been indicated on the charts. While comparisons of variable mean scores for educational aspiration groups with the original score dimensions may be interesting and useful, it should be emphasized that the educational aspiration groups are made up of equal representation from the several SES and race groups. The groups, then, are not "normative" samples. This feature enhances the ability to determine whether or not differences among educational aspiration groups depend on race or SES. However, the emphasis is on differences among educational aspiration groups rather than on the absolute level of the group means. Where such differences depend on race or SES, this interaction has been shown in a separate graph. Finally, the reader will notice that some of the state-sex profiles have been designated as being nonsignificant. This means that the differences among the educa-

(Illinois Males)

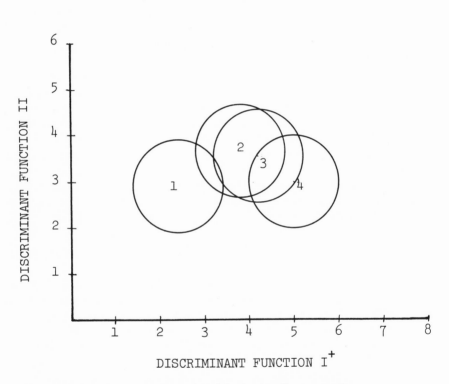

DISCRIMINANT FUNCTION I⁺

Chart 2-2. Separation of Educational Aspiration Groups on the Basis of Attitudes Toward School, Academic Behavior, and Achievement Variables*

*Educational aspiration groups are: 1–high school graduation only; 2–limited college; 3–graduation from a four-year college; 4–postgraduate attendance.

⁺Discriminant functions I and II summarize the ways in which the educational aspiration groups are distinguished on the basis of this variable set. The scales are in terms of standard deviation units with aspiration group 4 set at points (5, 3). The circles represent the estimated dispersion of approximately 50 percent of the students in each aspiration group.

tional aspiration groups were not large enough to justify generalizing from the sample results to the population of high school seniors in the state-sex group. Nevertheless, there are cases where several state-sex groups have similar, although nonsignificant trends, in which such a generalization is tentatively suggested. The level of significance adopted for all hypotheses was .05.

DISCRIMINANT ANALYSIS

If the educational aspiration groups are different from each other in terms of a variable set, it is possible mathematically to abstract a small number of uncorrelated variables which best reproduce the differences among the groups. These abstracted variables are discriminant functions, each of which is a weighted combination of the variables in the variable set. In most cases in the present SCOPE analyses, almost all of the differences among the educational aspiration groups could be represented or reproduced by two such discriminant functions in each variable set. In order to show the extent of differences among the educational aspiration groups, the means of each group on each discriminant function were obtained. These means can then be plotted in a bivariate graph much like a scatterdiagram in such a way as to depict graphically which groups are differentiated from each other by the variable set, and the extent of the differentiation.

Such diagrams will be called separation graphs, an example for explanatory purposes is Chart 2-2. The horizontal axis represents the first discriminant function and the vertical axis represents the second discriminant function. The means of all four educational aspiration groups on both discriminant functions are plotted in the space with reference to the two axes. The circles represent the estimated dispersion of 50 percent of the subjects in each group. Suffice it to say, that the discriminant function analysis provides a scheme by which the extent and direction of differences or discrimination among educational aspiration groups can be viewed graphically. One additional feature should be pointed out. In some analyses, the constellation of variables contributing most heavily to a discriminate function, as determined from weights associated with each variable, provides an interpretable dimension or factor in conceptual as well as in mathematical terms. Where this is the case, the factor will be interpreted conceptually.

The remainder of this publication is organized on the basis of the variable sets. In general, the reporting of conclusions regarding a variable set will be presented once to give the general picture across the several state-sex groups, rather than reporting conclusions from each of the eight state-sex analyses individually. Graphs and displays will usually show the most typical results from among the analyses. Of course, where important state or sex differences are apparent, such findings will be presented.

Chapter Three

Attitudes Toward School, Academic Behavior, and Achievement

INTRODUCTION

Academic attributes are generally of primary concern when considering the differential characteristics of high school seniors having differing educational aspirations. It seems self-evident that differing attitudes toward education, levels of ability and achievement, and academic striving behaviors would have a great deal to do with how long students aspire to stay in school; and such factors are known to be highly related to educational outcomes after high school. Therefore, this study of how the high school experience, personal attitudes, the influence of others, certain problem areas, and other student characteristics are related to levels of educational aspirations will begin with school-related attitudes and attributes. The substantive concerns in this chapter can be classed into four broad areas: values concerning education, academic striving, self-evaluation of academic ability, and measured aptitude and achievement.

REVIEW OF THE LITERATURE

The literature was examined not only for studies of the relationship of these academic attitudes and behaviors to educational aspirations, but also for their relationship to educational outcomes, such as differential college attendance. This latter seems to be a predominant focus of studies in this area reflecting the long interest in predicting educational outcomes from measures of school abilities and achievements. Thus, in part, this chapter examines the extent to which the academic attitudes and behaviors of high school students with varying educational aspirations are similar to the attitudes and behaviors of students who eventually attain the corresponding outcomes. In addition, the identification of the ways by which students in the several aspiration groups can be characterized by differing academic attitudes and behaviors should be of use to educational planners and high school personnel who are interested in designing high school programs to fit students as they really are and to facilitate their growth and fulfillment.

Values Concerning Education

Purpose of Education.   In a review of literature including three statewide surveys in Indiana, Arkansas, and Wisconsin, Beezer and Hjelm (1961) concluded that the mental set to continue or not continue one's education is important in determining whether or not one will attend college. In addition, Beezer concluded that preparing for a vocation is a dominant motive of college-goers. This finding was later reaffirmed by Project Talent (Flanagan, et al. 1964). Trent and Medsker (1968) found that most college persisters (in college for four years) had stated as high school seniors that the most important purpose of college education is "general education" rather than vocational preparation, whereas, the majority of bright non-attenders and of students who withdrew from college (withdrawals) had indicated vocational preparation as the most important purpose of education.

Slocum (1968), in a study of high school students, obtained a positive relationship between both educational aspirations and educational expectations and the number of elective "academic courses" that students choose to take. Conversely, there was a negative relationship between both of these goal-orientation variables and the number of semester hours in vocational courses. While these results are not a direct expression of the purpose of education, they do suggest a value orientation. In brief, it suggested that high school students who are academically oriented are more inclined to pursue higher education than those who are not.

Importance of Education.   Trent and Medsker (1968) asked high school seniors in 1959 how much they liked school, the importance of education, and about the importance and likelihood of graduating from college. The responses of high school seniors to these items were highly related to their "educational status" four years later. Nearly three-quarters of the college persisters had said as high school seniors in 1959 that education is "extremely important," as opposed to 44 percent of the withdrawals and 14 percent of those who did not attend college during the four years subsequent to high school graduation. Similarly, many more of the persisters had indicated as high school seniors that they liked school "very much" and similar results were obtained concerning the likelihood and importance of graduating from college. In a discriminant analysis, the importance of college (answered when the students were high school seniors) proved to be the most important in predicting the educational status of these students four years later (Trent, 1970).

It is quite evident from these results that the responses of high school seniors concerning attitudes and values about education are highly related to their later college attendance.

Academic Striving

The high positive relationships between the academic striving of students and both their success in school and their subsequent decisions about college have been well documented by such longitudinal studies as Project Talent, the Educational Testing Service Growth Studies, and earlier findings from the SCOPE Project itself. Furthermore, the studies of McClelland and his colleagues have demonstrated high correlations of need achievement with measures of success in school (McClelland, 1953). *Beyond High School* documented the continuing relationship between striving and achievement into the college years. For example, even when controlled for ability and time spent in employment, students who persisted in college spent significantly more time studying than did those who dropped out along the way (Trent and Medsker, 1968).

SCOPE's annual studies (grades ten, eleven, and twelve) have shown for both boys and girls from the four project states consistent and very strong positive relationships between aspirations for education beyond high school and such indexes of academic striving as time spent on homework, grades students try to get, and the importance they place on learning in school (Tillery et al., 1967 and 1969; Staff working paper, 1971).

Self-Evaluation of Academic Ability

Bailey (1966) found that "academic self-concept," a scale constructed from several items assessing self-evaluation of ability, was positively related to college attendance. Even when ability levels were held constant, college-goers had, when they were high school seniors, a higher academic self-concept than did noncollege-goers. (This outcome measure, college versus noncollege, was obtained one year after high school.) Similar results were obtained when comparing students who persist in college for one year beyond high school to students who dropped out of college during the first year, except that for students of low ability academic self-concept was not related to persistence in college (Bailey, 1966). Trent (1970) obtained a similar result, showing that high school seniors who said they had college ability were more likely to persist in college for four years. Thus, college-goers and college-persisters have high self-estimates of college ability.

In the same vein, Slocum (1968) obtained a positive relationship between both educational aspirations and educational expectations and academic self-concept: the higher the academic self-concept, the higher the level of aspirations and expectations. The relationship was stronger with expectations than with aspirations, and it was stronger with boys than with girls. For girls, the relationship between aspirations and academic self-concept was not statistically significant.

This literature supports the notion that students who have a higher assessment of their own academic ability are more likely to attend and persist in college. In addition, there is evidence that high school students who think more highly of their academic ability are more likely to indicate that they aspire and expect to attend college.

Measured Aptitude and Achievement

School College and Ability Test (SCAT) scores have been shown to be highly related to college attendance (Trent and Medsker, 1968, 1970). Furthermore, persons with high ability are more likely to persist in college for four years. Bailey (1966) found that within high, middle, and low SCAT groups, college-attenders (one year after high school) had higher SCAT scores than non-attenders. Within the high and middle SCAT groups, students who persisted in college for one year had higher SCAT scores than students who withdrew during the first year; SCAT scores did not distinguish between low ability persisters and low ability nonpersisters. Beezer (1961) concluded from his survey of several studies that there is a positive relationship between measured achievement (high school rank) and the proportion of high school graduates who attend college. Similarly, Bailey (1966) obtained a positive relationship between high school grade point average and educational outcomes. This was true when ability (SCAT) was held constant.

Bailey (1966) also presented results indicating that measured ability (SCAT) is positively related to the educational expectations of high school seniors. Furthermore, in a longitudinal study of students in high school from the eighth through the eleventh grades, it was found that educational aspirations and educational expectations are both positively correlated with high school grade point average. Educational expectations has a consistently higher correlation with high school grade point average over the four years than does educational aspirations. The obtained correlations between educational expectations and grade point average and between educational aspirations and grade point average were (Brookover, Erickson, and Joiner, 1967, p. 396):

	EXP.-GPA	APS.-GPA
Eighth grade	.38	.35
Ninth grade	.32	.22
Tenth grade	.31	.25
Eleventh grade	.30	.23

Thus, the research shows that measured ability is positively related to not only college attendance and persistence, but also the educational aspirations and expectations of high school seniors.

This review of related literature has provided evidence that the attitudes and values of high school seniors concerning education are related to their educational goal projections and to educational outcomes. A general academic orientation appears to be characteristic of students aspiring or expecting to go to college and of students who attend and persist in college. In contrast, students who are not college-oriented tend to be more concerned with vocational preparation. In addition, the college-oriented students have a more positive attitude toward the importance of education than do those who are not college-oriented. Similarly, it has been found that academic self-concept, or self-evaluation of academic ability, is positively related to both educational goal projections and educational outcomes. The amount of time high school seniors spend studying is related to later educational outcomes. Finally, measured aptitude and achievement are positively related to the educational goal projections of high school seniors and to later educational outcomes.

The SCOPE study addressed itself directly to the relationship of these aspects of the high school experience to the educational aspirations expressed by students as they complete their high school studies. The findings confirm previous research results concerning the relationship of measured achievement and ability, students' self-assessment of ability, and students' educational value orientations to their goal projections. Furthermore, the findings present a more complete view of the relationships between educational aspirations and the attitudes and behaviors of high school seniors concerning education. The study also suggests that such characteristics of different aspiration groups are similar to those for corresponding outcome groups.

THE VARIABLE SET

This variable set consists of sixteen variables as measures of values concerning education, academic striving and self-evaluation, and measured aptitude and achievement. A complete specification of these sixteen variables, as scored for analysis, is provided in Appendix A. A summary of these variables follows:

I.   Values and Attitudes Concerning Education
  1. How important to you now is getting good grades?
  2. How important to you now is learning as much as possible in school?
  3. How much influence would believing that the important things in life aren't learned in college have on a decision not to go to college?
  If you had the opportunity, how much would you like to attend each of the following types of colleges?:
  4. Academic-intellectual orientation
  5. Friendly/student activity type of college
  6. Philosophically-oriented college
  7. Activist college
  8. Occupationally-oriented college
  9. School spirits type of college

II. Academic Striving
   10. What grades do you try to get?
   11. About how many hours each week during the school year do you spend doing homework?
   12. Which of the following statements best describes your attitude toward school work in grade 12? (These have to do with how hard one tried in his course work.)
III. Self-Evaluation of Academic Ability
   13. In general, do you feel you can do college work?
IV. Measured Aptitude and Achievement
   14. Verbal score on the Academic Aptitude Test
   15. Math score on the Academic Aptitude Test
   16. Self-report of high school grades

   This set of sixteen variables was analyzed with each of the eight state-sex groups, using multivariate analysis of variance (manova) and discriminant analysis (see Chapter 2 on the design of the study). The results of these eight analyses were quite similar.

THE MULTIVARIATE ANALYSES OF VARIANCE

To give the most generalized picture first, high school students of varying educational aspirations were found to differ from each other in terms of the sixteen variables taken simultaneously. This is true regardless of race and regardless of SES (no interactions). Caucasians as a group, however, tend to be different from non-Caucasians in terms of the sixteen variables as a set, and females of different SES levels tend to be differentiated from each other with respect to this set of variables, but there is no evidence for saying the same of males. It should be remembered, however, that the scope and focus of this report limit discussion of race and SES differences except where such differences affect the interpretation of relative differences among educational aspiration groups. The multivariate and univariate statistics resulting from the eight state-sex analyses of this variable set are presented in Appendix B.

   Thus, students who have aspirations for different levels of education are different in their academic values and behaviors. The pattern and extent of this differentiation will be discussed in the section on discriminant analysis. As a prelude to this interpretation, the groups' differences in terms of the individual variables in the three substantive subcategories are discussed. These are: values concerning education, academic striving and self-evaluation, and measured achievement and aptitude.

Values Concerning Education
   We have keyed variables 1 and 2 (the importance of getting good grades and of learning as much as possible in school), and variable 3 (believing

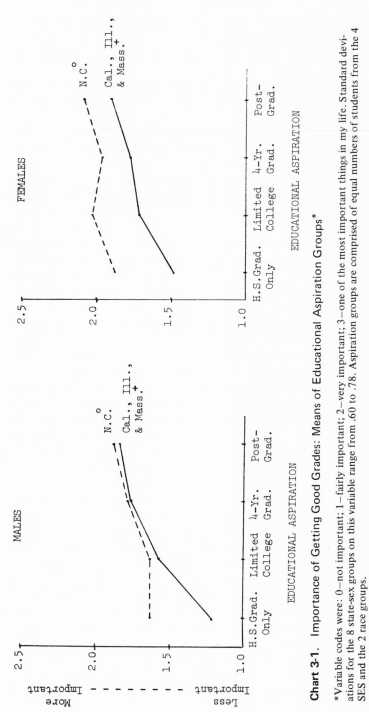

Chart 3-1. Importance of Getting Good Grades: Means of Educational Aspiration Groups*

*Variable codes were: 0—not important; 1—fairly important; 2—very important; 3—one of the most important things in my life. Standard deviations for the 8 state-sex groups on this variable range from .60 to .78. Aspiration groups are comprised of equal numbers of students from the 4 SES and the 2 race groups.

+State composites are used when differences among the educational aspiration groups in those states are similar.

°Not significant at .05 level of probability.

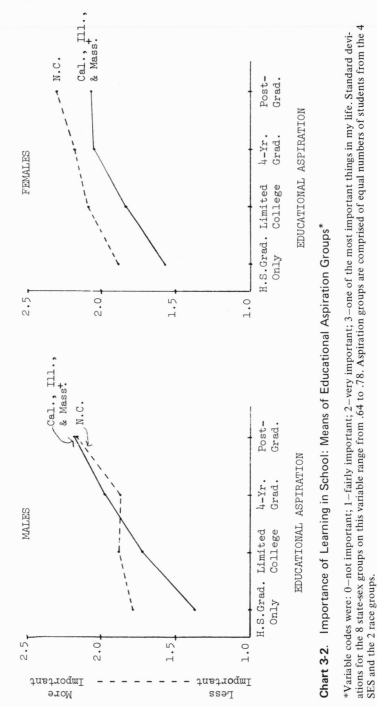

Chart 3-2. Importance of Learning in School: Means of Educational Aspiration Groups*

*Variable codes were: 0—not important; 1—fairly important; 2—very important; 3—one of the most important things in my life. Standard deviations for the 8 state-sex groups on this variable range from .64 to .78. Aspiration groups are comprised of equal numbers of students from the 4 SES and the 2 race groups.

+State composites are used when differences among the educational aspiration groups in those states are similar.

that the important things are not learned in school) as indicative of positive versus negative orientations toward college education.

The belief that the important things in life are not learned in college is not very much related to how long seniors say they want to stay in school. Since students in the four educational aspiration groups tended to answer this item the same way, such attitudes do not seriously affect aspirations but may do so in the ultimate decisions about college. However, it is generally true that high school seniors with extensive educational aspirations tend to place more importance on getting good grades and on learning as much as possible in school than do those of lesser aspirations. The means on these two discriminating variables for the aspiration groups are graphed in Charts 3-1 and 3-2. Since the results for students in California, Illinois, and Massachusetts were very similar, the overall average of students in these three states is presented. This composite gives a clearer picture of the relative differences among aspiration groups. It can be seen from looking at these graphs that students in North Carolina are somewhat different from the general result stated above. Male high school seniors in North Carolina, regardless of their educational aspirations, showed similar attitudes about grades and learning in school. This was also true of North Carolina women who, in addition, tended to regard grades and learning in school as being considerably more important than did the females in the other three states.

These results allow the conclusion that there is a positive relationship between positive values about education and the educational aspirations of high school seniors. This relationship appears to be somewhat stronger for males than for females, and does not appear to be true of students in North Carolina.

Another facet of the attitudes and values of students concerning education had to do with the preference for various types of colleges. SCOPE's measure of this question was the extent to which students say they would like to go to colleges with distinctive environments, based on short descriptions in the questionnaire. One of these can be thought of as an occupationally-oriented college and another as a highly academically-oriented college (variables 4 and 8). The graphs of group means for these two types of colleges are shown in Charts 3-3 and 3-4. It is clear that the longer students want to stay in school, the greater the attractiveness of academically-oriented colleges. Seniors aspiring to four or more years of college tend to reject the occupationally-oriented college, as do students not aspiring to go to college. The students most strongly favoring the occupational orientation are those with limited college aspirations (two years). Other SCOPE working papers demonstrate that most of these students who do, in fact, attend college enter junior colleges. This institution was the prototype for the questionnaire description. One anomaly in the results is that females in Illinois with two-year aspirations favored the academic orientation (Chart 3-3) least of any group—less so than the females in Illinois who did not aspire to go to college. The analysis indicated that this is a true population difference. On the

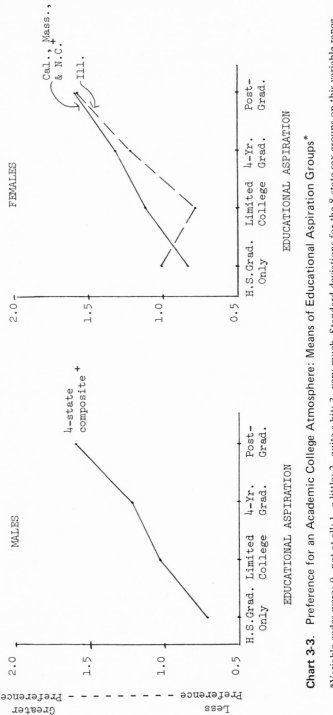

Chart 3-3.   Preference for an Academic College Atmosphere: Means of Educational Aspiration Groups*

*Variable codes were: 0—not at all; 1—a little; 2—quite a bit; 3—very much. Standard deviations for the 8 state-sex groups on this variable range from .83 to .92. Aspiration groups are comprised of equal numbers of students from the 4 SES and the 2 race groups.

+State composites are used when differences among the educational aspiration groups in those states are similar.

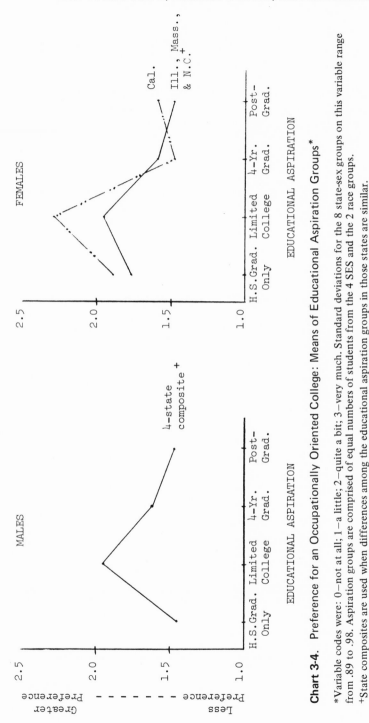

Chart 3-4. Preference for an Occupationally Oriented College: Means of Educational Aspiration Groups*

*Variable codes were: 0—not at all; 1—a little; 2—quite a bit; 3—very much. Standard deviations for the 8 state-sex groups on this variable range from .89 to .98. Aspiration groups are comprised of equal numbers of students from the 4 SES and the 2 race groups.

+State composites are used when differences among the educational aspiration groups in those states are similar.

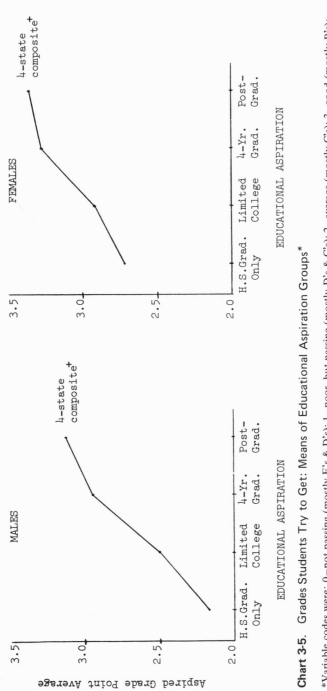

Chart 3-5. Grades Students Try to Get: Means of Educational Aspiration Groups[*]

[*]Variable codes were: 0–not passing (mostly F's & D's); 1–poor, but passing (mostly D's & C's); 2–average (mostly C's); 3–good (mostly B's); 4–excellent (mostly A's). Standard deviations for the 8 state-sex groups on this variable range from .69 to .92. Aspiration groups are comprised of equal numbers of students from the 4 SES and the 2 race groups.

[+]State composites are used when differences among the educational aspiration groups in those states are similar.

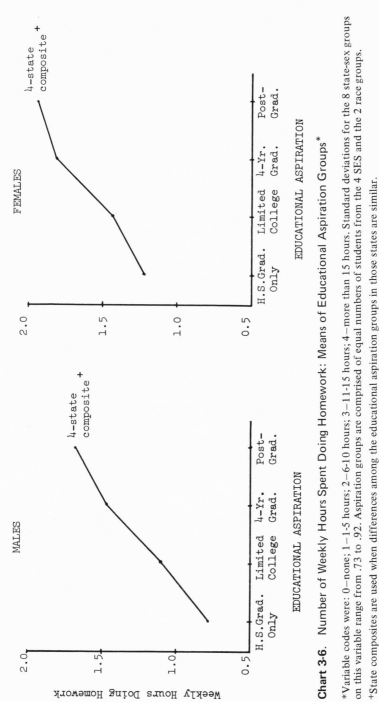

Chart 3-6. Number of Weekly Hours Spent Doing Homework: Means of Educational Aspiration Groups[*]

[*]Variable codes were: 0—none; 1—1-5 hours; 2—6-10 hours; 3—11-15 hours; 4—more than 15 hours. Standard deviations for the 8 state-sex groups on this variable range from .73 to .92. Aspiration groups are comprised of equal numbers of students from the 4 SES and the 2 race groups.
[+]State composites are used when differences among the educational aspiration groups in those states are similar.

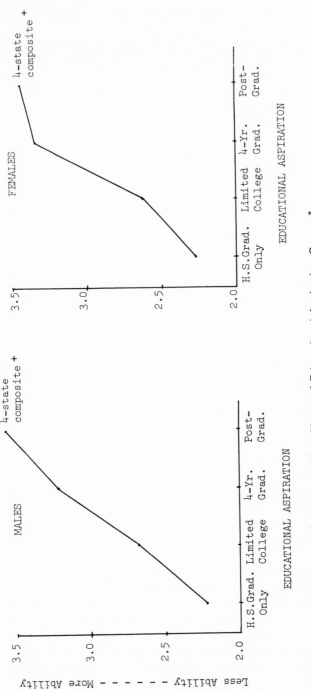

Chart 3-7. Self-Assessment of College Ability: Means of Educational Aspiration Groups*

*Variable codes were: 0—I don't know; 1—I definitely do not have the ability; 2—I probably do not have the ability; 3—I probably have the ability; 4—I definitely have the ability. Standard deviations for the 8 state-sex groups on this variable range from .95 to 1.12. Aspiration groups are comprised of equal numbers of students from the 4 SES and the 2 race groups.

+State composites are used when differences among the educational aspiration groups in those states are similar.

other hand, it was the California females of limited college aspirations who most strongly favored the occupationally-oriented college.

This study will not focus on students' responses concerning the other four types of schools since no clear-cut results were apparent. It can be concluded that students who aspire to go to college less than four years (junior college, business school, or special schools) are most interested in vocational-orientation institutions and students with more extensive educational aspirations are most interested in institutions which have more academic and intellectual environments.

Academic Striving

The means of the aspiration groups on variables 10 (grades tried for) and 11 (hours per week on homework) are shown in Charts 3-5 and 3-6 respectively. There is a very clear relationship for each of these two variables which were keyed to provide measures of academic striving and students' educational aspirations. Variable 12 (students' reports of how hard they tried with their course work) was not significantly related to their educational aspirations and is, therefore, not displayed. However, the results on variables 10 and 11 lead to the conclusion that the relationship of academic-striving behaviors to educational aspiration precurses a similar relationship of such behaviors to the actual educational outcomes of seniors as reflected in other SCOPE findings and related research. High school students with more extensive educational aspirations manifest a greater degree of academic orientation in their school endeavors than do students with less extensive educational aspirations. The reader will not be surprised to note, as in other studies, the relatively higher academic striving of girls as compared with boys.

Self-Evaluation of Academic Ability

The more extensive a student's educational aspirations, the higher his self-estimate while in high school of ability to do college work. This result, shown in Chart 3-7, is consistent with previous findings concerning academic self-concept. The relationship is quite linear and quite strong—somewhat more so for men than for women. Students' academic self-evaluations have a great deal to do with the educational goal projections they make as high school seniors.

Measured Aptitude and Achievement

As expected, there is a general positive relationship between the measures of aptitude and achievement, and educational aspirations. The means for the groups are shown in Charts 3-8, 3-9, and 3-10. Students in North Carolina tend to score lower on traditional measures of academic ability than students in the other three states. This is most evident in the AAT-Verbal scores (Chart 3-8). However, the same is not true when it comes to grades (Chart 3-10),

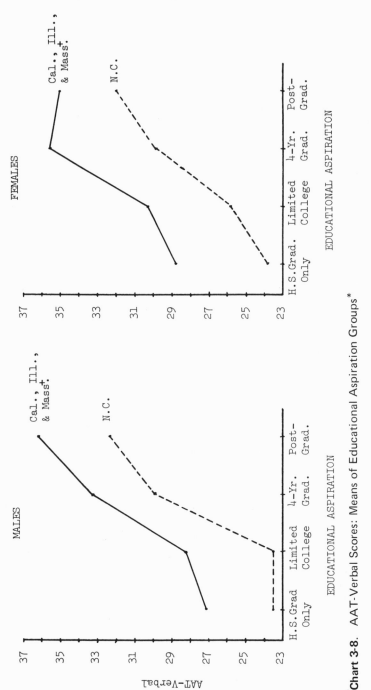

Chart 3-8. AAT-Verbal Scores: Means of Educational Aspiration Groups*

*Standard deviations for the 8 state-sex groups on this variable range from 7.70 to 9.12. Aspiration groups are comprised of equal numbers of students from the 4 SES and the 2 race groups.

+State composites are used when differences among the educational aspiration groups in those states are similar.

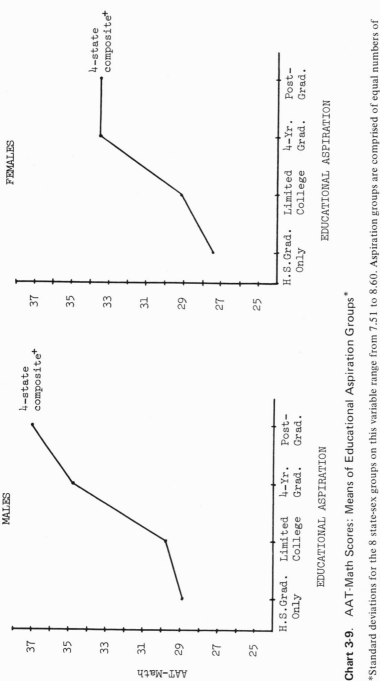

Chart 3-9. AAT-Math Scores: Means of Educational Aspiration Groups*

*Standard deviations for the 8 state-sex groups on this variable range from 7.51 to 8.60. Aspiration groups are comprised of equal numbers of students from the 4 SES and the 2 race groups.

+State composites are used when differences among the educational aspiration groups in those states are similar.

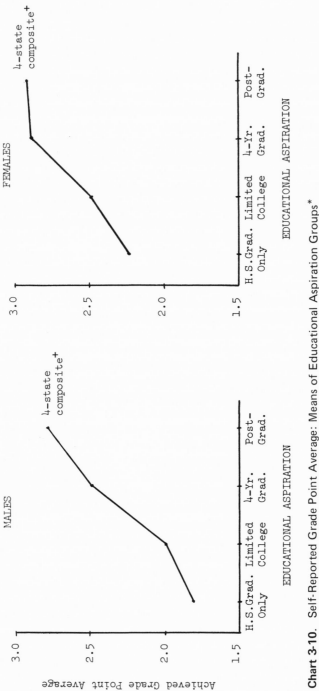

Chart 3-10. Self-Reported Grade Point Average: Means of Educational Aspiration Groups*

*Variable codes were: 0–not passing (mostly F's and D's); 1–poor, but passing (mostly D's & C's); 2–average (mostly C's); 3–good (mostly B's); 4–excellent (mostly A's). Standard deviations for the 8 state-sex groups on this variable range from .70 to .80. Aspiration groups are comprised of equal numbers of students from the 4 SES and the 2 race groups.
+State composites are used when differences among the educational aspiration groups in those states are similar.

although this may reflect differential grading practices as well as the high value North Carolina's students put on getting good grades.

Grades and measures of academic abilities remain the primary evidence used in advising students about college choice and in the policies and practices of institutional admission. Great differences exist among the mean scores of college student bodies on these measures and among types of institutions as determined by degree level and other factors (Darley, 1962; Tillery, 1973).

THE DISCRIMINANT ANALYSES

Considering the entire variable set as a whole, the analyses indicate that groups of students with differing educational aspirations are distinguished from each other relatively well on the basis of their academic attitudes and behaviors. A good example is that of Massachusetts males and the extent and pattern of differentiation among educational aspiration groups in this state-sex group as shown in Chart 3-11. In other state-sex groups, except California males, degrees of discrimination and the patterns of differentiation were similar but not identical.

Before discussing these patterns, it would be well to mention that with this variable set, the two discriminant functions obtained formed interpretable dimensions or factors in all of the eight analyses. In each case, the first discriminant function can be described as an academic orientation. The most consistent contributing variables across the eight state-sex groups are the hours spent on homework (variable 11), self-estimate of college ability (variable 13), and for males, the AAT-Verbal score (variable 14). In five of the state-sex groups, the attractiveness of an occupationally-oriented college (variable 8) contributes moderately in a negative direction to discriminant function one—in other words, high scorers on this function tend not to be attracted to this type of college. Discriminant function two has some contribution from academic factors, but not in any consistent fashion across state-sex groups, and even within a state-sex analysis, some academic variables contribute positively and others contribute negatively. The most consistent feature is that high scorers on this function tend to prefer the occupational type of college (variable 8) or the school spirit type of college (variable 9). Thus, this might be called a college orientation which is nonacademic, with possible emphasis on occupational preparation.

In Chart 3-11, the bivariate plot of educational aspiration groups according to discriminant function scores, it can be seen that the more extensive the educational aspirations, the higher the scores on the first discriminant function (horizontal axis), indicating a greater degree of academic orientation. This is characteristic of all state-sex groups. Looking at group differences along the vertical axis, it is evident that students with limited (two-year) and baccalaureate

(Massachusetts Males)

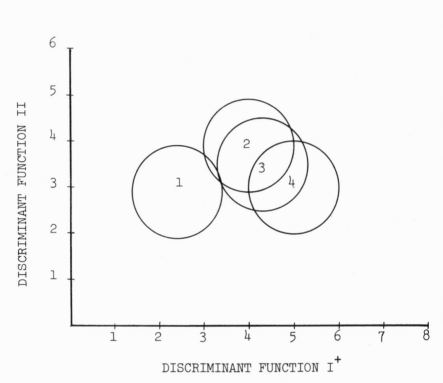

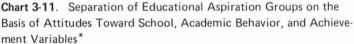

DISCRIMINANT FUNCTION I⁺

Chart 3-11. Separation of Educational Aspiration Groups on the
Basis of Attitudes Toward School, Academic Behavior, and Achievement Variables*

*Educational aspiration groups are: 1—high school graduation only; 2—limited college;
3—graduation from a four-year college; 4—postgraduate attendance.
⁺Discriminant functions I and II summarize the ways in which the educational aspiration
groups are distinguished on the basis of this variable set. The scales are in terms of standard
deviation units with aspiration group 4 set at points (5, 3). The circles represent the estimated dispersion of approximately 50 percent of the students in each aspiration group.

educational aspirations score highest on the nonacademic college-occupational
dimension. It is interesting to note that noncollege aspirants and postgraduate
aspirants score at about the same low point on this function; the function is *not*
a noncollege dimension, but high scorers evidently are oriented toward a different type of college experience as compared to the high scorers on the first discriminant function. This, of course, is consistent with the contributions of preference for school spirit colleges and occupational colleges to the second function.

For California males (Chart 3-12), function two shows very little

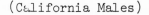

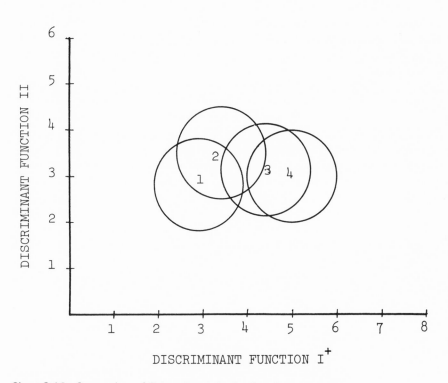

DISCRIMINANT FUNCTION I$^+$

Chart 3-12. Separation of Educational Aspiration Groups on the Basis of Attitudes Toward School, Academic Behavior, and Achievement Variables*

*Educational aspiration groups are: 1—high school graduation only; 2—limited college; 3—graduation from a four-year college; 4—postgraduate attendance.

$^+$Discriminant functions I and II summarize the ways in which the educational aspiration groups are distinguished on the basis of this variable set. The scales are in terms of standard deviation units with aspiration group 4 set at points (5, 3). The circles represent the estimated dispersion of approximately 50 percent of the students in each aspiration group.

discrimination among the groups although limited college aspirants are slightly more oriented to nonacademic college environments. What is noteworthy is the greater similarity on function one (academic orientation) for the noncollege group and the limited college group.

CONCLUSION

In general, those students with more extensive educational aspirations score higher on measures of positive attitudes toward school and tend to have a more academic-intellectual orientation towards school than do students with less extensive educational aspirations. They tend to be more diligent in their academic striving, to have more confidence in their ability to do college work, and to have higher measured ability and achievement. Thus, the kinds of relationships which have been shown in previous research to exist between variables in this area and educational outcomes pertain also to the educational aspirations of high school students.

Much of this information should be of use in thinking about and planning high school programs. One feature of these results, which probably corroborates the informal observations of people who work with high school students, suggests that many students who do not aspire to go to college or who have limited college aspirations are "turned off" to traditional education. This is reflected in the responses concerning the importance and value of education. Some attention should be given to providing ways of making the high school experience more interesting and stimulating to students who do not exhibit a strong academic orientation. Education can be more tailored to the specific interests and needs of students if ways can be found to assess and develop a wider array of human talents and goals than is generally true of contemporary educational practice.

Chapter Four

Personal Propensities and Values

Although certain attitudes and behaviors concerning education have been shown to be related to the educational aspirations of high school seniors, it is obvious that this is certainly not the entire story. There are many students of high ability and with positive attitudes toward education who do not go to college and those with questionable commitments and achievements who do.

REVIEW OF THE LITERATURE

Trent and Medsker (1968) emphasize that ability and SES do not account completely for the differential performance of students in college or for the differences between college persisters and non-attenders. Earlier, Lavin (1965) stressed that ability was inadequate to account for differential academic performance and that a fruitful avenue for research would be in the area of personality and value dimensions. It is not a very large extrapolation to apply the same reasoning when educational aspirations is the criterion rather than college attendance or academic performance. Certainly it is reasonable to hypothesize that certain personality orientations and features of an individual's outlook on life and the world around him are integrally connected with the aspirations he will set for himself. Knowing something about the nature of such relationships should have important implications concerning the needs of high school students and how they can be met.

SCOPE has centered on three aspects of this large and complex area in its study of twelfth graders and their educational aspirations. Broadly stated, these are: (1) Intellectual Orientation (as measured by personality instruments), (2) Work Ethic and Identification with the Establishment, and (3) Attitudes Toward Social Issues. The literature review which follows by no means exhaustive, provided no direct empirical evidence of the relationship of individual characteristics in these areas to educational aspirations. However, it did provide a groundwork which enabled us to pose certain research questions in looking at the analyses of this variable set.

Intellectual Orientation

The Omnibus Personality Inventory (OPI) has been developed under the auspices of the Center for Research and Development in Higher Education as an instrument to measure the personality characteristics, attitudes, and values relevant to normal ego functions and intellectual activity. As part of the research and validation of the OPI, two factor analyses of sixteen OPI scales yielded five factors, one of which was labeled a scholarly orientation factor. There were four OPI scales which contributed to this factor: Thinking Introversion (TI), which measures preference for reflective, abstract thinking; Theoretical Orientation (TO), which reflects an interest in science, problem-solving, and logical thinking; Estheticism (Es), which indicates interests in artistic matters and activities, and Complexity (Co), which measures extent of intellectual curiosity and tolerance for ambiguity. The Autonomy (Au) scale, which measures independence of authority as traditionally imposed through social institutions and opposition to infringements on the rights of individuals, was associated with the Scholarly Orientation factor to a lesser degree.

The Scholarly Orientation factor was described as follows:

> The high loadings on (TI, TO, Es, and Co) indicate that high scorers have an interest in thinking and dealing with abstractions, appreciate freedom of thought, and are interested in scientific and artistic problems. Both cognitive and affective aspects of personality are mobilized, in the high scorer, in the services of problem solving, to judge from the diversity of the correlating scales [Omnibus Personality Inventory–Research Manual, CSHE, 1962, p. 26].

In further confirmation of a general scholarly orientation factor, Maddison and Studdiford (1963) have shown that all of these scales have significant correlations with the grade point averages of Princeton freshman. Two of these scales, Au and TI, had a significant unique contribution to the prediction of grades. Trent and Medsker (1968) found that some of the measures of scholarly orientation, four years after high school graduation, were related to college attendance. These included TI and Au. However, OPI scholarly orientation measures obtained four years previously, when the subjects were high school seniors, were not as highly related to later educational outcomes (college attendance), with the exception of TI.

In the meantime, continued research with the OPI resulted in a refined measurement of learning orientation. This new measure, called Intellectual Disposition Categories (IDCs), consists of eight categories on a continuum of inventoried interest in and commitment to general learning and intellectual activity. In addition to the four scales previously used to define Scholarly Orientation (TI, TO, Es, and Co), the IDCs utilize two scales as secondary or conditional criteria. These two additional scales are Au and Religious Orientation (RO). The assumption underlying the inclusion of the two additional scales is that an expressed interest in intellectual involvement may well be attenuated by authoritarian thinking or lack of freedom in independent thinking. A considerable amount of information has been amassed in support of the construct validity of the IDCs. Students with differing academic interests, values and aspirations, occupational values, intellectual and cultural interests, and religious attitudes are differentiated on the IDCs in ways which are supportive of its validity. Particularly relevant to the concerns of the present study, it has been found that students who, as college freshmen, aspire to graduate schooling have higher median IDC scores than students who intend to terminate their formal education at the baccalaureate level. Also, students with a vocational orientation toward education obtain relatively low median IDC scores (Heist and Yonge, 1968).

Of interest in the present study is the extent to which students with differing aspirations on the SCOPE four-level educational aspiration factor are differentiated in their intellectual orientations. SCOPE did not administer the complete OPI but has developed short scales which are considered to be indices of intellectual predisposition or orientation.

Work Ethic and Identification with the Establishment

The Protestant Ethic is generally traced to the development of Calvinism (cf. Weber, 1930; Parsons, 1935). Its manifestation in America has variously been called, for example, the American Dream and the American work ethic (e.g., Strodtbeck, 1958, Rosen, 1959). It is in this context that the terms *work ethic* and *identification with the establishment* are being used.

Strodtbeck (1958) identified three elements as being integral to the "American work ethic": (1) man's responsibility to control his own destiny, (2) the importance of loyalty to a larger collective than the family (willingness to leave home to make one's way in life), and (3) a preference for individual rather than collective credit for work accomplished. Facets of the "work ethic" have been measured by scales of "mastery" over one's fate and "active-passive" orientation (mostly related to the first element), "independence of family," "individualistic-collectivistic orientation," and "present-future orientation" (Strodtbeck, 1958, Rosen, 1959).

In other empirical work with these aspects of work ethic, Rosen (1959) showed that active-passive orientation, individualistic-collectivistic orientation, and present-future orientation are related to achievement. These interact with SES and ethnicity (Rosen, 1959; Strodtbeck, 1958).

Gough (1965) correlated his adjective checklist (Gough and Heilbrun, 1965) with his college attendance equation based on the California Personality Inventory. Adjectives correlating positively with the college attendance equation for males included: mature (.32), ambitious (.31), capable (.30), responsible (.30), and foresighted (.25); for females: dominant (.36), determined (.29), aggressive (.29), confident (.26), forceful (.26), and assertive (.24). On the face of it, these adjectives appear to describe traits involved in the work ethic as here conceived. Trent and Medsker (1968) found that the greatest proportion of young people who described themselves as a "leader" was among the men and women college-persisters and the smallest proportion was among the nonattenders.

Thus, qualities involved in the "work ethic" are related to achievement, and are related to educational outcomes. Rosen's (1959) work suggests that persons with high achievement values will also have high educational and occupational aspirations. The present study incorporates a look at the relationship of a measure of work ethic to the educational aspirations of high school seniors.

Attitudes Toward Social Issues

It takes only a casual reading of the newspapers to be aware that there has been an immense upsurge of student activism and campus unrest during the past decade. We can point to such landmarks as the free speech movement in Berkeley, the violence at Columbia University, the War Moratoriums, the response to the Cambodian crisis on college campuses. These are only some of the more publicly noted manifestations. This phenomenon has been studied by a number of investigators, perhaps the foremost of which is the President's Commission on Campus Unrest. The report of that investigation, *Campus Unrest* (the "Scranton Report"), points to basic social and philosophic movements and a fundamental shift in student culture as underlying causes. Whittaker and Watts have described one activist population as being "alienated from conventional values, . . . a protest against society . . . and against the dehumanizing influences of modern institutions and a materialistic way of life; . . . politically, it tends from the independent liberal to the radical left; . . . it appears to be intellectually sophisticated and culturally aware . . . " (Whittaker and Watts, 1969, p. 66).

This student activism is also a part of the high school and junior high school scene in many communities in the U.S. (Birmingham, 1970); Gorton, 1970; Liberale and Seligson, 1970). Also Dagenais and Marascuilo (1971), studying the involvement of Berkeley high school students in protest demonstrations, found that such involvement is related to I.Q., race, SES, religious attendance, and political orientation. In summary, high school students more extensively involved in social issues are more likely to be white, articulate, and intelligent, of good academic standing, live in a middle class home, have political beliefs that are left of center, be nonchurch-goers, and believe that the effects of demonstrations are positive. These students are sensitive to social, political, and economic injustices. In the Berkeley high school, 42 percent had participated in demonstrations opposed to the Vietnam war, 37 percent in demonstrations to save the environment, and 29 percent were involved in the cause of the grape pickers. With their high ability and good academic standing, it can be speculated that a high proportion of high school student activists will go to college (Dagenais and Marascuilo, 1971). The present study includes a consideration of the relationship of students' attitudes toward certain political-social issues, which can be thought of on a liberal-conservative dimension, to their educational aspirations.

In brief, this review of literature has lead to the following propositions: (1) high school seniors aspiring to go to college will have a greater degree of intellectual orientation, as measured by OPI items, than students not aspiring to go to college, (2) students with more extensive educational aspirations will be likely to report a greater degree of endorsement of work ethic values than students with less extensive educational aspirations, and (3) students having more extensive educational aspirations will be more likely to have attitudes concommitant with the type of social involvements discussed by Dagenais and Marascuilo than students with less extensive educational aspirations.

THE VARIABLE SET

A complete outline of the variables in this set appears in Appendix A.

Intellectual Orientation

Because of considerations of questionnaire length, SCOPE did not administer any single complete OPI scales. Instead, 31 OPI items were selected which were the strongest discriminators on the Au, TI, and TO scales. A factor analysis of these items using SCOPE data gathered in a pilot study showed that these items clustered as follows: The fifteen items selected from the Au scale formed a single factor. The six items from the TO scale formed two three-item factors, one appearing to consist of a science orientation, the other a problem-solving orientation. The nine items selected from the TI scale also formed two factors. One of these, a three-item affair, has to do with a musical orientation; the other, consisting of six items, may be called an analytical orientation. One item has been omitted.

Cross (1968), using these items and SCOPE pilot study data, obtained clear differentiations between groups of young people not attending college and those attending two-year or four-year colleges.

Given the results of previous research with the OPI scholarly-orientation scales, the OPI IDCs, Cross' findings, and the results of SCOPE's factor analysis, the following scales will be considered collectively as indices of intellectual orientation. The term *intellectual orientation* is being used to avoid confusion with the OPI Intellectual Disposition Categories.

1. Autonomy—based on fifteen items from the OPI Au scale.
2. Theoretical Orientation-science—based on three TO items.
3. Theoretical Orientation-problem solving—based on three TO items.
4. Thinking Introversion-music—Three TI items.
5. Thinking Introversion-analysis—six TI items.

Work Ethic and Identification with the Establishment

According to the research reviewed earlier in this chapter, the following items appear to tap aspects of the work ethic. The three-item work ethic scale (variable 12) was derived by Fred Dagenais, who has been associated with the SCOPE staff, on the basis of a priori considerations (content validity) and factor analytic studies. These variables are:

The importance of

6. being a leader
7. being able to do at least one thing very well
8. putting up a good fight when competing with others

Agreement that

9. by high school graduation people should know where they are headed in life
10. I expect the best of others
11. I like people who are hard workers
12. Work Ethic scale—consisting of three items:

    a.   the most important qualities of a husband are determination and ambition
    b.   every wage earner should be required to save a certain part of his salary each month so that he will be able to support himself and his family in later years
    c.   more than anything else, it is good hard work that makes life worthwhile

13. Agreement that it is more important to work for the good of the community than for one's own self-interests.

Attitudes Toward Social Issues

The following four items are included as assessments of attitudes toward certain social issues:

Agreement that

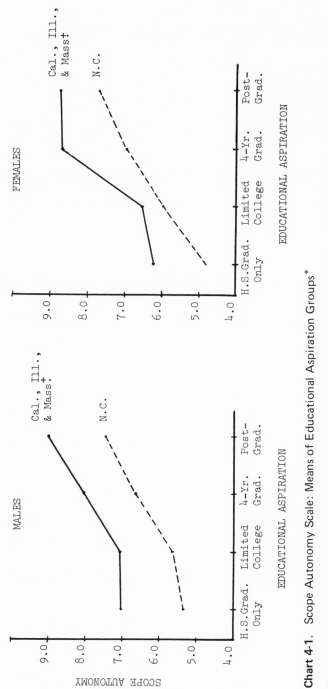

Chart 4-1. Scope Autonomy Scale: Means of Educational Aspiration Groups*

*Standard deviations for the 8 state-sex groups on this variable range from 3.00 to 3.48. Aspiration groups are comprised of equal numbers of students from the 4 SES and the 2 race groups.

†State composites are used when differences among the educational aspiration groups in those states are similar.

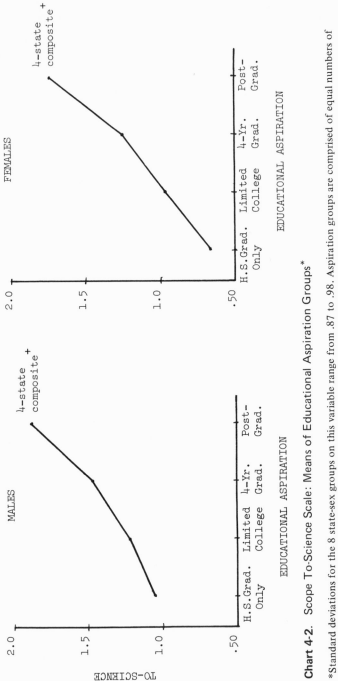

Chart 4-2.   Scope To-Science Scale: Means of Educational Aspiration Groups*

*Standard deviations for the 8 state-sex groups on this variable range from .87 to .98. Aspiration groups are comprised of equal numbers of students from the 4 SES and the 2 race groups.

+State composites are used when differences among the educational aspiration groups in those states are similar.

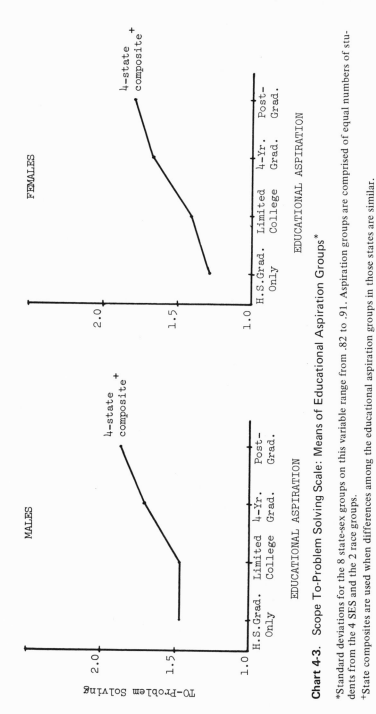

Chart 4-3. Scope To-Problem Solving Scale: Means of Educational Aspiration Groups*

*Standard deviations for the 8 state-sex groups on this variable range from .82 to .91. Aspiration groups are comprised of equal numbers of students from the 4 SES and the 2 race groups.

+State composites are used when differences among the educational aspiration groups in those states are similar.

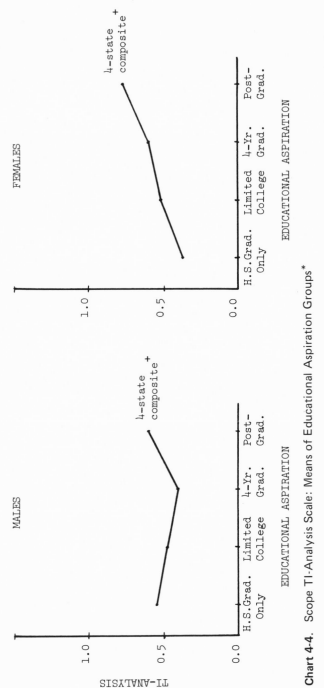

Chart 4-4. Scope TI-Analysis Scale: Means of Educational Aspiration Groups[*]

[*]Standard deviations for the 8 state-sex groups on this variable range from .74 to .83. Aspiration groups are comprised of equal numbers of students from the 4 SES and the 2 race groups.

[+]State composites are used when differences among the educational aspiration groups in those states are similar.

14. Student protest movements do more harm than good
15. Attending religious meetings regularly is necessary to lead a good life.
16. It is morally wrong for a person to refuse to fight in Vietnam even if doing so violates his beliefs.
17. Disrespect for law and order is the major problem in society today.

THE MULTIVARIATE ANALYSES OF VARIANCE

This set of seventeen variables distinguished among the four educational expectation groups in all eight state-sex groups. In all cases, the ways in which high school seniors with differing educational expectations were different from each other in terms of this variable set did not depend on SES, race, sex, or state of residence. The emphasis in the following will be to discuss the particular ways in which the educational aspiration groups differed from each other with respect to intellectuality, work ethic values, and attitudes toward social issues. Sex and state differences will be mentioned in this discussion.

Intellectual Orientation

Charts 4-1, 4-2, 4-3, and 4-4 depict the means of the four educational aspiration groups on the SCOPE Au, TO-science, TO-problem solving, and TI-analysis scales. Each of these variables shows a clear relationship to educational aspirations—students with more extensive educational aspirations tend to have higher scores. This effect is remarkably similar in all of the four states. Therefore the figures show the averaged means, for males and for females. There is one exception to this: students in North Carolina as a group have relatively lower Au scores, shown separately in Chart 4-1, although the same positive relationship between autonomy and educational aspirations is apparent. The educational aspiration groups were not notably different from each other on the three-item TI-music scale.

The results shown in Charts 4-1 through 4-4 are striking evidence that high school students who aspire to go to college have a stronger intellectual orientation than those who do not, as measured by several short scales constructed from OPI items. The more extensive the educational aspirations, the greater the intellectual orientation.

Work Ethic and Identification with the Establishment

Two variables, 6 and 12, showed clear and consistent relationships with educational aspirations. The more extensive the educational aspirations, the greater the emphasis on the importance of being a leader. This relationship was essentially the same in all eight state-sex groups, and the means are graphed accordingly (averaged across states) in Chart 4-5. Work ethic values as measured by the three-item work ethic scale vary the same way with educational aspira-

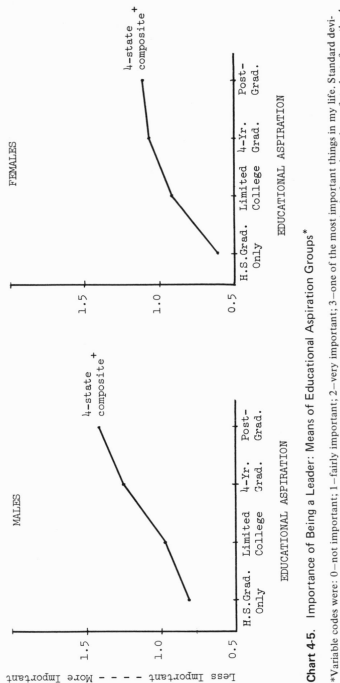

Chart 4-5. Importance of Being a Leader: Means of Educational Aspiration Groups*

*Variable codes were: 0—not important; 1—fairly important; 2—very important; 3—one of the most important things in my life. Standard deviations for the 8 state-sex groups on this variable range from .77 to .87. Aspiration groups are comprised of equal numbers of students from the 4 SES and the 2 race groups.

+State composites are used when differences among the educational aspiration groups in those states are similar.

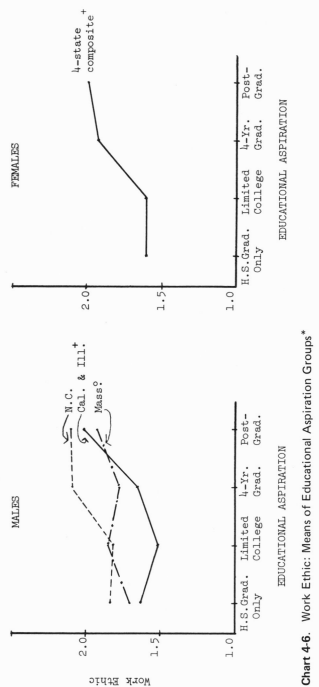

Chart 4-6. Work Ethic: Means of Educational Aspiration Groups*

*Standard deviations for the 8 state-sex groups on this variable range from .86 to .99. Aspiration groups are comprised of equal numbers of students from the 4 SES and the 2 race groups.

+State composites are used when differences among the educational aspiration groups in those states are similar.

°Not significant at .05 level of probability.

tions—the more extensive the educational aspirations, the greater the endorsement of work ethic values (this was not true for males in Massachusetts). The
means for this variable are shown in Chart 4-6. On both of these variables, there
was a slight tendency for students in North Carolina to show the greatest and for
Californians to show the least extent of work ethic and leadership values. These
differentiations were small and were not preserved on the graphs except in the
case of North Carolina males on the three-item work ethic scale (Chart 4-6).

Variables 10 and 11, "with friends I like people who are hard workers" and "with friends I expect the best of others" showed slight positive relationships with educational aspirations in four of the state-sex groups. The corresponding means are not shown because of the weakness of the relationships.

The means on variable 9, "by high school graduation people should
know where they are headed in life," are graphed in Chart 4-7. Males of varying
educational aspirations were not different on this variable except that males in
Massachusetts who do not aspire to go to college tend to have much less agreement with this statement. Among the females, there is a tendency for agreement
with the statement to be less strong as educational aspirations increase. This
seems to be in contradiction with our general hypothesis concerning work ethic
values; however, it is reasonable that students aspiring to go to college would be
willing to spend more time determining their life goals. They are not under the
immediate pressure probably felt by many high school seniors not planning to go
to college. Again there was a tendency for North Carolinians as a group to have a
stronger endorsement of this statement, in the direction of a stronger work
ethic.

The results on the item 13, "it is more important to work for the
good of the community than for . . . self-interests," were a little more complex
(Chart 4-8). Male students in Illinois and Massachusetts tend to agree more as
educational aspirations increase. This is not in support of the general work ethic
hypothesis, since the work ethic involves an individualistic rather than col-
lectivistic emphasis. However, it is quite congruent with the increasing concern
with social issues which has been observed among young people. Males in California tend to endorse this statement more strongly if they have limited educational aspirations or if they aspire to graduate from a four-year college (groups
two and three). Males and females in North Carolina tend to show stronger endorsement of the statement regardless of their educational aspirations, which
again is not consistent with the work ethic hypothesis. On the other variables,
North Carolinians tend to show the strongest work ethic values. But in this case
the strongest community interest is shown by North Carolinians. Illinois females
show stronger agreement if they aspire to continue their education beyond four
years of college. The females in the other states did not differ on this item
according to their educational aspirations. Thus the results on this item are
mixed; there is a tendency toward a positive relationship with educational aspirations in some state-sex groups but not in others, and students in North Carolina

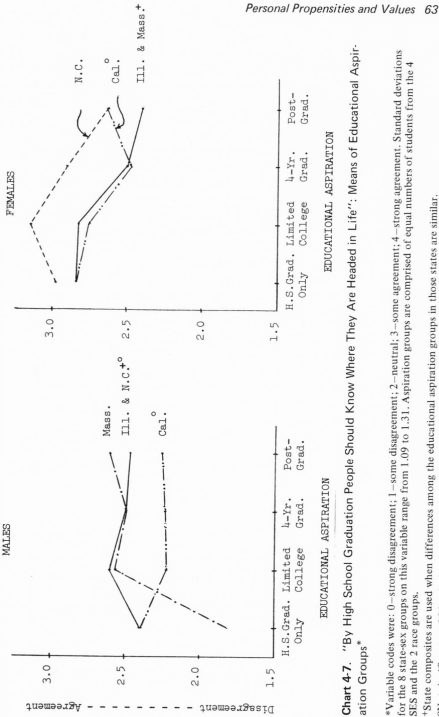

Chart 4-7. "By High School Graduation People Should Know Where They Are Headed in Life": Means of Educational Aspiration Groups*

*Variable codes were: 0—strong disagreement; 1—some disagreement; 2—neutral; 3—some agreement; 4—strong agreement. Standard deviations for the 8 state-sex groups on this variable range from 1.09 to 1.31. Aspiration groups are comprised of equal numbers of students from the 4 SES and the 2 race groups.

+State composites are used when differences among the educational aspiration groups in those states are similar.

oNot significant at .05 level of probability.

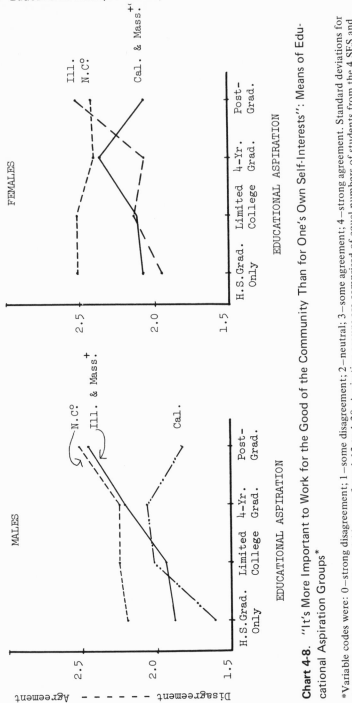

Chart 4-8. "It's More Important to Work for the Good of the Community Than for One's Own Self-Interests": Means of Educational Aspiration Groups*

*Variable codes were: 0–strong disagreement; 1–some disagreement; 2–neutral; 3–some agreement; 4–strong agreement. Standard deviations for the 8 state-sex groups on this variable range from 1.12 to 1.20. Aspiration groups are comprised of equal numbers of students from the 4 SES and the 2 race groups.

+State composites are used when differences among the educational aspiration groups in those states are similar.

°Not significant at .05 level of probability.

appear to profess stronger agreement regardless of their educational aspirations. It is possible that North Carolinian responses to this item were more influenced by regional social values rather than by striving for individual credit for accomplishments, which is a component of work ethic.

Students with differing educational aspirations did not differ, as groups, in their responses to variables 7 and 8, the importance of being able to do at least one thing very well and the importance of putting up a good fight when competing with others. The findings for these variables are not displayed.

Thus there is strong support for the hypothesis that endorsement of work ethic values is positively related to educational aspirations from the three-item work ethic scale and from the item concerning the importance of being a leader. The items " . . . I like people who are hard workers" and " . . . I expect the best of others" were also positively related to educational aspirations, though the differences among the groups on these items were not large. The results on the other items were mixed. It appears that high school students with more extensive educational aspirations in general have stronger work ethic values, but do not necessarily adopt certain facets of what has been taken to be the work ethic, such as an individualistic as opposed to a community orientation, being able to do at least one thing well, or putting up a good fight in competition. In addition students in North Carolina tend to more strongly endorse work ethic ideals, regardless of their educational aspirations.

Attitudes Toward Social Issues

The means on the four variables concerning social issues are shown in Charts 4-9, 4-10, 4-11, and 4-12. These variables are not as highly related to students' educational aspirations as might be expected. This is especially true for men. California males with intermediate educational aspirations (limited or four year) tend to be somewhat more conservative regarding issues of student protest movements and law and order (variables 14 and 17, Charts 4-9 and 4-12) than other students. Agreement that it is morally wrong to refuse to fight in Vietnam (variable 16) is negatively related to educational aspirations for Illinois males. Otherwise there is no evidence for concluding that the attitudes of male high school students regarding these issues are linearly related to their levels of educational aspirations.

For women, agreement with these value statements (which is being taken as the more conservative orientation), other than the one concerning religious meetings, seems generally to be negatively related to educational aspirations. Specifically, this is true for females in California, Illinois, and North Carolina regarding protest movements and law and order (Charts 4-9 and 4-12), and for Illinois females regarding the morality of refusing to fight in Vietnam (Chart 4-11). On this latter issue, Massachusetts females with four-year aspirations are most conservative and those with postgraduate aspirations are least conservative.

It can be noted also that North Carolinians tend generally to adopt

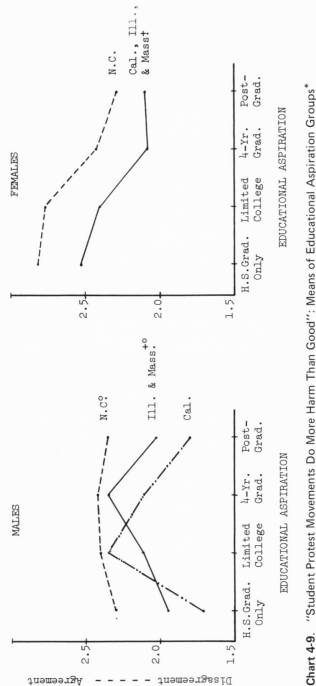

Chart 4-9. "Student Protest Movements Do More Harm Than Good": Means of Educational Aspiration Groups*

*Variable codes were: 0–strong disagreement; 1–some disagreement; 2–neutral; 3–some agreement; 4–strong agreement. Standard deviations for the 8 state-sex groups on this variable range from 1.26 to 1.33. Aspiration groups are comprised of equal numbers of students from the 4 SES and the 2 race groups.

[+]State composites are used when differences among the educational aspiration groups in those states are similar.

[o]Not significant at .05 level of probability.

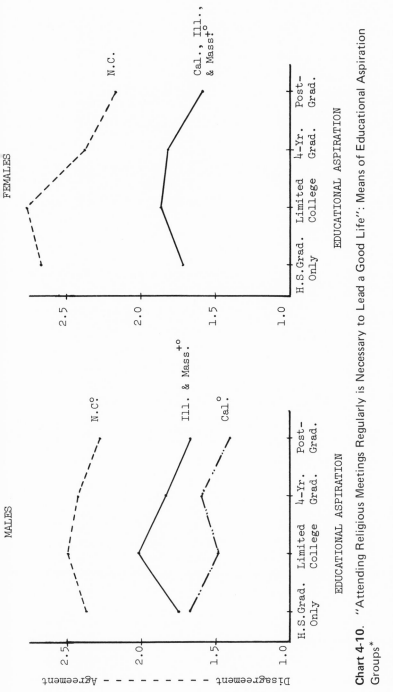

Chart 4-10. "Attending Religious Meetings Regularly is Necessary to Lead a Good Life": Means of Educational Aspiration Groups*

*Variable codes were: 0—strong disagreement; 1—some disagreement; 2—neutral; 3—some agreement; 4—strong agreement. Standard deviations for the 8 state-sex groups on this variable range from 1.21 to 1.34. Aspiration groups are comprised of equal numbers of students from the 4 SES and the 2 race groups.

+State composites are used when differences among the educational aspiration groups in those states are similar.

°Not significant at .05 level of probability.

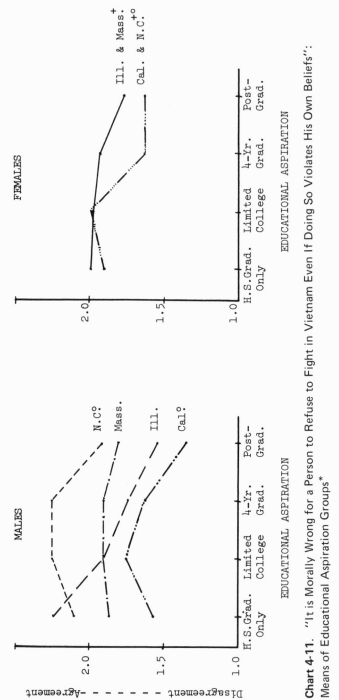

Chart 4-11. "It is Morally Wrong for a Person to Refuse to Fight in Vietnam Even If Doing So Violates His Own Beliefs": Means of Educational Aspiration Groups*

*Variable codes were: 0—strong disagreement; 1—some disagreement; 2—neutral; 3—some agreement; 4—strong agreement. Standard deviations for the 8 state-sex groups on this variable range from 1.30 to 1.46. Aspiration groups are comprised of equal numbers of students from the 4 SES and the 2 race groups.

+State composites are used when differences among the educational aspiration groups in those states are similar.

°Not significant at .05 level of probability.

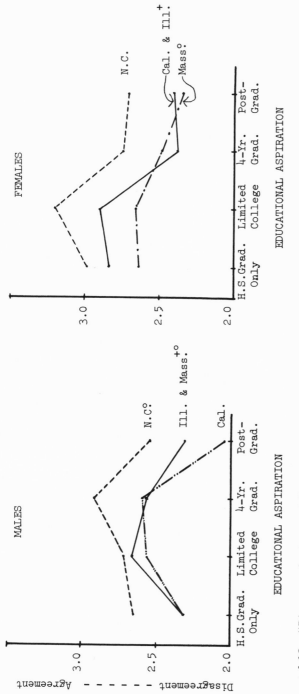

Chart 4-12. "Disrespect for Law and Order Is The Major Problem in Our Society Today": Means of Educational Aspiration Groups*

*Variable codes were: 0—strong disagreement; 1—some disagreement; 2—neutral; 3—some agreement; 4—strong agreement. Standard deviations for the 8 state-sex groups on this variable range from 1.17 to 1.28. Aspiration groups are comprised of equal numbers of students from the 4 SES and the 2 race groups.

+State composites are used when differences among the educational aspiration groups in those states are similar.

°Not significant at .05 level of probability.

(Massachusetts Females)

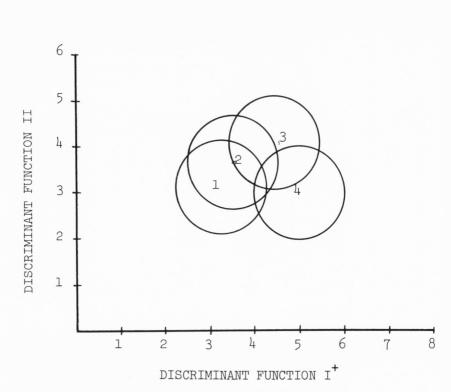

DISCRIMINANT FUNCTION I[+]

Chart 4-13. Separation of Educational Aspiration Groups on the Basis of Personal Propensities and Values[*]

[*]Educational aspiration groups are: 1–high school graduation only; 2–limited college; 3–graduation from a four-year college; 4–postgraduate attendance.
[+]Discriminant functions I and II summarize the ways in which the educational aspiration groups are distinguished on the basis of this variable set. The scales are in terms of standard deviation units with aspiration group 4 set at points (5, 3). The circles represent the estimated dispersion of approximately 50 percent of the students in each aspiration group.

the most conservative attitudes on these issues and that the item about religious worship is related to educational aspirations only for North Carolina females, who tend to value religious worship less if they expect to complete four or more years of college (but still much more than students in any of the other three states).

Thus these results are certainly mixed, and there is no clear-cut linear relationship between the attitudes high school seniors admit to concerning these social issues and their educational aspirations, especially for males. The lack of such a relationship for males is surprising when considering the results

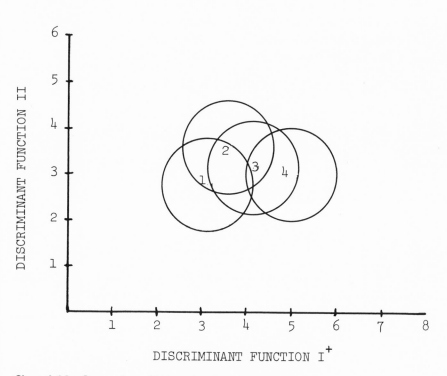

Chart 4-14. Separation of Educational Aspiration Groups on the Basis of Personal Propensities and Values*

*Educational aspiration groups are: 1—high school graduation only; 2—limited college; 3—graduation from a four-year college; 4—postgraduate attendance.
+Discriminant functions I and II summarize the ways in which the educational aspiration groups are distinguished on the basis of this variable set. The scales are in terms of standard deviation units with aspiration group 4 set at points (5, 3). The circles represent the estimated dispersion of approximately 50 percent of the students in each aspiration group.

obtained by Dagenais and Marascuilo, as well as others. The expected relationships were obtained in some cases for females, but not consistently.

THE DISCRIMINANT ANALYSES

It has been shown that the variable set "Personal Propensities and Values" does differentiate among students with differing educational aspirations and the nature of this differentiation has been discussed in terms of specific variables. A look at the discriminant analyses and the extent of the differentiation follows.

(North Carolina Males)

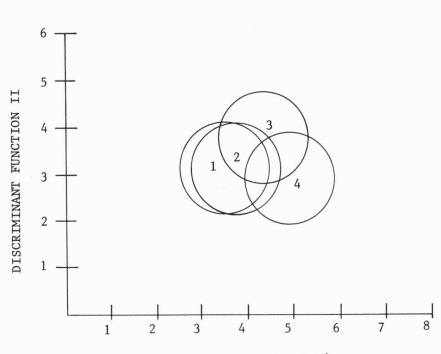

DISCRIMINANT FUNCTION I[+]

Chart 4-15.   Separation of Education Aspiration Groups on the Basis of Personal Propensities and Values[*]

[*]Educational aspiration groups are: 1—high school graduation only; 2—limited college; 3—graduation from a four-year college; 4—postgraduate attendance.
[+]Discriminant functions I and II summarize the ways in which the educational aspiration groups are distinguished on the basis of this variable set. The scales are in terms of standard deviation units with aspiration group 4 set at points (5, 3). The circles represent the estimated dispersion of approximately 50 percent of the students in each aspiration group.

In discussing specific variables, there were a number of instances in which the distinctions among educational aspiration groups are stronger for females than for males. As might be expected, then, the analyses showing the greatest differentiations among students of differing educational expectations were of females; specifically, Massachusetts females. The separation graph for this state-sex group is in Chart 4-13.

In all of the state-sex groups, it can be said that the first discriminant function is primarily an intellectual orientation factor with an additional strong contribution from leadership values (the importance of being a leader). In Chart

4-13, the more extensive the educational aspirations, the higher the position on the function (horizontal axis). The second discriminant function (vertical axis) is less easily interpreted. It is a factor which has contributions from autonomy and negative work ethic. However, this is not as consistent across the eight state-sex groups; in two of the groups, the contribution of autonomy is replaced by theoretical orientation-science, and in one case the three-item work ethic is not involved. In Chart 4-13 groups two and three (intermediate aspirations) are slightly higher on this dimension.

All of the eight state sex groups showed very similar patterns of differentiation among the educational aspiration groups. The male group with the greatest degree of differentiation, shown in Chart 4-14, was Massachusetts males. The group with the least extent of differentiation was North Carolina males. The separation graph for North Carolina males is given in Chart 4-15.

Looking again at Charts 4-14 and 4-15, high school students expecting to complete more than four years of college are fairly well distinguished from seniors not expecting to go to college at all. This differentiation is due largely to the intellectual orientation and importance of leadership factor (first discriminant function). Groups two and three are intermediate on intellectual orientation, but the clarity of distinction is aided by some differentiation on the second discriminant function.

North Carolina males (Chart 4-15) was the only state-sex group in which educational aspiration groups one and two look almost identical in terms of this variable set. There is still some differentiation of students aspiring to complete four years of college and students aspiring to complete more than four years (groups three and four).

CONCLUSION

Students with aspirations for extensive education beyond high school also have stronger intellectual orientations than do their peers who aspire to less formal education beyond high school. There is a clear linear relationship between how long students aspire to stay in school and the importance they place on intellectual values. High school seniors aspiring to go to college are also more likely to ascribe to work ethic ideals. These ideals have particular reference to the importance of leadership; the need for hard work, determination, and ambition. As a group, these students do not necessarily put self-interests above those of community needs. In fact, the high aspirant is more inclined to be committed to community interests than are low aspirants. The intellectual orientation and leadership values appeared to be the most pervasive qualities differentiating the educational aspiration groups in the discriminant analysis, taking the entire variable set as a whole.

Women who have aspirations for extensive higher education tend more than other groups in this study to deviate from conservative middle class values. For example, more of them agree that protest movements are beneficial, that it is not wrong to refuse to fight in Vietnam, and that disrespect for law and order is not the major problem in American society. Fewer men of comparable educational aspirations share these attitudes. This difference between the sexes seems congruent with recent research which shows that young women are more extensively involved in student protests movements than are young men (Dagenais and Marascuilo, 1971). In view of the special barriers to continuing education for women it is likely, indeed, that such high aspirants would be independent of mind and committed to social change (Tillery, 1962).

The results of this analysis call for greater recognition of the varying needs students have in relation to their quite different educational and life goals. The predominant academic orientation of many high schools simply does not fit the practical, "now" orientation of many young people, especially those not having extensive educational aspirations. However, this lack of fit is not restricted to those young people who reject college, but would seem to be characteristic of many potential new students to higher education with limited educational aspirations and with little orientation to intellectual or scholastic values (Cross, 1971). No more adequate is the schismatic nature of many high school programs which grossly divides students into the college-bound with traditional academic experiences and the work-bound who are often deprived of opportunities for fuller development of their talents and the exploration of options.

The challenges to curriculum and guidance leaders and to practitioners in serving the diversity of young people who do in fact have extensive options for education beyond high school or for individual development quite outside formal educational institutions are profound. The student who does not aspire to attend college is perhaps handicapped in today's society and institutions by his lower autonomy and intellectual orientations and the fact that he is less oriented to the work ethic. He needs new opportunities to explore alternatives for personal identity and for developing talents and skills. Among the possibilities are early explorations of self and of experiences which help develop special abilities. Part of this process would involve far greater information for students about college and other opportunities beyond high school.

College-aspiring students generally are more intellectually oriented, place greater importance on work ethic, and are more liberal in their attitudes. However, this is a continuum; two-year aspirants are generally more like noncollege aspirants than like their peers who aspire to graduate school. These diverse value orientations have meaning not only for where they go to college, for what kinds of education, and for how long, but should also influence the nature of developmental programs while in high school. The traditional academic fare is not necessarily the best way to prepare many of the new students who will enter American colleges. A wider range of skills, abilities, and interests is being and will increasingly be honored in higher education. This suggests the need for new patterns of articulation between school and college.

The concerns which many young people have for social issues should influence the development of programs which promote constructive and satisfying expression of such concerns. These might include studies of ethnic groups; the changing roles of women in contemporary societies; and ecological issues such as pollution, population, and urban renewal. In brief, enrichment of school programs and services seems inevitable if meaning is to be given to the identification, nurture, and development of a wider range of talents, interests, and opportunities for youth who have varying intellectual and value orientations.

Finally, an interesting state difference in attitudes and values of high school students should be pointed out. In general, when compared with the other three states, high school students in North Carolina appear to be more conservative and conventional. They are, in short, quite supportive of American middle class values. They also are more committed to the work ethic and are less autonomous than are students from the other states. This finding seems congruent with the relatively low urban development of North Carolina and with its traditions of social conservatism.

The area of personal values and attitudes has proved to be useful in helping to explain differences among students who have different educational aspirations. There are implications for high school programs, and there may be features of the high school experience which have led to the differentiations that have been observed among students with differing educational expectations.

Chapter Five

Information-Gathering Behavior

It has been shown that high school seniors with differing educational aspirations can be differentiated in terms of their academic attitudes and behaviors, and that in doing so two dimensions were primarily involved. One of these was interpreted as an academic-intellectual dimension; the second was interpreted as a dimension of college orientation which is nonacademic, with emphasis on occupational preparation. This theme was then extended by findings concerning personality and value differences. For example, students' dispositions toward intellectual values were shown to be positively related to their educational aspirations. It would seem useful at this point, then, to examine the ways in which educational aspirations, bearing in mind their manifest relationships with academic and intellectual orientations, are in turn related to information gathering about college and about jobs. In doing so, attention is being focused more directly on developmental phenomena in the maturation of youth.

REVIEW OF THE LITERATURE

Information-gathering behavior has been studied extensively in the context of vocational development (Super et al., 1957; Super and Overstreet, 1960; Crites, 1965; Gribbons and Lohnes, 1969). Specificity of information about preferred occupations was one of the indices of vocational maturity defined by Super in the Career Pattern Study (Super and Overstreet, 1960). Similarly, Gribbons and Lohnes (1969) developed two informational variables, one concerning occupations and the other concerning curricula, as a part of their Readiness for Vocational Planning Index. Information-gathering behavior is conceived of as an important facet in the development of adolescents. In the conceptualization of vocational development, adolescents are in the "exploration" stage; their needs, interests, capacities, values, and opportunities begin to be synthesized, and reali-

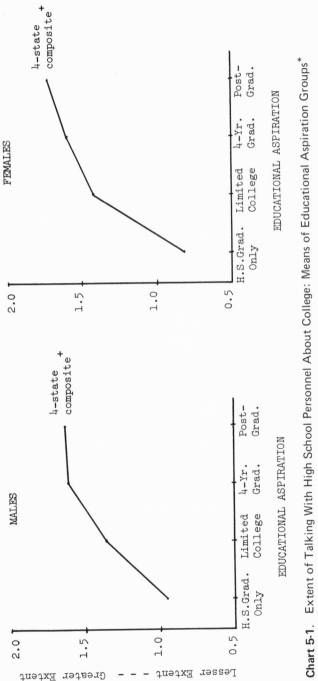

Chart 5-1. Extent of Talking With High School Personnel About College: Means of Educational Aspiration Groups*

*Standard deviations for the 8 state-sex groups on this variable range from .69 to .77. Aspiration groups are comprised of equal numbers of students from the 4 SES and the 2 race groups.

+State composites are used when differences among the educational aspiration groups in those states are similar.

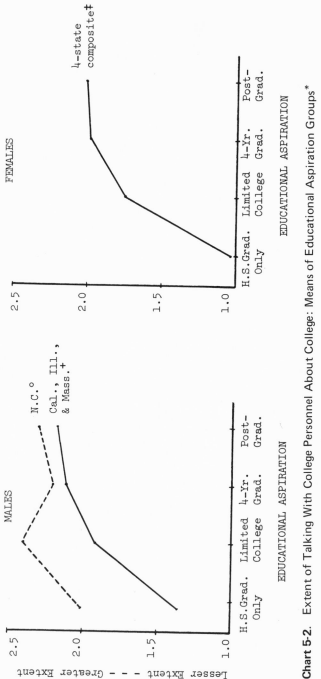

Chart 5-2. Extent of Talking With College Personnel About College: Means of Educational Aspiration Groups*

*Standard deviations for the 8 state-sex groups on this variable range from 1.12 to 1.46. Aspiration groups are comprised of equal numbers of students from the 4 SES and the 2 race groups.

+State composites are used when differences among the educational aspiration groups in those states are similar.

○Not significant at .05 level of probability.

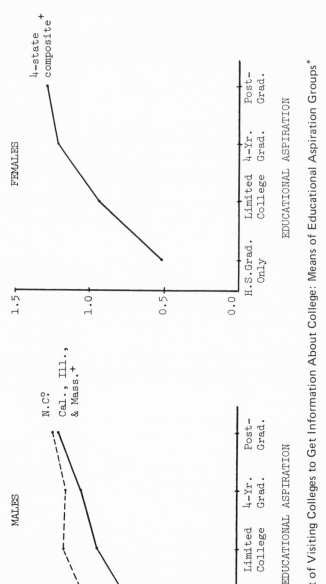

Chart 5-3.   Extent of Visiting Colleges to Get Information About College: Means of Educational Aspiration Groups*

*Standard deviations for the 8 state-sex groups on this variable range from .73 to .84. Aspiration groups are comprised of equal numbers of students from the 4 SES and the 2 race groups.

+State composites are used when differences among the educational aspiration groups in those states are similar.

°Not significant at .05 level of probability.

ty considerations need to be given more weight. A large element involved in such reality testing is the gathering of factual information.

As an indication of the importance of information gathering and of vocational maturity, in an eleven-year follow-up study, Gribbons and Lohnes (1969) administered their eight Readiness for Vocational Planning scales to junior high school students. There was a strong relationship between these measures and the educational plans (college versus noncollege) when the students were tenth graders and when they were twelfth graders. In addition, the eighth grade Readiness for Vocational Planning measures were effective predictors of college versus noncollege outcomes two and four years after high school graduation. In each case, the strongest relationship was with the "factors in curriculum choice" scale, which is primarily an extent-of-information dimension.

In the present study, it was expected that the educational aspirations of high school seniors would be mirrored by the extent of their information-gathering activities about college and about jobs.

THE VARIABLE SET

This variable set consists of six variables, three having to do with information about college and three having to do with information about jobs. However, these are assessments not of the amount of knowledge held by students about jobs and about college, but rather assessments of the extent to which they have engaged in information-gathering activities. The information-gathering variables follow.

Information Gathering About College

1. Talking with teachers and counselors at the high school level regarding college
2. Talking with college students, admissions officers, financial aid counselors, and representatives of college athletic departments
3. Visiting and taking tours of college campuses

Information Gathering About Jobs

4. Talking with teachers and counselors about jobs
5. Learning about jobs from television, radio, or printed matter
6. Visiting, talking with, and watching people working at jobs of interest or talking with prospective employers

In each case, the measure obtained is an assessment of the extent of the specified activity. A more complete description of these six variables is in Appendix A.

THE MULTIVARIATE ANALYSES OF VARIANCE

The variable set as a system differentiated among educational aspiration groups in all state-sex groups regardless of race or SES. The multivariate and univariate statistics are shown in Appendix B.

Information Gathering About College

The results show that high school seniors with differing educational aspirations differ in the extent to which they engaged in activities to gather information about college. The more extensive the educational aspirations, the more extensive the information-gathering activity. This is true regardless of race, SES, state of residence, or sex, except that males in North Carolina of differing educational aspirations did not differ from each other regarding talking with college personnel or visiting college campuses. Instead, students not aspiring to go to college engaged in these activities just as much as those with more extensive educational aspirations. The means for the educational aspiration groups on these three variables are graphed in Charts 5-1, 5-2, and 5-3.

Information Gathering About Jobs

As a rule, the educational aspiration groups do not differ in the extent of information-gathering activities about jobs. The means of the groups on variables 4, 5, and 6 are shown in Charts 5-4, 5-5, and 5-6. Here again the male students in North Carolina reported engaging in more information-gathering behavior than other groups. This difference between North Carolina males and the male students in the other three states is not large, but it does occur consistently.

Although information gathering about jobs was not shown to be related to students' educational aspirations, the elevation of students' scores on variables 4, 5, and 6 as compared to variables 1, 2, and 3 indicates that students in all of the aspiration groups engaged in at least as much information-gathering activity about jobs as did students with extensive educational aspirations about college. This is perhaps difficult to see on the charts, since the means are not standardized and the several variables do not all have the same range of possible scores. However, variables 1, 3, 4, and 6 had the same range (0 to 2) and variables 2 and 5 had the same range (0 to 4). Rough comparisons between college information-gathering activities and job information-gathering activities can be made within these two sets. Thus, comparing variables 1 and 3 (Charts 5-1 and 5-3) to variables 4 and 6 (Charts 5-4 and 5-6), it is evident that the amount of information gathering undertaken by all students concerning jobs is roughly the same as the amount of information gathering undertaken by postgraduate aspirants about colleges. A similar observation can be made in comparing variable 2 (Chart 5-2) to variable 5 (Chart 5-5).

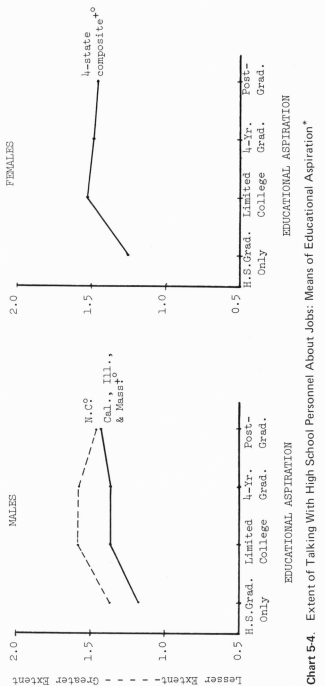

Chart 5-4. Extent of Talking With High School Personnel About Jobs: Means of Educational Aspiration*

*Standard deviations for the 8 state-sex groups on this variable range from .69 to .84. Aspiration groups are comprised of equal numbers of students from the 4 SES and the 2 race groups.

+State composites are used when differences among the educational aspiration groups in those states are similar.

°Not significant at .05 level of probability.

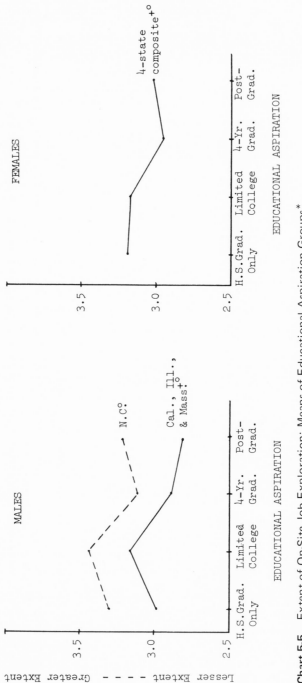

Chart 5-5. Extent of On-Site Job Exploration: Means of Educational Aspiration Groups*

*Standard deviations for the 8 state-sex groups on this variable range from 1.13 to 1.31. Aspiration groups are comprised of equal numbers of students from the 4 SES and the 2 race groups.

+State composites are used when differences among the educational aspiration groups of those states are similar.

°Not significant at .05 level of probability.

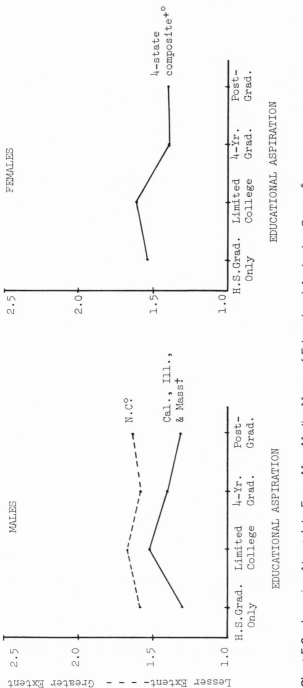

Chart 5-6. Learning About Jobs From Mass Media: Means of Educational Aspiration Groups*

*Standard deviations for the 8 state-sex groups on this variable range from .63 to .78. Aspiration groups are comprised of equal numbers of students from the 4 SES and the 2 race groups.

+State composites are used when differences among the educational aspiration groups in those states are similar.

°Not significant at .05 level of probability.

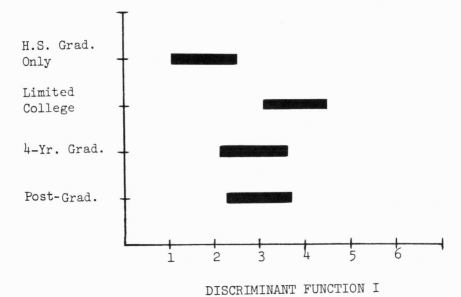

DISCRIMINANT FUNCTION I

Chart 5–7. Separation of Educational Aspiration Groups on the Basis of Information-Gathering Behavior*

*This graph depicts the relative separation of the educational aspiration groups on discriminant function I. The scale is in terms of standard deviation units with the Post-Grad group set at point 3. The length of the bars represents the estimated range, on discriminant function I, of the dispersion of 50 percent of the students in each educational aspiration group.

THE DISCRIMINANT ANALYSES

The extent of differentiation among educational expectation groups in terms of this variable set was relatively small. The second discriminant function in each of the eight analyses was noninterpretable and provided essentially no distinctions among the groups. For this reason, the usual kind of separation graph will not be employed. Instead, the estimated dispersion of 50 percent of the students in each group on the first discriminant function is displayed by bars above a horizontal axis representing the first function.

The greatest differentiation occurred with Illinois females. This is

(Massachusetts Females)

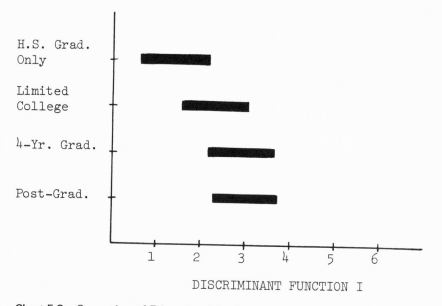

DISCRIMINANT FUNCTION I

Chart 5-8. Separation of Educational Aspiration Groups on the Basis of Information Gathering Behavior*

*This graph depicts the relative separation of the educational aspiration groups on discriminant function I. The scale is in terms of standard deviation units with the post-grad group set at point 3.

The length of the bars represents the estimated range, on discriminant function I, of the dispersion of 50 percent of the students in each educational aspiration group.

shown in Chart 5-7. This pattern of differentiation, with group 1 the lowest and group 2 the highest, was unusual. The other seven state-sex groups had a pattern similar to that shown in Charts 5-8 and 5-9. Chart 5-8, Massachusetts females, shows a relatively large (for this variable set) extent of differentiation. Chart 5-9 depicts California males with a smaller degree of differentiation among the groups.

The first discriminant function appears to be a bipolar college-job factor, except in the case of North Carolina males. What is different about men in North Carolina is that they report engaging in more information-gathering activities about college even when not aspiring to go to college. In the other

(California Males)

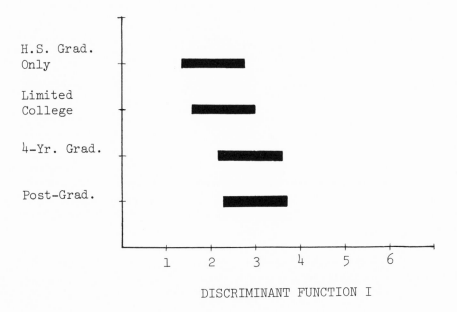

H.S. Grad.
Only

Limited
College

4-Yr. Grad.

Post-Grad.

1   2   3   4   5   6

DISCRIMINANT FUNCTION I

Chart 5-9. Separation of Educational Aspiration Groups on the
Basis of Information Gathering Behavior*

This graph depicts the relative separation of the educational aspiration groups on discriminant function I. The scale is in terms of standard deviation units with the post-grad group
set at point 3.
The length of the bars represents the estimated range, on discriminant function I, of the
dispersion of 50 percent of the students in each educational aspiration group.

seven state-sex groups, information-gathering activities about college contribute
heavily and, to a lesser degree, information-gathering activities about jobs contribute negatively. As seen above (with the exception of Illinois females), this
dimension is positively related to educational aspirations: students with extensive educational aspirations score more highly on this dimension than do students with less extensive educational aspirations. The negative contribution of
information-gathering activities about jobs suggests that job information gathering is in some way inversely related to educational aspirations, a notion that was
clearly not apparent in examining the means of the educational aspiration groups
on the individual variables. The probable explanation for this lies in the moderate positive correlation which exists in the data between information gathering

about jobs and information gathering about college. Even though there are essentially no educational aspiration group mean differences in job information gathering, the discriminant analysis takes advantage of the positive correlation to aid in the discrimination. An idealized example of how this works is shown in Chart 5-10. This shows the four educational aspiration groups in a scatterdiagram of the relationship between job information gathering and college information gathering. The slant of the elipses of each of the aspiration groups represents the positive relationship between the two information-gathering variables, showing that individuals who have high scores on one of the variables tend to have high scores also on the other variable, and vice versa. Also, the diagram shows the aspiration group differences in information gathering about college and the lack of group differences in job information-gathering behavior. Now, it can be seen that, even though there are no group differences in job information gathering, for individuals scoring at the points designated X, Y, or Z on college information gathering, knowing whether they have a high or a low score on job information gathering aids in distinguishing aspiration group membership. For example, if an individual scoring at point X on college information gathering has a high score on job information gathering, he would be distinguished as a member of the noncollege aspiration group (group 1). But if an individual scoring at point X on college information gathering has a low score on job information gathering, he would be a member of the limited college aspiration group (group 2).

Thus, in the context of the entire variable set, the extent of job information gathering can be a useful discriminator of the educational aspiration groups, even though there are no group mean differences in such behavior.

CONCLUSION

The extent to which students engage in activities to gather information about college is positively related to their educational aspirations. The aspiration groups do not differ in the extent of information gathering about jobs. However, this aspect of vocational maturity is still predictive of educational aspiration groups membership because of the kinds of relationships illustrated in Chart 5-10.

The positive relationship between college information gathering and educational aspirations is a natural manifestation of the differing academic and intellectual orientations, and of the realities of the situation in which college aspirants are more likely to be actually anticipating college attendance and have need of information about college, whereas this is not the case for noncollege aspirants. The relatively high level of job information gathering for all aspiration groups also makes sense in that most individuals ultimately need to be concerned with job choice, although this is not such an immediate need for college-goers except as it may affect their choice of college program.

The relatively high information-gathering activities reported by

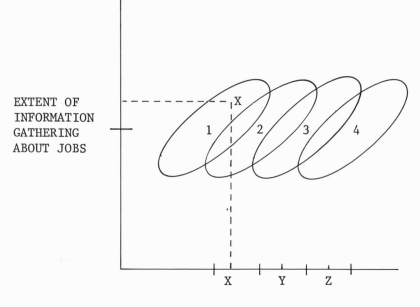

EXTENT OF INFORMATION
GATHERING ABOUT COLLEGE

Chart 5-10. Hypothetical Scatterdiagram of Correlation Between Job Information-Gathering and College Information-Gathering, Showing Job Information-Gathering as an Educational Aspiration Group Discriminator

NOTE: Aspiration groups are: 1—high school graduation only; 2—limited college; 3—four-year graduation; and 4—postgraduate degree.

North Carolina seniors can be partially understood by their generally positive attitudes toward the helpfulness of others in educational and career matters which has been seen consistently in SCOPE data through the years. Since information gathering usually involves other people, such activities would very likely be facilitated by the perceived helpfulness of others.

Interestingly, the type of mechanism illustrated in Chart 5-10 suggests that for some individuals, a higher degree of vocational maturity, as manifested in the extent of job information-gathering activity, is likely to be concomitant with less extensive educational aspirations, and vice versa. It is probably not inappropriate that some college aspirants may be less concerned about job information than peers with less extensive educational aspirations. One function of college going, at least initially, is that of exploration among different fields of endeavor. In this sense, the less extensive the educational aspirations, the greater the immediate need for such vocational maturity.

Chapter Six

Problems and Conflicts

INTRODUCTION

Adolescence is widely recognized as a period of problems, doubts, questions, and dissonance in the transition from childhood to adulthood. This transition involves movement from dependence to independence and the development of adult roles and identity. The problems and conflicts of adolescence are common themes in the writings of a number of developmental theorists. This chapter, then, extends the concern with developmental phenomena to a broader context than in previous chapters.

The purpose of this chapter is to report SCOPE's findings about the relationships of some problems and conflicts, as reported by high school seniors, to their aspirations for education beyond high school. As far as the SCOPE staff has determined, there has been no other research dealing with this relationship. It seems self-evident, however, that knowing more about how certain problems experienced by students in the prime of adolescence are related to educational aspirations could be useful to high school personnel as they endeavor to understand and to work with students. These problems and conflicts are broadly grouped into two classes: personal and interpersonal. Brief attention will also be given to the relative helpfulness of certain significant others with a broad spectrum of problems confronting high school students. Thus, this chapter reports the analyses of three variable sets: Personal Problems and Conflicts, Interpersonal Problems and Conflicts, and Helpfulness of Others. Included in these variable sets are measures assessing whether or not certain potential problems have been or are manifest, the immediacy of certain problems, and the extent of agreement with significant others regarding social issues. Together these variables can be identified under three broad problem areas—college and academic problems, job choice, and personal-social issues.

Because the theories of Erikson have been useful in this study of adolescent decision making, some of his most relevant ideas will be briefly discussed. Some attention will also be given to other research on problems of adolescence, although such literature review is by no means exhaustive.

REVIEW OF THE LITERATURE ON ADOLESCENT DEVELOPMENT

Erikson (1956) sees the primary developmental task of adolescence to be identity formation. The adolescent process is complete only when the individual has subordinated his childhood identifications to a new kind of identification. Erikson (1959) believes that the final identity is superordinated to any single identification with individuals of the past: It includes all significant identifications but it also alters them in order to make a unique and reasonably coherent whole. These new identifications force the young individual into choices and decisions which will, with increasing immediacy, lead to a more final self-definition, to "irreversible" role patterns, and thus to commitments "for life."

In short, adolescence is a life stage in which a lasting pattern of "inner identity" is developed from previous significant identifications. This is for most young adults a formidable task fraught with problems and conflicts. Most high school seniors are probably in the throes of this battle and consequently experiencing problems concerning what kind of person to be. In addition, their altering of previous identifications, particularly those in the home, may bring about differences between themselves and significant others with respect to issues which are of importance to them.

Erikson (1956) sees the development of identity as consisting of a number of more specific developmental tasks. These have to do with such things as vocational identity, sexual identity, ideology, and self-certainty, among others. The danger of inadequately coping with various developmental tasks in adolescence is what Erikson refers to as identity confusion or identity diffusion (Erikson, 1962, 1963).

Marcia (1966, 1967, 1968), building directly on Erikson, has done some work towards operationalizing and measuring stages of ego identity in adolescence. This was done, using an interview technique, in terms of two parameters which are important in Erikson's conceptualizations: crisis and commitment. The four ego identity statuses measured by Marcia are ego identity, moratorium, foreclosure, and identity diffusion. Each of these are defined and measured in terms of crisis and commitment. Ego identity involves having experienced a period of crisis (serious doubt and questioning) and having resolved the crisis in terms of a definite commitment. Moratorium is a stage of crisis in which an individual has only vague commitments. Foreclosure is characterized by very strong commitment arrived at without any serious questioning or crisis, probably through appropriating parental values. And identity diffusion, which may or may not involve crisis, can be described as a striking lack of commitment.

Marcia measured ego identity statuses with respect to occupation and ideology, using college students as subjects who were in stages of very late adolescence if not early adulthood. Studying correlates of ego identity stages, he found that individuals who have achieved ego identity and those in moratorium are better at concept attainment tasks. They changed their opinions of themselves with personality-relevant feedback less than did individuals characterized by foreclosure or identity diffusion. Foreclosed individuals, according to Marcia's findings, tend to have the most authoritarian views and to set unrealistically high goals. Persons in moratorium are most anxious.

In the context of identity formation and the development of roles, Barbara Sherman, co-director of the SCOPE Project, has done a detailed analysis, using SCOPE data, of role explorations underlying the decision-making processes of eleventh graders (Sherman, 1971). An important consideration in her approach is the integration of role theory with developmental theory. Sherman's paper provides a substantial treatment of some of the processes involved in the changing role identifications of adolescents. Among other things, her findings indicate that there are certain "stabilizing" roles which are extended from interactions with parents to interactions with peers and school personnel. On the other hand, it is in relations with peers that young people seem to find the most opportunity for experimenting with new roles. Teachers and counselors in a sense occupy a special position: There was an apparent identification on the part of students with teachers and counselors in terms of "prototypic child roles." It was hypothesized that this identification with the child aspects of significant others may play an important part in the development of adult roles, in which case teachers and counselors have the potential of offering themselves as attractive adult role models.

REVIEW OF OTHER RELEVANT LITERATURE

Turning to some examples of research dealing specifically with inventoried problems and agreement with significant others on certain issues, Adams (1964), in a cross-sectional study of students ranging in age from ten to nineteen, asked four thousand boys and girls to report the problem causing them the greatest difficulty, and the most important problem encountered by peers. Through the latter inquiry he sought to elicit problems students might be reluctant to report about themselves. The most frequently occurring problem areas were those associated with school, with interpersonal relationships, with family, and with financial matters. School problems were by far the most frequently mentioned, usually involving difficulties with academic work. From age eleven on, academic problems were of major concern for boys, perhaps because of increased emphasis on science and engineering and on college preparation, but such problems were of less concern to girls. Girls were much more concerned with interpersonal problems than boys. After age thirteen or fourteen, there was a tendency for problems with peers to decrease. Although problems of work were of less frequency overall and were seldom mentioned before ages fourteen to fifteen, after age seventeen the choice of a vocation was the major problem for both sexes (Adams, 1964).

Trent and Medsker (1968) found that students who withdrew from college tended to indicate more personal problems than did persisters, especially in the areas of social life and finances. In addition, four-year persisters who did not attain a degree reported more such problems than did four-year persisters who did earn a degree. Similarly, these degree earners had fewer academic problems. However, those not earning a degree indicated more problems than did those who withdrew. The predominant academic problem was "learning how to study" (Trent and Medsker, 1968).

Kandel and Lesser (1969) studied the agreement of high school students with best friend and mother on educational plans. The results indicate that agreement with mother is higher than agreement with best friend. However, agreement with parents on educational goals goes together with agreement with friends, whereas adolescents who disagree with their parents are also likely to disagree with their friends. The authors concluded that interactions with peers support the values of parents (Kandel and Lesser, 1969).

Some aspects of the upheaval and reorientation during adolescence have been described. In this chapter the emphasis is on adolescent problems rather than crisis per se. It is likely, however, that problems in the areas of college, job choice, and personal-social issues are reflections of what Erikson and others have referred to as crisis. As such, the experiencing of problems is an important part of the adolescent process. The extent of agreement with significant others is also an important facet of this process which is related to changing role identifications.

In looking at the relationship of problems and conflicts of high school seniors to their educational aspirations, no attempt has been made to determine the extent of identity formation or changing role identifications. The data are not suitable for this purpose. For example, indication of the existence of problems or the immediacy of problems may suggest crisis, but does not indicate the resolution. In addition, where problems associated with college or work are concerned, it is not known whether this represents a concern because the high school years are nearly over—with the concommitant pressure to decide what one will do immediately after high school—or whether it represents a serious questioning which will lead to strong educational or career commitments. Nevertheless, viewing the results in the context of identity crisis and formation is likely to enhance the understanding of the problems and conflicts of high school students as related to their educational aspirations.

THE VARIABLE SETS

Appendix A provides a complete specification of the variables in these analyses. In brief, the three variable sets are as follows:

Problems and Conflicts—Personal

A. College and Academic Variables
1. Is deciding what your college major will be a problem now?
2. Extent of incongruity between actual and aspired high school grades.
3. Is deciding what kind of student to be a problem now?
4. Has finding out which college best suits your abilities and interests been a problem?
5. Has deciding what to do if rejected by first choice college been a problem?
6. When will it be (has it been) most difficult to choose between going to college to develop a philosophy of life or to prepare for a job? (immediacy of problem)
7. When will it be (has it been) most difficult to choose between applying for a job which is now available or going to school to prepare for a better job? (immediacy of problem)

B. Job and Career Variables
8. Congruence between first choice, second choice, and actual anticipated occupation.
9. Has deciding what to do if you don't get the job you want been a problem?
10. Has learning how your interests fit with different jobs been a problem?
11. Has finding out about job requirements been a problem?
12. Has finding out where to train for the job you want been a problem?

C. Personal-Social Issue Variables
13. Is where you stand on politics a problem now?
14. Is where you stand on religion a problem now?
15. Is what kind of person to be a problem now?
16. When will it be (has it been) most difficult to choose between trying to control what happens to you or taking things as they come? (immediacy of problem)
17. When will it be (has it been) most difficult to choose between doing something you know you're good at or trying something you've never done before? (immediacy of problem)
18. When will it be (has it been) most difficult to choose between keeping problems to yourself or talking to others who might help you? (immediacy of problem)

Problems and Conflicts—Interpersonal

A. College Choice Variables
1. Has working out difficulties with your parents about which college to attend been a problem?
2. When has it been most difficult to decide between choosing between a

major you like or choosing a major your parents want for you? (immediacy of problem)

3. Extent of agreement with parents on choice of major.
4. Extent of agreement with counselor and best-liked teacher on choice of major.

B. Occupational Variable
5. Extent of agreement with parents on aspired career.

C. Personal-Social Issue Variables
The following five variables assess agreement with significant others on six personal-social issues. The six issues are:

By high school graduation people should know where they are headed in life and what they want to become.

Student protest movements do more harm than good.

It is more important to work for the good of the community than for one's own self interests.

Attending religious meetings regularly is necessary to lead a good life.

It is morally wrong for a person to refuse to fight in Vietnam even if doing so violates his own beliefs.

Disrespect for law and order is the major problem in our society today.

6. Extent of agreement with mother on above issues.
7. Extent of agreement with father on above issues.
8. Extent of agreement with best-liked teacher on above issues.
9. Extent of agreement with best-liked girl on above issues.
10. Extent of agreement with best-liked boy on above issues.

Helpfulness of Others

The following five variables assess the relative helpfulness of significant others with fourteen selected potential problems, many of which are the same problems inventoried in the previous two variable sets. The list of the fourteen problems and specific scoring procedures for these variables is in Appendix A. The variables indicate relative overall helpfulness of:

1. Best-liked teacher
2. Counselor
3. Mother
4. Father
5. Peers

THE MULTIVARIATE ANALYSES OF VARIANCE:
PROBLEMS AND CONFLICTS—PERSONAL

In each of the eight state-sex groups, personal problems and conflicts distinguish among students of differing educational aspirations. This relationship does not depend on race or SES except in the case of North Carolina females. For North Carolina females, the ways in which educational aspiration groups differ depend on the level of SES and on race. Attention will be given to these phenomena with respect to the individual variables involved. The multivariate and univariate statistics for these eight analyses are summarized in Appendix B.

College and Academic Factors

Two of the seven variables concerning academic problems did not distinguish at all among educational aspiration groups. There is very little incongruity, on the average, between actual and aspired grades (variable 2) regardless of students' educational aspirations. Similarly, choosing between going to college to develop a philosophy of life versus to prepare for a job (variable 6) is, on the average, not an immediate concern of high school seniors. This is a problem that students have very likely either dealt with earlier or expect to deal with in the future. The variable, as an index of immediacy, does not distinguish between these two possibilities.

Few seniors designated "deciding what kind of student to be" (variable 3) as much of a problem. However, males in Illinois with limited (two-year) educational aspirations indicated that this is more of a problem than did other groups. For females in North Carolina, this variable is negatively related to educational aspirations, so that North Carolina females with limited or no college aspirations seemed to be quite concerned about what kind of student to be. The respective means on this variable are graphed in Chart 6-1, with Illinois males and North Carolina females shown separately. It may seem somewhat odd that for some groups concern about what kind of student to be is negatively related to educational aspirations. This may reflect the possibility that students with more extensive educational aspirations have long ago settled this issue or experienced relatively few problems in this regard, whereas more high school seniors with relatively limited aspirations are still struggling with how to be a student. In the other six state-sex groups, however, "deciding what kind of student to be" appears not to be a problem for most students, and is not related to students' educational aspirations.

With the other college-related variables, it can be observed that, in general, problems concerning college and academic factors are related to educational aspirations as might be expected (Charts 6-2, 6-4, 6-5, and 6-7). In particular, the extent to which deciding upon a college major (variable 1) is a problem,

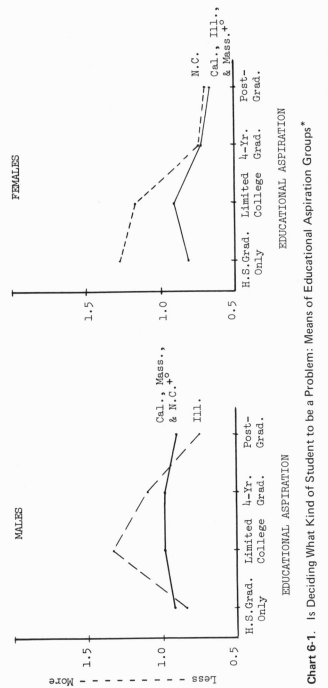

Chart 6-1. Is Deciding What Kind of Student to be a Problem: Means of Educational Aspiration Groups*

*Variable codes were: 0—not at all; 1—a little; 2—quite a bit; 3—very much. Standard deviations for the 8 state-sex groups on this variable range from .86 to .98. Aspiration groups are comprised of equal numbers of students from the 4 SES and the 2 race groups.
+State composites are used when differences among the educational aspiration groups in those states are similar.
oNot significant at .05 level of probability.

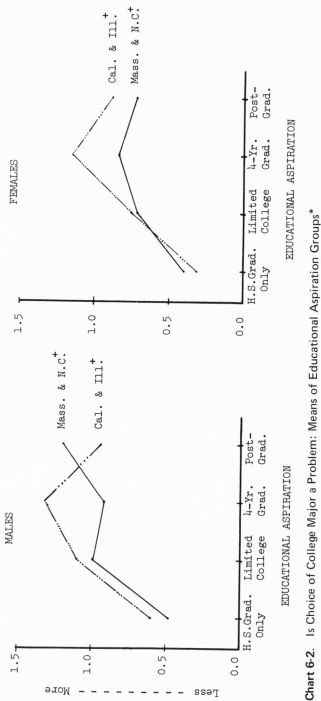

Chart 6-2. Is Choice of College Major a Problem: Means of Educational Aspiration Groups*

*Variable codes were: 0—not at all; 1—a little; 2—quite a bit; 3—very much. Standard deviations for the 8 state-sex groups on this variable range from .88 to .98. Aspiration groups are comprised of equal numbers of students from the 4 SES and the 2 race groups.
+State composites are used when differences among the educational aspiration groups in those states are similar.

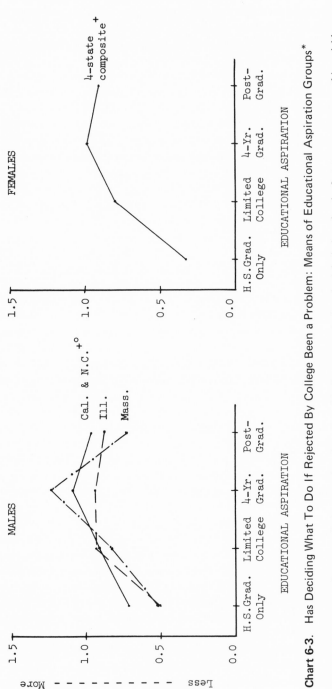

Chart 6-3.   Has Deciding What To Do If Rejected By College Been a Problem: Means of Educational Aspiration Groups*

*Variable codes were: 0—not at all; 1—somewhat; 2—quite a bit; 3—very much. Standard deviations for the 8 state-sex groups on this variable range from .86 to 1.08. Aspiration groups are comprised of equal numbers of students from the 4 SES and the 2 race groups.

+State composites are used when differences among the educational aspiration groups in those states are similar.

°Not significant at .05 level of probability.

and the extent to which finding out which college best suits one's interests and abilities (variable 4) or deciding what to do if rejected by one's first choice college (variable 5) have been a problem are all positively related to educational aspirations.

There are some modifications to this generalization. Students in California and Illinois who aspire to obtain a baccalaureate degree seem to be more concerned with choice of a college major than students with the same aspiration in North Carolina and Massachusetts. But males in Illinois and California with postgraduate aspirations are less concerned, presumably having settled the problem of choice of major. For both sexes similar profiles were obtained by students in Illinois and California, on one hand, and by students in North Carolina and Massachusetts on the other. Thus, for display purposes the means for Massachusetts and North Carolina were averaged and the means for California and Illinois were averaged. These are shown in Chart 6-2.

The extent to which deciding what to do about college rejection has been a problem does not differentiate among males with differing educational aspirations in California and North Carolina, although there is a slight trend towards a positive relationship with educational aspirations. Males in Massachusetts with postgraduate aspirations tend to be less worried about college rejection. The means are shown in Chart 6-3.

For females in North Carolina, where low-cost education, although accessible, may not be easily financed by some, the relationship of both of these variables to educational aspirations depends on the socioeconomic level of family (SES). This dependency is not characteristic of the other state-sex groups. The two interactions are shown in Charts 6-4 and 6-5, in which the educational aspiration profiles for the four SES groups are depicted separately. The reader will note that these results look complex and are not easily explained. In fact, by comparison with the same interactions in the other state-sex groups, which were "nonsignificant," it is apparent that these interactions contain a fair amount of random variation. There are a few salient features which can be pointed out. For women in North Carolina of low and low-mid SES, there is a direct positive relationship between concern about being rejected by the college of choice and educational aspirations (Chart 6-4). Students with limited economic resources who aspire to college are most vulnerable to being rejected. They may be hoping to attend the nearest public institution or may be depending on a scholarship at a particular institution. However, students of high SES who aspire to postgraduate education also have found this to be a problem. One can speculate that students of high SES who aspire to postgraduate education make multiple applications to colleges, perhaps hope to attend an elite institution, and are therefore sensitive to rejection.

Turning again to North Carolina women of low and low-mid SES, it is apparent that concern with choice of college major has not been a very troublesome problem for these students, regardless of their educational aspira-

(North Carolina Females)

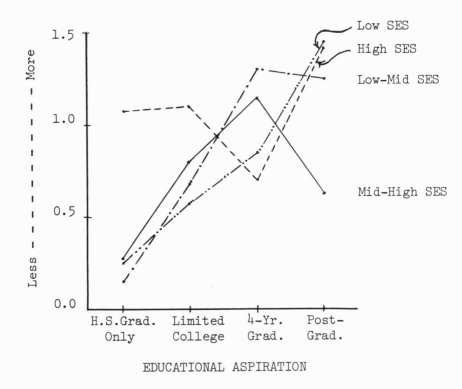

EDUCATIONAL ASPIRATION

Chart 6-4. Has Deciding What To Do If Rejected By College Been a Problem: Interaction of Educational Aspiration and SES*

*Variable codes were: 0—not at all; 1—somewhat; 2—quite a bit; 3—very much.
This graph shows the 4 SES groups separately for North Carolina Females; the ways in which educational aspiration groups differed depended upon the level of SES.

tions (Chart 6-5). If it is true that these students are particularly vulnerable to college rejection, it may be that they are not concerning themselves very much with their choice of major before being accepted by a college. It can also be observed in Chart 6-5 that students of mid-high SES with baccalaureate aspirations seem to be very concerned with choice of major. This, to a lesser degree, was also true in several of the other state-sex groups. Now it must be emphasized that the results in these interactions and the accompanying possible explanations are not clear-cut. And one has to ask why these interactions were not characteristic of North Carolina males or, indeed, of any of the other state-sex groups.

(North Carolina Females)

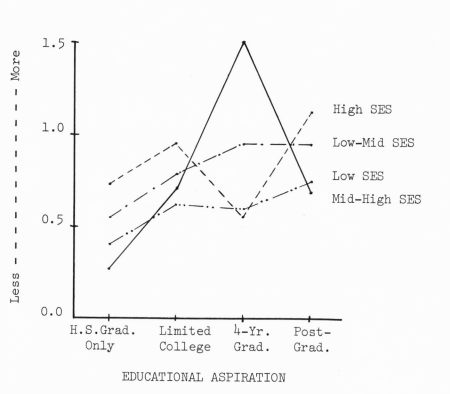

EDUCATIONAL ASPIRATION

Chart 6-5. Is Choice of College Major a Problem: Interaction of Educational Aspiration and SES*

*Variable codes were: 0—not at all; 1—a little; 2—quite a bit; 3—very much.
This graph shows the 4 SES groups separately for North Carolina Females; the ways in which educational aspiration groups differed depended upon the level of SES.

The generalization that there is a consistently positive relationship between aspiration and the extent to which finding out about which college suits one's interests and abilities is mitigated by the fact that males in California with differing educational aspirations are not significantly differentiated on this variable (Chart 6-6). The reason for this appears to be that males in California who do not aspire to go to college have been almost as concerned about this problem as students who have college aspirations. The wide availability of low cost colleges in California, particularly its extensive community college system, seems related to this finding. Many students in California who, at grade twelve, do not

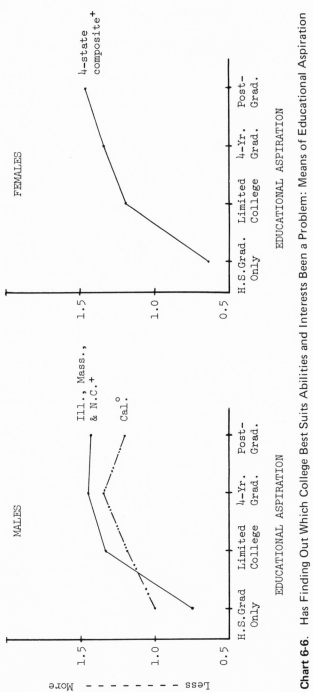

Chart 6-6. Has Finding Out Which College Best Suits Abilities and Interests Been a Problem: Means of Educational Aspiration Groups*

*Variable codes were: 0—not at all; 1—somewhat; 2—quite a bit; 3—very much. Standard deviations for the 8 state-sex groups on this variable range from .97 to 1.07. Aspiration groups are comprised of equal numbers of students from the 4 SES and the 2 race groups.

+State composites are used when differences among the educational aspiration groups in those states are similar.

°Not significant at .05 level of probability.

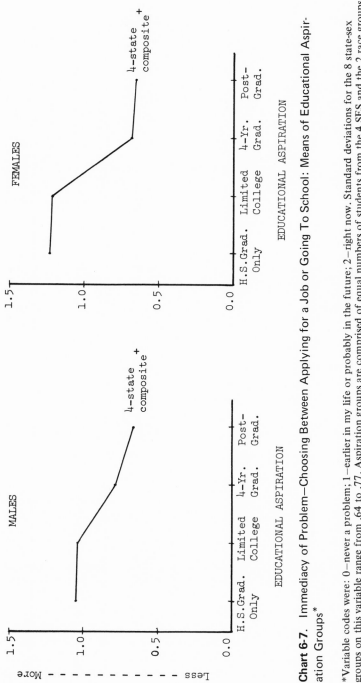

Chart 6-7. Immediacy of Problem—Choosing Between Applying for a Job or Going To School: Means of Educational Aspiration Groups*

*Variable codes were: 0—never a problem; 1—earlier in my life or probably in the future; 2—right now. Standard deviations for the 8 state-sex groups on this variable range from .64 to .77. Aspiration groups are comprised of equal numbers of students from the 4 SES and the 2 race groups. +State composites are used when differences among the educational aspiration groups in those states are similar.

(North Carolina Females)

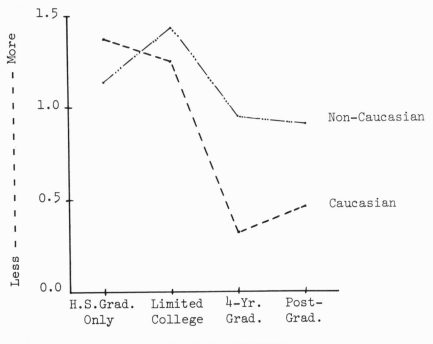

EDUCATIONAL ASPIRATION

Chart 6-8. Immediacy of Problem—Choosing Between Applying for a Job or Going to School: Interaction of Educational Aspiration and Race*

*Variable codes were: 0-never a problem; 1—earlier in my life or probably in the future; 2—right now.
This graph shows the 2 race groups separately for North Carolina Females; the ways in which educational aspiration groups differed depended upon race.

aspire to college may have done so earlier or may still be holding that option open.

While not all of the college and academic variables were related to educational aspirations, and others were not related in all of the state-sex groups, there is some evidence that the extent of concern with potential college and academic problems varies positively with students' educational aspirations. This is most true with problems relating to college choice factors (variables 1, 4, and 5).

Variable 7, which assesses the immediacy of the problem of choosing between an available job versus going to school to prepare for a better job, may be considered a transition variable between problems concerning college and problems concerning work. The profiles of all eight state-sex groups were almost identical. The averages of all males and of all females are shown in Chart 6-7, indicating a distinct negative relationship with educational aspirations. Students with more extensive aspirations tend not to have seen this as a problem; students with limited or no college aspirations find this to be a more immediate problem. Thus it can be said that students with less extensive educational aspirations are more likely to be bothered by the question of work versus school at some time.

For females in North Carolina, this relationship is modified some-what when looking at Caucasians and non-Caucasians separately (Chart 6-8). The main finding is that non-Caucasians, even with college aspirations, are more likely to be concerned with this question than are their Caucasina peers.

Job and Career

The extent of concern with potential problems related to work, as represented in this variable set, is not very highly related to students' educational aspirations. More specifically, these variables are not related to educational aspirations for females in California or in Illinois and only one of these variables is related to educational aspirations for males in California; on the other hand, these variables are more consistently related to educational aspirations in the case of males in North Carolina.

Congruence between ideal and anticipated actual occupations (variable 8) tends to increase with educational aspirations for males in California and for females in Massachusetts (Chart 6-9). Illinois males with postgraduate aspirations tend to indicate a greater degree of congruence while Illinois males with four-year aspirations only tend to have low congruence between ideal and antici-pated actual occupation. These differences are really quite small. The other state-sex groups also show a slight positive relationship on this variable with educational aspirations, but the differences were not large enough for use in drawing conclusions.

Deciding what to do if one doesn't get the job he wants (variable 9) has been more of a problem for males with less extensive educational aspirations in North Carolina (Chart 6-10). Males in California and females in North Caro-lina and Massachusetts exhibit a similar trend, but a weaker one. Differential employment opportunities in the several states as related to availability of low cost, postsecondary educational opportunities would seem related to these find-ings.

The extent to which learning how one's interests fit with different jobs has been a problem (variable 10) is not related to educational aspirations except in the case of North Carolina males. It is apparent from the findings

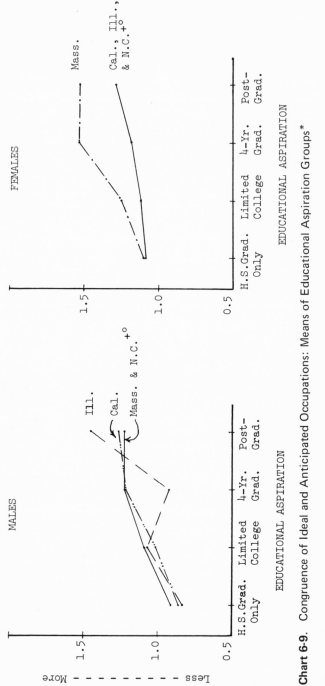

Chart 6-9. Congruence of Ideal and Anticipated Occupations: Means of Educational Aspiration Groups*

*Standard deviations for the 8 state-sex groups on this variable range from .84 to .93. Aspiration groups are comprised of equal numbers of students from the 4 SES and the 2 race groups.

+State composites are used when differences among the educational aspiration groups in those states are similar.

°Not significant at .05 level of probability.

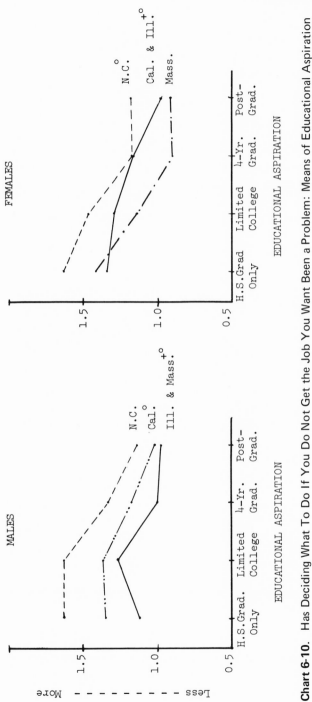

Chart 6-10. Has Deciding What To Do If You Do Not Get the Job You Want Been a Problem: Means of Educational Aspiration Groups*

*Variable codes were: 0—not at all; 1—somewhat; 2—quite a bit; 3—very much. Standard deviations for the 8 state-sex groups on this variable range from 1.00 to 1.07. Aspiration groups are comprised of equal numbers of students from the 4 SES and the 2 race groups.

+State composites are used when differences among the educational aspiration groups in those states are similar.

°Not significant at .05 level of probability.

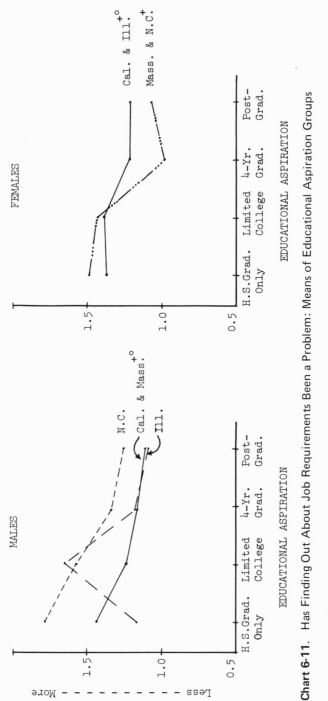

Chart 6-11. Has Finding Out About Job Requirements Been a Problem: Means of Educational Aspiration Groups

*Variable codes were: 0—not at all; 1—somewhat; 2—quite a bit; 3—very much. Standard deviations for the 8 state-sex groups on this variable range from .98 to 1.09. Aspiration groups are comprised of equal numbers of students from the 4 SES and the 2 race groups.

+State composites are used when differences among the educational aspiration groups in those states are similar.

°Not significant at .05 level of probability.

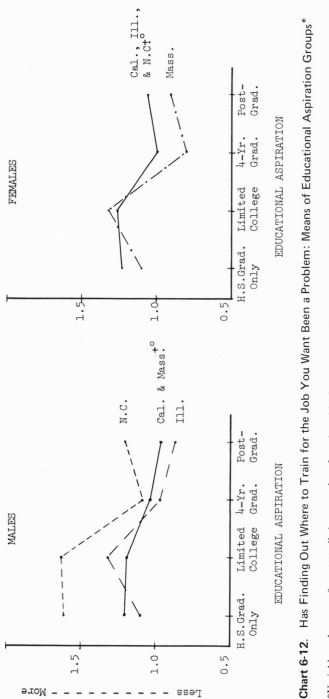

Chart 6-12. Has Finding Out Where to Train for the Job You Want Been a Problem: Means of Educational Aspiration Groups*

*Variable codes were: 0—not at all; 1—somewhat; 2—quite a bit; 3—very much. Standard deviations for the 8 state-sex groups on this variable range from .99 to 1.10. Aspiration groups are comprised of equal numbers of students from the 4 SES and the 2 race groups.
⁺State composites are used when differences among the educational aspiration groups in those states are similar.
ºNot significant at .05 level of probability.

(chart not shown) that more of the males in North Carolina with limited or no college aspirations experience this problem than do their peers. Most students across the states simply do not indicate that this has been much of a problem. The extent to which finding out about job requirements and finding out where to train for desired jobs have been problems (variables 11 and 12) is clearly inversely related to the educational aspirations of males in North Carolina. On both of these variables, males in California and Massachusetts show a slight trend in the same direction (Charts 6-11 and 6-12). Illinois males show more concern with this problem if they have two-year educational aspirations. Similar relationships are present for females in Massachusetts and North Carolina on variable eleven (Chart 6-11) and for Massachusetts females on variable twelve (Chart 6-12).

It is somewhat surprising that, except for North Carolinians, concern with problems related to work is not more consistently related to students' educational aspirations. This is, however, consistent with the results of the analyses of the variable set: "Information-gathering Behavior" (Chapter 5), which show that the extent of information gathering about jobs is also unrelated to the educational aspirations of students.

Personal-Social Issues

The extent to which personal-social issues are perceived as problems does not appear to be highly related to students' educational aspirations. Nevertheless, the extent to which one's political stand is a problem (variable 13) is related to the educational aspirations of females in California, Illinois, and Massachusetts: The more education aspired to, the greater the concern (Chart 6-13). This is interesting in conjunction with the observation of Dagenais and Marascuilo (1971) that females tend to be more active politically than do males.

Both males and females in North Carolina with less extensive educational aspirations tend to be more concerned about their stand on religion (variable 14), again suggesting a more conservative-traditional stance on the part of these students. Interestingly, males in North Carolina with postgraduate aspirations, to a lesser degree, also reflect this concern. These findings are displayed in Chart 6-14. Some of this group may be interested in the ministry.

The other personal-social variables (15 to 18) were not associated with educational aspirations except in a few isolated instances: North Carolina females with limited or no college aspirations tended to show slightly more concern about what kind of person to be and indicated a slightly more immediate concern with choosing between trying to control what happens versus taking things as they come than students with more extensive educational aspirations. California females with four-year educational aspirations and Massachusetts females with two-year educational aspirations indicated slightly more immediate concern with choosing between doing something one is good at versus trying something new.

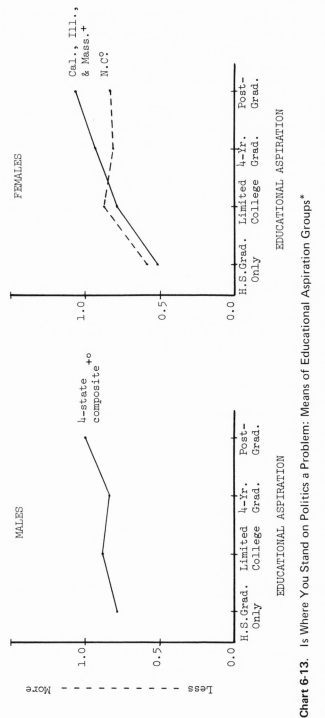

Chart 6-13. Is Where You Stand on Politics a Problem: Means of Educational Aspiration Groups*

*Variable codes were: 0—not at all; 1—a little; 2—quite a bit; 3—very much. Standard deviations for the 8 state-sex groups on this variable range from .81 to .98. Aspiration groups are comprised of equal numbers of students from the 4 SES and the 2 race groups.
+State composites are used when differences among the educational aspiration groups in those states are similar.
°Not significant at .05 level of probability.

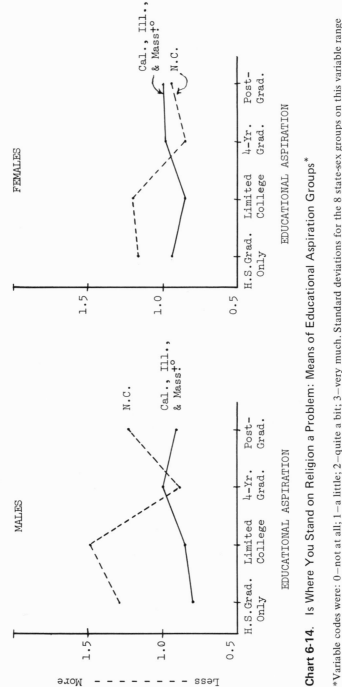

Chart 6-14. Is Where You Stand on Religion a Problem: Means of Educational Aspiration Groups*

*Variable codes were: 0—not at all; 1—a little; 2—quite a bit; 3—very much. Standard deviations for the 8 state-sex groups on this variable range from .91 to 1.08. Aspiration groups are comprised of equal numbers of students from the 4 SES and the 2 race groups.

+State composites are used when differences among the educational aspiration groups in those states are similar.

oNot significant at .05 level of probability.

(North Carolina Females)

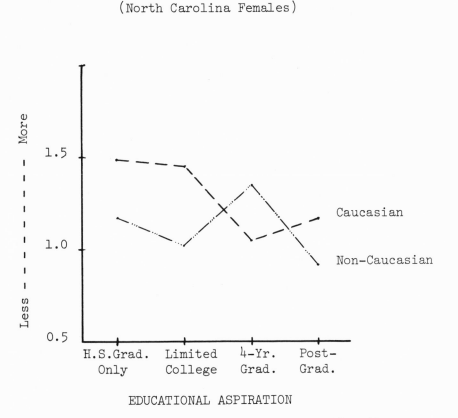

EDUCATIONAL ASPIRATION

Chart 6-15. Immediacy of Problem—Keeping Problems to Yourself or Confiding in Others: Interaction of Educational Aspiration and Race*

*Variable codes were: 0—never a problem; 1—earlier in my life or probably in the future; 2—right now.

This graph shows the 2 race groups separately for North Carolina Females; the ways in which educational aspiration groups differed depended upon race.

Variable 18, the immediacy of the problem of keeping problems to oneself versus talking to others who might be of help, was not related to students' levels of educational aspirations, except it can be noted that among North Carolina females, Caucasians with limited or no college aspirations tend to see this problem as being somewhat more immediately pressing than do non-Caucasians. The educational aspiration-race interaction on this variable is shown in Chart 6-15.

(Massachusetts Females)

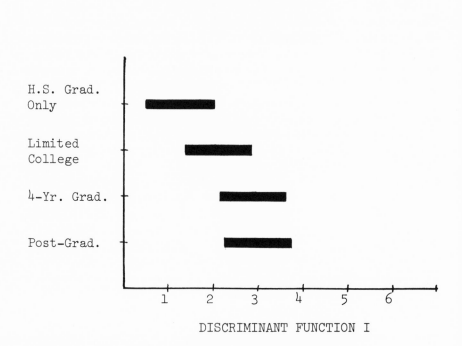

DISCRIMINANT FUNCTION I

Chart 6-16. Separation of Educational Aspiration Groups on the Basis of the Personal Problems and Conflicts Variable Set*

*This graph depicts the relative separation of the educational aspiration groups on discriminant function I. The scale is in terms of standard deviation units with the post-grad group set at point 3.

The length of the bars represents the estimated range, on discriminant function I, of the dispersion of 50 percent of the students in each educational aspiration group.

DISCRIMINANT ANALYSES: PROBLEMS AND CONFLICTS—PERSONAL

The variable set "Problems and Conflicts: Personal" taken as a whole provides moderate discrimination among the aspiration groups. In each of the eight analyses, most of the obtained discrimination is reproduced by the first discriminant function.

Some generalizations can be made about the nature of this function. Most of the contribution to the obtained discrimination comes from the variables assessing the extent of problems concerning college choice and academic behavior. Most consistently, variable 7 is weighted negatively on this function. It was observed that students with limited or no college aspirations are consistently higher on this variable. In each of the eight state-sex analyses, there are other variables about college problems which contribute positively to the overall discrimination among educational aspiration groups. To a lesser degree, problems concerning work also contribute, except in the case of California and Illinois females. The extent of congruence between ideal and anticipated jobs (variable 8) contributes positively; other problems concerning work are weighted negatively. For Massachusetts males and California females, problems concerning personal-social issues contribute marginally. These results, then, tend to coincide with the observations made when looking at the individual variables.

It happens that the extent of discrimination is somewhat greater for females and for males in North Carolina than for the other six groups. In each case the pattern of discrimination is the same: the no college group is the lowest, the limited college group is in between, and the senior college groups are the highest. There is essentially no differentiation between students with baccalaureate and students with postgraduate aspirations. Chart 6-16 is a bar graph showing the typical pattern of discrimination on the basis of this variable set as reproduced by the first discriminant function. The length of the bars represents the estimated range of the dispersion of 50 percent of the subjects in each group. The state-sex analyses used for display of this generalized finding is Massachusetts females.

THE MULTIVARIATE ANALYSES OF VARIANCE:
PROBLEMS AND CONFLICTS—INTERPERSONAL

This variable set, briefly described earlier, did not discriminate among educational aspiration groups for California males, nor for North Carolina males or females. In the other state-sex groups, students with differing educational aspirations were to some degree different with respect to interpersonal problems and conflicts. The multivariate and univariate statistics are shown in Appendix B. Part of the decision-strategy which has been adopted in using the multivariate analyses of variance is to consider educational aspiration group differences on individual variables only when the analysis indicates that there is strong enough evidence to conclude that the entire variable set, as a whole, discriminates among students with differing educational aspirations. Accordingly, in looking at the individual variables in this set which differentiate among educational aspirations groups, only Illinois males and females, Massachusetts males and females, and California females will be considered and shown in the charts. However, in many instances, California males, North Carolina females, and North Carolina males showed similar trends. An exception to this approach will be to show findings for North Carolina students on the three variables assessing agreement with significant adults on certain issues (variables 6, 7, and 8) because North Carolina students were quite different from other students on these variables.

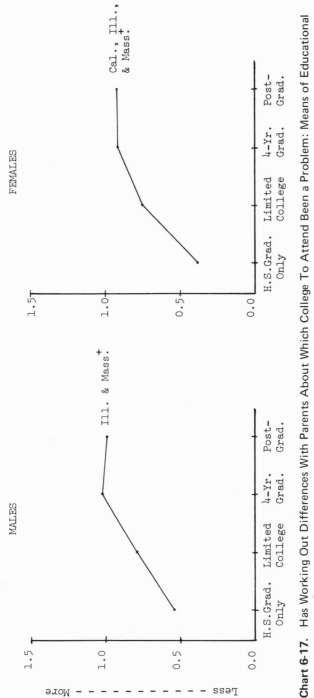

Chart 6-17. Has Working Out Differences With Parents About Which College To Attend Been a Problem: Means of Educational Aspiration Groups*

*Variable codes were: 0—not at all; 1—somewhat; 2—quite a bit; 3—very much. Standard deviations for the 8 state-sex groups on this variable range from .91 to 1.04. Aspiration groups are comprised of equal numbers of students from the 4 SES and the 2 race groups.
+State composites are used when differences among the educational aspiration groups in those states are similar.

College Choice and Academic Variables

The only college choice variable on which the aspiration groups consistently differed was variable 1, concerning the extent to which working out differences with parents about which college to attend has been a problem. The means, averaged for Illinois, Massachusetts, and California females and for Illinois and Massachusetts males, are graphed in Chart 6-17. As one might expect, students with more extensive educational goals tended to be more concerned about this problem.

Other differences on these variables are few and not very large. Massachusetts females with limited or no college aspirations tended to indicate a slightly greater degree of immediacy with the problem of choosing a major they like versus one their parents like (variable 2) than do their peers who aspire to senior college degrees. Massachusetts females with four-year college aspirations indicated a greater degree of congruence with parents on choice of major (variable 3) while Massachusetts females with limited educational aspirations had much less congruence with parents. Massachusetts females with four-year and postgraduate aspirations had slightly more congruence with school personnel on choice of major (variable 4) than Massachusetts females with limited or no college aspirations.

Occupational Variable

Congruence with parents on occupational choice (variable 5) is positively related to educational aspirations for Illinois and Massachusetts males and for Massachusetts females (Chart 6-18). These differences are modest, but there is some tendency for students with more extensive educational aspirations to be in greater agreement with their parents on their choice of occupation than students with less extensive aspirations.

Personal-Social Issues

The most salient feature of the results on the five variables (6 to 10) assessing agreement with significant others on social issues is that the means show a rather high degree of agreement in all cases. There is considerable variability about these means. There are some differences among educational aspiration groups, however, which merit comment.

On variables 6, 7, and 8, which measure extent of agreement with significant adults (mother, father, and best-liked teacher), there is a tendency for the male profiles to have the shape of an inverted U—showing more agreement for males with limited (two-year) or four-year educational aspirations than for the noncollege and postgraduate aspirants. These group differences are large enough to justify making an inference only for Illinois males, although Massachusetts males have similar profiles on these variables. It appears that students with postgraduate aspirations have the least agreement with parents on social issues. The agreement of females with parents is inversely related to their educa-

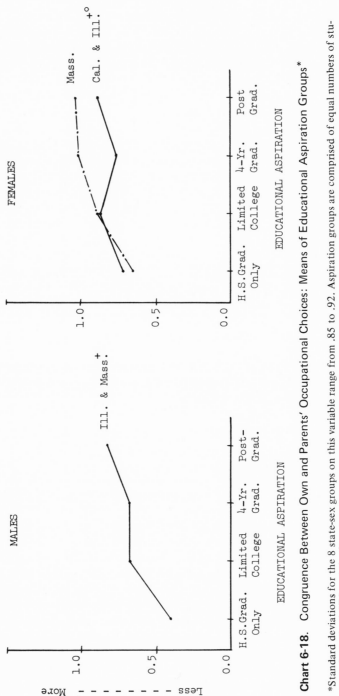

Chart 6-18. Congruence Between Own and Parents' Occupational Choices: Means of Educational Aspiration Groups*

*Standard deviations for the 8 state-sex groups on this variable range from .85 to .92. Aspiration groups are comprised of equal numbers of students from the 4 SES and the 2 race groups.

+State composites are used when differences among the educational aspiration groups in those states are similar.

°Not significant at .05 level of probability.

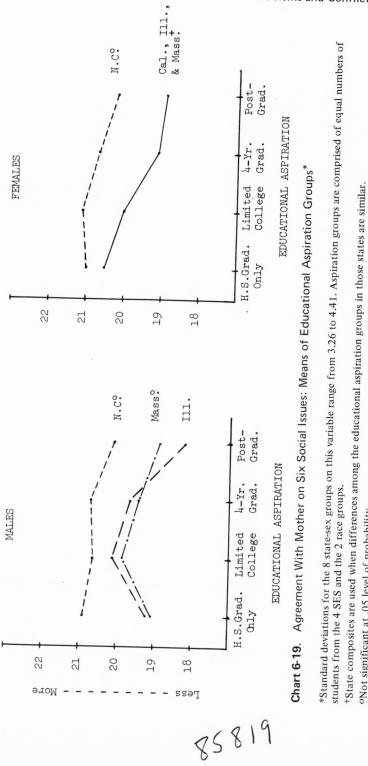

Chart 6-19. Agreement With Mother on Six Social Issues: Means of Educational Aspiration Groups*

*Standard deviations for the 8 state-sex groups on this variable range from 3.26 to 4.41. Aspiration groups are comprised of equal numbers of students from the 4 SES and the 2 race groups.

+State composites are used when differences among the educational aspiration groups in those states are similar.

°Not significant at .05 level of probability.

85819

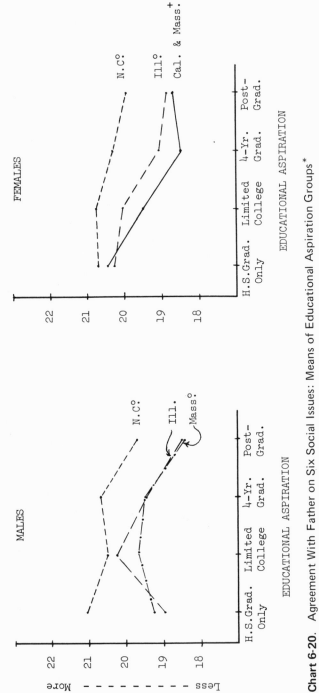

Chart 6-20. Agreement With Father on Six Social Issues: Means of Educational Aspiration Groups*

*Standard deviations for the 8 state-sex groups on this variable range from 3.59 to 4.60. Aspiration groups are comprised of equal numbers of students from the 4 SES and the 2 race groups.

+State composites are used when differences among the educational aspiration groups in those states are similar.

°Not significant at .05 level of probability.

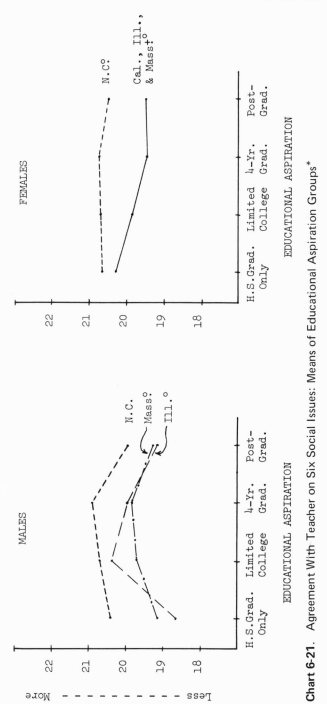

Chart 6-21. Agreement With Teacher on Six Social Issues: Means of Educational Aspiration Groups*

*Standard deviations for the 8 state-sex groups on this variable range from 3.14 to 3.86. Aspiration groups are comprised of equal numbers of students from the 4 SES and the 2 race groups.

+State composites are used when differences among the educational aspiration groups in those states are similar.

ºNot significant at .05 level of probability.

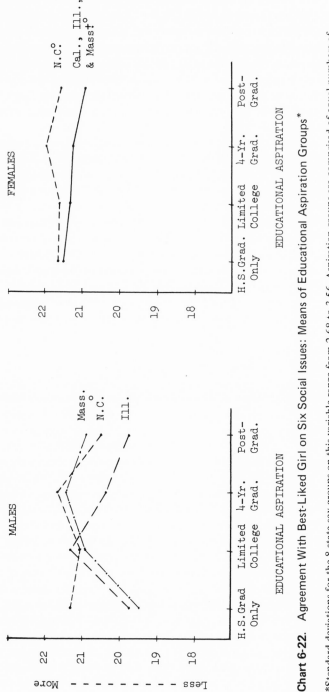

Chart 6-22. Agreement With Best-Liked Girl on Six Social Issues: Means of Educational Aspiration Groups*

*Standard deviations for the 8 state-sex groups on this variable range from 2.68 to 3.56. Aspiration groups are comprised of equal numbers of students from the 4 SES and the 2 race groups.

+State composites are used when differences among the educational aspiration groups in those states are similar.

oNot significant at .05 level of probability.

tional aspirations; the less extensive the educational aspirations, the greater the extent of agreement with parents. On the other hand, the extent to which girls agree with their best-liked teacher is not related to their educational aspirations. These results are shown in Charts 6-19, 6-20, and 6-21. North Carolina students are included on these graphs not because the extent to which they agreed with significant adults is related to their educational aspirations, but because they indicate a relatively high degree of agreement with significant adults when compared with students from other states.

Thus it might be suggested that students with very high educational aspirations experience a greater degree of questioning of values held by adults in their lives, leading to some divergence of views. A similar interpretation seems true of males without college aspirations. However, these results are not strong or consistent across the eight state-sex groups.

The extent to which girls agreed with best-liked boy and best-liked girl on social issues is not related to their educational aspirations. Males in Massachusetts with four-year or postgraduate aspirations were most likely to agree with their best-liked boy and best-liked girl. Males in Illinois with two-year educational aspirations were most likely to agree with their best-liked girl. These results, graphed in Charts 6-22 and 6-23, are not consistent across the eight state-sex analyses.

DISCRIMINANT ANALYSES: PROBLEMS AND CONFLICTS—INTERPERSONAL

The modest extent to which the educational aspiration groups differed on the basis of this variable set is manifested mostly in the first discriminant function. There is some consistency among the five state-sex groups being considered concerning the nature of this abstracted variable. It is positively weighted by the degree of problems students have in working out differences with parents about which college to attend and by the extent of agreement with parents concerning occupational choice. It is negatively weighted by the extent of agreement with parents on social issues. Caution is in order when interpreting this function, because the extent to which aspiration groups are discriminated from each other is small. However, the consistency of the nature of this discriminant function across the five state-sex groups, in conjunction with the results obtained on the individual variables most involved (especially variables 1, 5, 6, and 7), lends confidence to the conclusion that students with more extensive educational aspirations have experienced more problems with their parents in choosing a college, agree more with their parents concerning occupational choice, but disagree more with their parents on social issues. A typical example of the extent to which students with differing educational aspirations are differentiated is shown in Chart 6-24. This again is a bar graph showing the relative position of educational aspiration groups, with the length of the bars representing the estimated

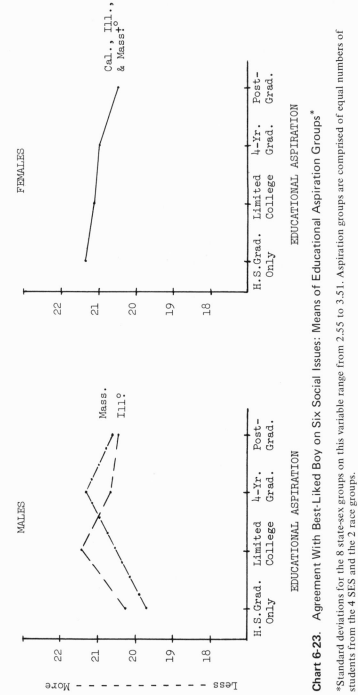

Chart 6-23. Agreement With Best-Liked Boy on Six Social Issues: Means of Educational Aspiration Groups*

*Standard deviations for the 8 state-sex groups on this variable range from 2.55 to 3.51. Aspiration groups are comprised of equal numbers of students from the 4 SES and the 2 race groups.

+State composites are used when differences among the educational aspiration groups in those states are similar.

°Not significant at .05 level of probability.

(Massachusetts Males)

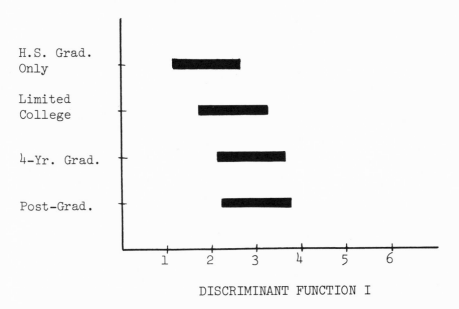

DISCRIMINANT FUNCTION I

Chart 6-24. Separation of Educational Aspiration Groups on the
Basis of the Interpersonal Problems and Conflicts Variable Set*

*This graph depicts the relative aspiration of the educational aspiration groups on discriminant function I. The scale is in terms of standard deviation units with the post-grad group set at point 3.

The length of the bars represents the estimated range, on discriminant function I, of the dispersion of 50 percent of the students in each educational aspiration group.

range of the dispersion, on the first discriminant function, of 50 percent of the individuals in each educational aspiration group. The state-sex group is Massachusetts males.

THE MULTIVARIATE ANALYSES OF VARIANCE: HELPFULNESS OF OTHERS

Having looked at problems and conflicts of high school seniors, as related to their educational aspirations, findings dealing with the relative helpfulness of significant others will now be reported.

This set of variables assesses the differential helpfulness of best-liked teacher, counselor, mother, father, and peers with respect to a list of fourteen potential problems (see Appendix A), many of which were part of the problems and conflicts variable sets. In the questionnaire, respondents were asked to check who was most helpful with each of the fourteen problems. The five scores in this variable set were constituted by counting how many times each of the five persons was identified as being most helpful. Therefore these variables represent relative helpfulness, not the extent of helpfulness, of significant others.

Although there was an overall difference among the educational aspiration groups in five of the eight state-sex groups on the basis of this variable set, the extent of this differentiation, where present, was small. As for other sets, the summary of the obtained statistics is in Appendix B. The upshot is that there is not very strong evidence for concluding that the relative helpfulness of significant others is related to students' educational aspirations. There are slight trends in the data, however, which are of interest and which are suggestive. The observations made on the basis of the observed means will involve comparisons of overall relative helpfulness (irrespective of educational aspirations), state-sex differences, and relationships of relative helpfulness to students' educational aspirations.

On the average, fathers and counselors tend to be reported as being most helpful by males, and mothers and counselors by females. This can be seen by observing the relative heights of the profiles in Charts 6-25 to 6-29. On the other hand, best-liked teacher tends to be reported as being least helpful. In addition to these overall differences, which do not depend on students' educational aspirations, the relative helpfulness of teachers tends to be inversely related to educational aspirations, so that students with more extensive educational aspirations tend to find teachers even less helpful than do students with noncollege aspirations. These differences were not large enough to allow generalization, but they were rather consistent across state-sex groups. The four-state averages presented in Chart 6-25 are thought to give a better estimate than any single state-sex profile.

A slight positive relationship between educational aspirations and helpfulness of counselors can be observed for North Carolina females and for males. This meets the decision criterion for making generalizations only in the case of North Carolina males (Chart 6-26). It can also be observed in Chart 6-26 that North Carolina females find counselors to be more helpful than do females in the other three states. Massachusetts males with limited educational aspirations tend to designate counselors as being more helpful than other males. Thus the picture regarding helpfulness of teachers and counselors is both mixed and tenuous. It can be suggested that teachers were not found overall to be very helpful to students regarding the potential problems sampled by SCOPE, and that counselors are relatively helpful to students, with the suggestion that in some cases counselors are more helpful to students who aspire to go to college. It is somewhat surprising that the greater helpfulness of counselors to males with

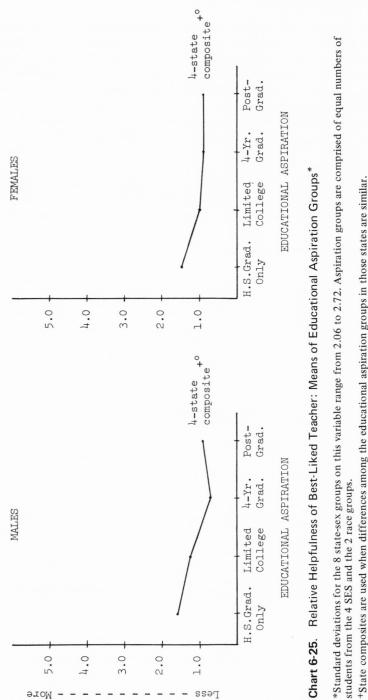

Chart 6-25. Relative Helpfulness of Best-Liked Teacher: Means of Educational Aspiration Groups*

*Standard deviations for the 8 state-sex groups on this variable range from 2.06 to 2.72. Aspiration groups are comprised of equal numbers of students from the 4 SES and the 2 race groups.

+State composites are used when differences among the educational aspiration groups in those states are similar.

°Not significant at .05 level of probability.

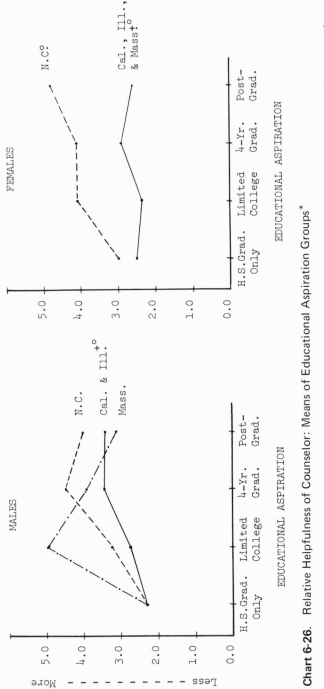

Chart 6-26.   Relative Helpfulness of Counselor: Means of Educational Aspiration Groups*

*Standard deviations for the 8 state-sex groups on this variable range from 3.19 to 4.12. Aspiration groups are comprised of equal numbers of students from the 4 SES and the 2 race groups.

+State composites are used when differences among the educational aspiration groups in those states are similar.

°Not significant at .05 level of probability.

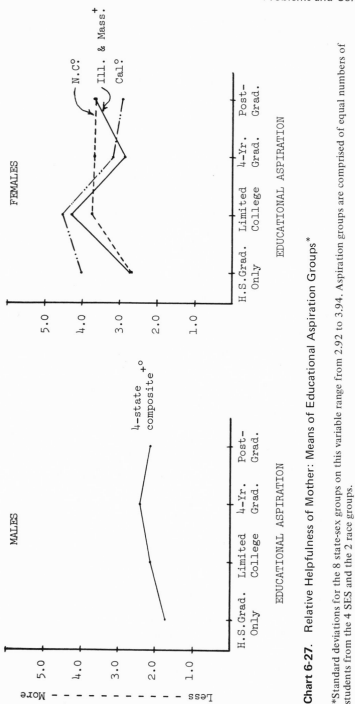

Chart 6-27. Relative Helpfulness of Mother: Means of Educational Aspiration Groups*

*Standard deviations for the 8 state-sex groups on this variable range from 2.92 to 3.94. Aspiration groups are comprised of equal numbers of students from the 4 SES and the 2 race groups.

+State composites are used when differences among the educational aspiration groups in those states are similar.

°Not significant at .05 level of probability. The profile for Massachusetts Females, averaged with Illinois Females because it was similar, also was not significant.

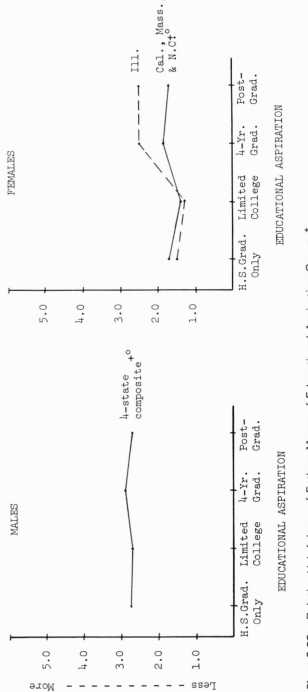

Chart 6-28. Relative Helpfulness of Father: Means of Educational Aspiration Groups*

*Standard deviations for the 8 state-sex groups on this variable range from 2.39 to 3.67. Aspiration groups are comprised of equal numbers of students from the 4 SES and the 2 race groups.

+State composites are used when differences among the educational aspiration groups in those states are similar.

°Not significant at .05 level of probability.

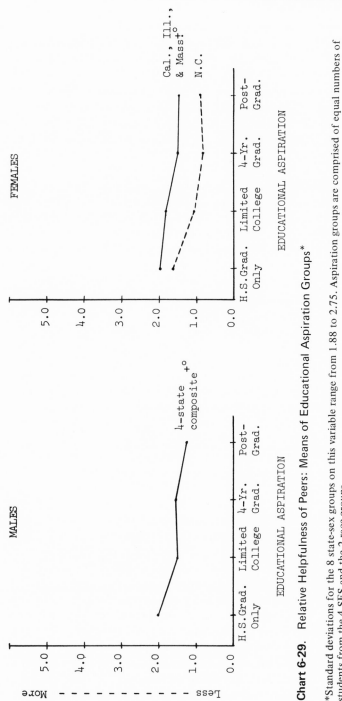

Chart 6-29. Relative Helpfulness of Peers: Means of Educational Aspiration Groups[*]

[*]Standard deviations for the 8 state-sex groups on this variable range from 1.88 to 2.75. Aspiration groups are comprised of equal numbers of students from the 4 SES and the 2 race groups.

[+]State composites are used when differences among the educational aspiration groups in those states are similar.

[o]Not significant at .05 level of probability.

two-year educational aspirations in Massachusetts was not true for males in California, since, of the SCOPE states, California has the greatest emphasis on comprehensive programs of postsecondary education in its extensive community college system.

The relative helpfulness of parents (Charts 6-27 and 6-28) to males is not related to their educational aspirations. The helpfulness of fathers to females is relatively low and is not related to their educational aspirations, except in the case of Illinois females. Females in Illinois with aspirations for the baccalaureate or postgraduate degree reported that fathers are somewhat more helpful than did other females. Overall, mothers tend to be relatively helpful to females. For females in Illinois, this is related to educational aspirations. The educational aspiration group means for Illinois females are almost the same as those for Massachusetts females, so those two state-sex groups are shown averaged together in Chart 6-27. The nature of this relationship is that mothers tend to be more helpful, relative to peers and other significant adults, to females with two-year educational aspirations and less helpful to females with four-year degree aspirations, but not to those who aspire to graduate degrees.

Peers (Chart 6-29), along with teachers, were reported as being relatively less helpful than parents and counselor. There is a suggestion that this is even more true for students as educational aspirations increase, but this relationship is generalizable only in the case of North Carolina females, shown separately on Chart 6-29.

It should be emphasized that each of these observations was strong enough to warrant generalization in only a few state-sex groups. One reason for this may lie in the fact that these variables represent an assessment of differential helpfulness across a spectrum of differing types of problems. If the fourteen problems had been subdivided into types of problems (e.g., academic, personal, etc.), there may have been greater discrimination in the relative helpfulness of significant others. As it is, the variables stand as a general index of differential helpfulness.

CONCLUSION

In viewing these results, let it be reemphasized that these analyses were not designed for the purpose of assessing the identity development of students as related to educational aspirations (although some implications along these lines will be suggested). Instead, since adolescence is a period of upheaval and transition one of the main features of which is "crisis" in a number of areas related to one's personhood, these analyses provide a look at a sampling of potential problems as related to students' educational aspirations in the areas of college, work, and personal-social issues. Adolescent development theory is an appropriate context for the consideration of such relationships.

The analyses of the two variable sets, Problems and Conflicts—

Personal and Problems and Conflicts—Interpersonal, affirm common sense impressions that the more extensive their educational aspirations, the more students are concerned about problems related to college. In contrast, problems concerning work are not much related to students' educational aspirations. There is also some evidence that college aspirants tend to be more concerned with working out differences with their parents regarding their college plans. Agreement with parents regarding occupational choice is positively related to educational aspirations. Problems concerning social issues are not stikingly associated with educational aspirations. Agreement with significant adults on social issues tends to be inversely related to educational aspirations for females. For males, agreement with significant adults, as well as with peers, tends to be greatest for students with two- or four-year college aspirations. For females, agreement with peers is not related to educational aspirations.

There are a number of things which seem surprising about these results. The potential problems about college and work represented in these variables primarily deal with immediate post-high school activities. Therefore, relationships with educational aspirations would be expected, aside from any considerations of ego identity development. However, few relationships between concerns about work, which are particularly immediate in nature as assessed by the variables in these analyses, and educational aspirations were revealed. One would expect that seniors not aspiring to go to college would be more concerned about work activities the following year. Indeed, Adams (1964) did find that for students late in high school (after age 17) the choice of a vocation was a major problem. It should be observed that the general level of problems in the occupational area was not low, relative to problems concerning college. This is similar to the findings that students in all aspiration groups engaged in about as much information gathering about jobs as the postgraduate aspirants did concerning college. Yet the absence of a relationship of vocational concerns to educational aspirations is bothersome, primarily because the less extensive one's educational aspirations, the sooner he will likely be dealing with the world of work. It would therefore be expected that noncollege aspirants would be considerably more affected by vocational concerns than college aspirants.

Adopting this viewpoint, these results may reflect an overemphasis on the part of high school counselors with college going, neglecting the needs of students who may in fact not go to college. The development of "work identity" is one of the major developmental tasks involved in the adolescent process as outlined by Erikson. A similar concern has been the subject of a monograph by Super (1963), who considers vocational choice and work to be the implementation of a self-concept, and is involved in the theory of vocational development and vocational maturity. The present data do not show that this development is not taking place among high school students; however, the question can certainly be raised as to the extent to which the vocational needs of students are being considered, particularly for students who will very likely be entering the world of work immediately after high school graduation. This concern is buttressed by the suggestion that best-liked teachers are seen by students as being relatively less helpful and that counselors are less helpful to students with noncollege or limited educational aspirations. Some of the things which high schools can do to facilitate the vocational development of students will be discussed in a later chapter.

There is another interesting facet to this problem. In considering the results of the SCOPE studies of twelfth graders, a feeling develops that many students who indicated limited postsecondary educational aspirations had not really made a decision. In other words, it may well be that many students with limited or no college aspirations (especially the latter) really would like to go to college but do not feel that it would be feasible for them to do so. Another explanation, which is not mutually exclusive, is that students without college aspirations may include students who simply do not plan ahead, so that as high school seniors there is still some ambiguity in their minds about going to college. One more direct indication of such a phenomenon is the finding in the analyses of Problems and Conflicts that the problem of choosing between applying for a job immediately or going to college is a more immediate problem for students with limited or no college aspirations. One possible implication, in addition to the considerations advanced about vocational development, is that there are many students, especially with less extensive educational aspirations, whose broader developmental needs have not been met, or who simply have not coped as effectively with certain developmental tasks. These students thus appear to be less certain as decisionmakers, less autonomous, and they appear to do less for themselves toward effective decision making.

Other evidence which can be seen as strengthening this possibility appears in the results of the three variables assessing agreement with significant adults on certain social issues. Sherman (1971) has suggested that adolescents maintain certain "stabilizing" roles with parents. However, the greatest degree of agreement with parents on social issues occurred with students with no college aspirations. It was already suggested that students with more extensive educational aspirations, who agreed less with significant adults, may have indulged in more serious thinking and questioning of their own, ending up with views that diverge more from those of significant adults in their lives. This is clearly speculative, especially since many of these results were not very strong. Yet the results are provocative enough to raise such questions. The work of Marcia, cited earlier, clearly suggests that students who have experienced "crisis" are less likely to hold the same views as significant adults in their lives. Given that these speculations are not off the mark, an interesting question is raised concerning ways in which the high school environment can be modified to better serve the developmental needs of students. The suggestions that students with less extensive educational aspirations find school personnel to be relatively less helpful is again relevant. It is likely that these very students are less active than students with

more extensive aspirations in seeking help. This, of course, makes it more important that school personnel strive to reach these students. To the extent that part
of the adolescent developmental process involves arriving at one's own stand on
issues and one's own way of thinking which may be different from the thinking
of adults involved in the lives of young people, this may involve some traumatic
soul-searching on the part of adults seeking to find ways of being more facilita-
tive of this process of identity development.

Chapter Seven

Barriers to Continued Education

INTRODUCTION

In seeking to understand the educational aspirations of high school students, it is important to study the extent to which there are perceived aspects of students' life spaces which constitute potential barriers to participation in higher education. Most of the variables being considered in this study of twelfth graders, such as academic factors, problems and conflicts, and personal values, could be placed under the rubric of barriers, In this sense, the classification is arbitrary. However, in the present chapter the concern will be centered on factors which students may see as obstacles to continued education. Students were asked to judge the extent to which each would influence a decision *not* to continue their education. Specifically, each item was asked in the context of the following question: "if in the future you decide you don't want to go to college or are unable to go, how much influence do you think the following would have on such a decision? If you have already decided not to go, how much influence did the following have on your decision?" Thus, the emphasis being considered is on factors which, as perceived by the student, would prevent college attendance.

The emphasis on *perceived* barriers is important. It is being posited that such perceptions are indicative of educational vulnerability. Educational vulnerability is a multidimensional concept which describes interrelationships between certain internal states of an individual and certain environmental presses. Actually, two types of educational vulnerability, which shall be termed psychological vulnerability and situational vulnerability, can be articulated. In either case, specific vulnerabilities can be assessed by means of specific individual-environment couplets. In the case of situational vulnerability, such couplets would involve observable facts about the individual and about his environment, such as the known cost of education at a specific school (environmental fact) and the known economic resources of the individual (individual fact). Another example would be the known academic demands of college going, such as required grade point average (environmental fact) and the measured academic ability of the student (individual fact) as interpreted in the light of the known correlation between academic achievement and measured academic ability.

Psychological vulnerability involves similar information as perceived by the individual, such as one's self-estimate of his academic ability and his estimate of the academic demands which will be placed on him in college. Thus, psychological vulnerability may differ from situational vulnerability; that is, it may be at variance with observable or measurable facts. Nevertheless, psychological vulnerability, being made up of an individual's perceptions and beliefs about himself and about his environment, constitutes the world as seen by the individual. Situational vulnerability per se will not influence one's decisions; psychological vulnerability is likely to have a large influence on one's decisions. It can, of course, be seen that the greater the congruence between the two types of vulnerability, the greater the amount of information in possession of the individual. In other words, if one's perceptions agree with observable facts, it is likely that he has obtained the relevant information and integrated it into his perceptions.

It is suggested that specific vulnerabilities (individual-environment couplets) are cumulative or additive, to comprise what might be referred to as generalized vulnerability.

Each of the ten potential barriers being studied in this chapter can be thought of as an individual-environment couplet in the assessment of psychological vulnerability. For example, implicit in a judgment of the potential influence of "not being able to earn enough money" on a decision not to go to college is an estimate of one's earning potential (individual) and an estimate of the cost of going to college (environment). Similarly, an assessment of the potential influence of "wanting to get married" implicitly involves a perception of one's own desires concerning marriage and a perception of the congruence of those desires with college going. Similar reasoning can be applied to the other potential barriers. Most students probably do not overtly engage in such reasoning when stating whether certain factors would prevent the continuation of their educations. Nevertheless, it is assumed that such self-environment equations are in effect present, even when not articulated, or if only be default. When a student indicates that wanting to get married would influence him to discontinue his education, he is in effect saying that, in his perceptions, getting married and going to college are mutually exclusive actions. This concern for vulnerability to education foreclosure grows out of related studies about why some students do not attend college.

REVIEW OF THE LITERATURE

Wright and Jung (1959) interviewed students, parents, and high school officials in an effort to determine why youths who ranked in the upper 10 percent of

their 1955 graduating classes in Indiana high schools did not continue their
schooling. It was concluded that financial burden, distant college locations, and
parental disinterest were primary reasons for failure to go to college. Marriage
was also a factor, especially for females. In a followup, the authors studied
matched pairs of students, one member of each pair having continued his education, the other having discontinued. The criteria for matching were that both
members of each pair (1) be from the same high school, (2) be in the upper 10
percent of the same class, and (3) be of the same sex. The continuers and the
noncontinuers were different on a number of factors. Overwhelmingly more
parents of the continuers had favorable attitudes toward college. Ninety-nine
percent of the continuers had educational plans to continue, as compared with
40 percent of the noncontinuers. Sixty-six percent of the continuers came from
families with annual incomes greater than $5000, as compared to 36 percent of
the noncontinuers. However, the estimated need for outside financial help, made
by parents and by school personnel, was the same for both groups. But three
times as many parents and two times as many students in the continue group
knew of community resources for financial help. In addition, more continuers
than noncontinuers knew about available scholarships. Since all of these students
were in the upper 10 percent of their classes, the factor of ability was controlled.
It appears that the most important reasons for not continuing included lack of
parental encouragement, lower family incomes, and less information about
sources of financial aid.

   In a study of the educational and occupational aspirations of high
school seniors in Virginia (CEEB, 1969), the most frequent reasons reported for
not attending college for males were: grades not good enough (31 percent),
military service (21 percent), rather get a job (14 percent), and lack of interest
(13 percent). For females, the most frequent responses were: rather get a job (33
percent), grades (20 percent), lack of interest (12 percent), don't know (11
percent), and too expensive (11 percent). Eight percent of the males gave too
expensive as a reason.

   In a longitudinal investigation of barriers to higher education
(SUNY, 1969), questionnaires were given to 5175 seniors in 101 randomly selected high schools in New York. About two-thirds of the subjects, more boys
than girls, reported plans to continue their educations the following year (September 1968). Seven percent of the students in the upper fourth of their graduation class failed to apply for admission to any college. SES was positively related to the submission of applications. Those seniors planning to continue received more individual counseling than did those who were not college bound.
Students not continuing their education sought counsel from sources external to
the high school establishment. It was concluded that parents exerted the greatest
influence on students' future plans, with the college bound feeling significantly
more parental influence than the noncollege bound. It was determined that over
half of the students would require financial assistance during the first year of
college, and that parents were somewhat more reluctant to assume financial

obligations for daughters than for sons. A sex difference is manifested also in the finding that boys showed a greater willingness to borrow or work part time in order to finance their educations. It was concluded that the financial barrier did not seem to prevent enrollment plans, but may be more related to college attrition than to the go/no go decision.

Shill (1968) studied the educational aspirations, educational expectations, and abilities of rural male high school seniors in Mississippi. There were 517 subjects, 400 of whom had one or more years of vocational-agricultural (vo-ag) training and 117 of whom had no vo-ag training. As part of the study, each student was asked to indicate the reason for not continuing his education beyond high school *or* the probable reason he would not be able to reach his aspiration level *if* something were to stop him in the future. In both groups (vo-ag and nonvo-ag), the leading reason for not being able to reach their educational goal would probably be lack of finances (about 44 percent of the cases). Lack of interest was given in about 30 percent of the cases, and lack of ability in about 25 percent of the cases. There were no significant differences between the vo-ag and nonvo-ag groups.

Beezer and Hjelm (1961), in an effort to summarize factors related to college attendance, did a review of statewide surveys in Arkansas, Indiana, and Wisconsin. Some of the findings are relevant to the present study. The surveys indicated that class rank and mental ability are positively related to college attendance. The mental set to continue or not to continue appears to be of extreme importance in determining whether or not an individual enrolls in college. The ability to pay the cost is definitely related to college attendance. This is difficult to evaluate, however, because the effect of finances appears to be highly related to other factors, such as motives or desire for going to college. The data indicate that financial aid is more readily accepted by the more capable students than by the less capable. There are also indications that boys accept financial aid more readily than girls. Being married or planning to get married reduces the probability of college enrollment. This is more so for girls than for boys, and also more so for low ability students than for high ability students. The military, of course, attracts a large number of boys graduating from high school, many of whom will receive training in the service. This 1961 survey's findings further indicate that an attitude of indifference or discouragement toward higher education on the part of an individual's parents is extremely difficult to overcome. In addition, teenagers tend to exert considerable influence on each other.

Trent and Medsker (1968), in their four-year longitudinal study of high school graduates, found that parental encouragement to attend college was highly related to college attendance and persistence, even when level of SES is controlled. The amount of discussion with parents about college attendance and parental praise of achievements were also related to college going. The likelihood of graduation from college as reported by students, which can be taken as a kind of probability of success estimate, was related to college attendance and persistence with grade point average controlled. The reasons most frequently given by withdrawals for leaving college were academic difficulties, financial problems, preference for working, and marriage or pregnancy. However, there was a large percentage of nonrespondents to this item.

In the main, the studies cited have identified lack of parental encouragement or parental disinterest, lack of finances or lack of information about available financial aids, lack of interest, low academic ability, military service (for boys), and marriage (more for girls) as reasons for discontinuing education. It is suggested that lack of financial resourses as a reason is difficult to evaluate because it is influenced by other factors, such as lack of motivation. Some sex differences were also indicated. Girls are more likely to be influenced by the possibility of marriage and by the lack of financial resources. Parents are less likely to encourage girls to continue their education or to assume financial obligation toward their daughters' college education.

For the most part, these findings represent efforts to discover the actual reasons for not going to college. They might be thought of as explorations primarily of situational vulnerability, although the distinction is not that precise since most of the data rely on students' perceptions of the situation. The present SCOPE investigation is concerned more directly with students' perceptions of factors that could lead to discontinuance of their education, or which have already led to a decision not to go to college. It will be inferred that those students who perceive more potential barriers to continued education are psychologically more vulnerable in attaining continuing education than students who perceive fewer potential barriers. It must be noted that these perceptions may accurately reflect the students' situations, or may be realistic assessments of the possibilities, closely reflecting situational vulnerability as it has been defined. The present analyses do not test this possibility.

THE VARIABLE SET

The variable set consists of eleven items which, as the preceding literature review shows, are potential barriers to college attendance. In the following list, the first three variables are concerned with economic factors, variables 4, 5, and 6 deal with academic factors, variables 7 and 8 reflect the influence of others, and variables 9, 10 and 11 are concerned with values and other alternatives. As described, respondents were asked to assess the potential influence of each item on a possible future decision to discontinue education, or to assess the influence of each item on the actual decision not to go to college if such a decision had already been made. Variable 1, which simply asks the students if they would have enough money to go to college next year, is an exception to this. A complete description of the variable set is in Appendix A. The items follow:

1. If you want to attend college next year, would you have the money to do so?

The influence on a no-go decision of:

2. My parents not having enough money.
3. Not being able to earn enough money to go.
4. Thinking that my grades aren't good enough.
5. Being afraid I might not make it.
6. Not being admitted to the college I wanted to attend.
7. Not getting much encouragement to go.
8. Not being given the right advice on what courses to take.
9. Believing that the important things in life aren't learned in college.
10. Wanting to get married.
11. Wanting to make money.

THE MULTIVARIATE ANALYSES OF VARIANCE

This variable set differentiated among educational aspiration groups in all eight state-sex groups. For California males, the nature of this differentiation was dependent on SES. In addition, the variable set differentiated among the SES groups for North Carolina females and between the race groups for North Carolina females and California females. These main effects of race and SES are beyond the scope of this report. The multivariate and univariate statistics are reported in Appendix B. In the following, the specific differentiations among educational aspiration groups, in terms of the individual variables, will be delineated.

The results on variables 1, 2, and 3 indicate that the perception of economic barriers to continued education is directly related to the educational aspirations of high school seniors. The means of the educational aspiration groups on these variables are shown in Charts 7-1, 7-2, and 7-3. As expected, the more extensive their educational aspirations, the more likely students are to state that they would have enough money to go to college. This relationship was nearly identical in all eight state-sex groups (Chart 7-1). However, parents not having enough money and not being able to earn enough money were seen as potential barriers more by those aspiring to attend college in contrast to those who do not (Charts 7-2 and 7-3). Thus, while noncollege aspirants are more likely to indicate a lack of financial resources necessary for college attendance than college aspirants, they are less likely to cite economic factors as having an influence on a decision not to go to college.

Economic factors may not be the primary influence in determining the noncollege or limited college aspirations of students. But the students aspiring to college—even for limited duration—apparently foresee potential economic

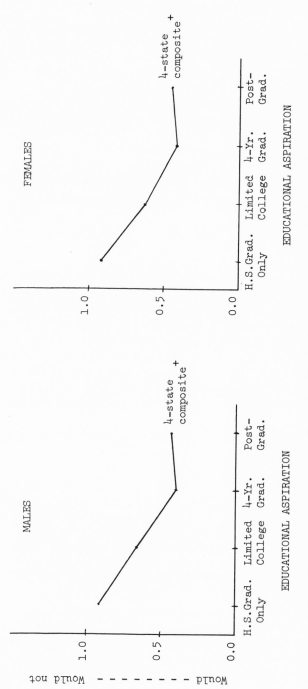

Chart 7-1. If You Wanted To Attend College Next Year Would You Have the Money?: Means of Educational Aspiration Groups*

*Variable codes were: 0—I would have the money; 1—I'm not sure I'd have the money; 2—I wouldn't have the money. Standard deviations for the 8 state-sex groups on this variable range from .61 to .70. Aspiration groups are comprised of equal numbers of students from the 4 SES and the 2 race groups.

+State composites are used when differences among the educational aspiration groups in those states are similar.

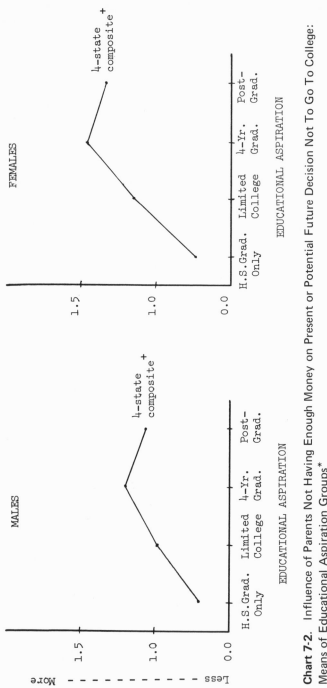

Chart 7-2. Influence of Parents Not Having Enough Money on Present or Potential Future Decision Not To Go To College: Means of Educational Aspiration Groups*

*Variable codes were: 0—no influence; 1—a little influence; 2—some influence; 3—a great deal of influence. Standard deviations for the 8 state-sex groups on this variable range from 1.00 to 1.17. Aspiration groups are comprised of equal numbers of students from the 4 SES and the 2 race groups.

+State composites are used when differences among the educational aspiration groups in those states are similar.

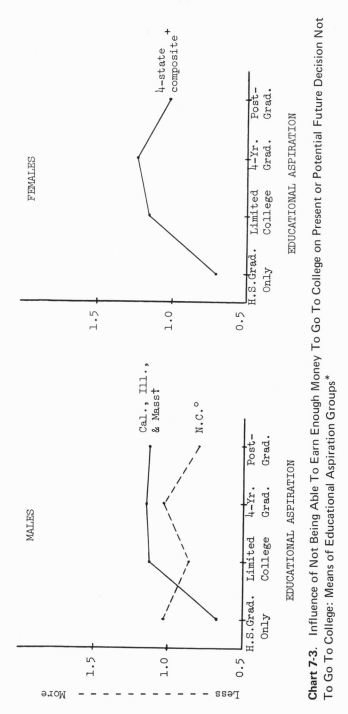

Chart 7-3. Influence of Not Being Able To Earn Enough Money To Go To College on Present or Potential Future Decision Not To Go To College: Means of Educational Aspiration Groups*

*Variable codes were: 0—no influence; 1—a little influence; 2—some influence; 3— a great deal of influence. Standard deviations for the 8 state-sex groups on this variable range from .94 to 1.01. Aspiration groups are comprised of equal numbers of students from the 4 SES and the 2 race groups.

+State composites are used when differences among the educational aspiration groups in those states are similar.

°Not significant at .05 level of probability.

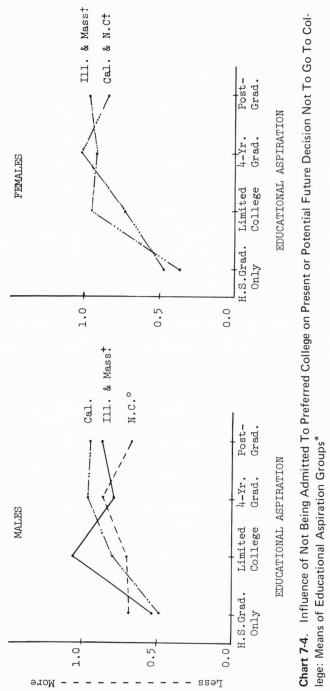

Chart 7-4. Influence of Not Being Admitted To Preferred College on Present or Potential Future Decision Not To Go To College: Means of Educational Aspiration Groups*

*Variable codes were: 0—no influence; 1—a little influence; 2—some influence; 3—a great deal of influence. Standard deviations for the 8 state-sex groups on this variable range from .90 to .98. Aspiration groups are comprised of equal numbers of students from the 4 SES and the 2 race groups. State composites are used when differences among the educational aspiration groups in those states are similar.
+Not significant at .05 level of probability.

barriers to the realization of their aspirations. This relationship is somewhat stronger for females than for males, which corroborates other research indicating that economic factors affect girls more than boys.

Students' perceptions of the influence of academic factors as barriers to continued education are not as highly related to their educational aspirations (variables 4, 5, and 6) as are the economic variables. The possibility of not being admitted to the preferred college as a potential barrier does not differentiate among the several college aspiration groups, although college aspirants generally perceive this more as a barrier than do noncollege aspirants (Chart 7-4). This could well be because most noncollege-bound students do not apply for college admission.

A trend shown in Chart 7-4 is of some interest because it is characteristic of boys and to some extent girls in both Illinois and Massachusetts who aspire to two years or less of college. Boys with limited educational aspirations in these two states perceive not being admitted to the preferred college as a more serious potential barrier than do students in other groups. While this group of girls in the two states is relatively high on this variable (as compared to girls with limited educational aspirations in the other two states), they seem similar to senior college aspirants. The aspiration of women in these states to enter private liberal arts colleges and high cost proprietary schools may be a factor in these results.

The perceived influence of fear of failing in college on a possible decision not to go to college does not differentiate generally among students with differing educational aspirations (Chart 7-5). Boys in Illinois, Massachusetts, and North Carolina provide exceptions to this. In these states males with postgraduate aspirations tend to perceive fear of failing as having less potential influence on possible discontinuance of their education than do other students. In addition, males in Illinois with two-year educational aspirations appear to be considerably more threatened by possible failure. Whether this represents anticipation of senior college grading standards at junior colleges or the expectation of entering competitive senior colleges is not known. Differences among educational aspiration groups in the other state-sex groups were not large enough to permit generalizations. However, all state-sex groups are shown separately in Chart 7-5, and it can be observed that the female educational aspiration group profiles tend to be rather similar to the male profiles. As a group, females are more fearful of not making it than are males.

Variable 4, the influence of thinking that one's grades aren't good enough (not displayed), also did not generally differentiate among groups, but the results were similar to being afraid of not making it in college, as shown in Chart 7-5. However, for males in California, the relationship of the grade variable to students' educational aspirations depends on the socioeconomic level of family. This interaction is displayed in Chart 7-6. The predominant features appear to be as follows: California males of low SES with senior college aspira-

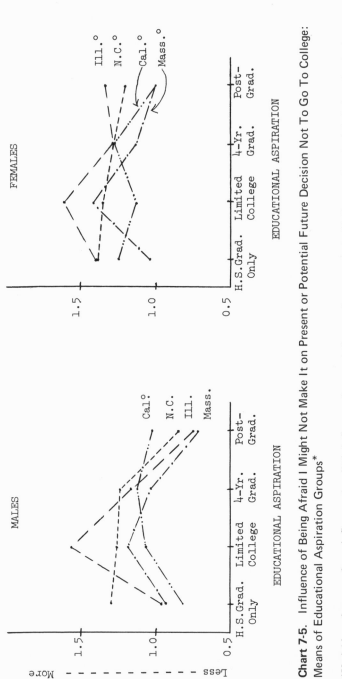

Chart 7-5. Influence of Being Afraid I Might Not Make It on Present or Potential Future Decision Not To Go To College: Means of Educational Aspiration Groups*

*Variable codes were: 0—no influence; 1—a little influence; 2—some influence; 3—a great deal of influence. Standard deviations for the 8 state-sex groups on this variable range from .90 to 1.05. Aspiration groups are comprised of equal numbers of students from the 4 SES and the 2 race groups.

+State composites are used when differences among the educational aspiration groups in those states are similar.

°Not significant at .05 level of probability.

(California Males)

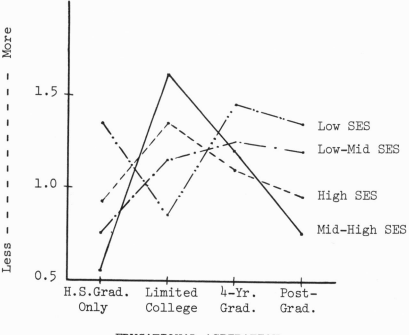

EDUCATIONAL ASPIRATION

Chart 7-6. Influence of Thinking Grades Are Not Good Enough on Present or Potential Decision Not To Go To College: Interaction of Educational Aspiration and SES*

*Variable codes were: 0—no influence; 1—a little influence; 2—some influence; 3—a great deal of influence.

This graph shows the 4 SES groups separately for California Males; the ways in which educational aspiration groups differed depended upon the level of SES.

tions tended to see insufficient grades as a potential barrier to their continuing education, more so than did students in the other SES groups with similar educational aspirations. California males of low SES with noncollege aspirations also scored high on this variable, apparently seeing grades as a reason for not aspiring to go to college. But California males of low SES with limited (two-year) aspirations were relatively secure about their grades. On the other hand, students of

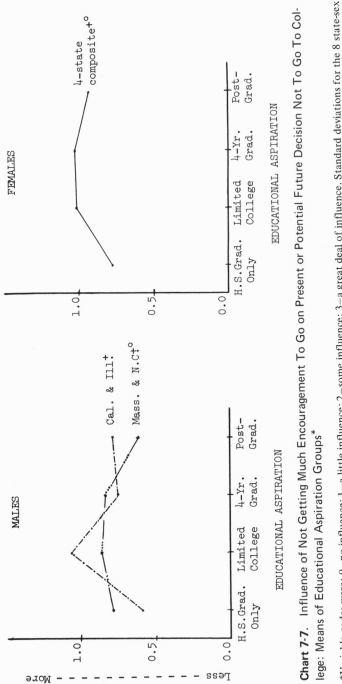

Chart 7-7. Influence of Not Getting Much Encouragement To Go on Present or Potential Future Decision Not To Go To College: Means of Educational Aspiration Groups[*]

[*]Variable codes were: 0—no influence; 1—a little influence; 2—some influence; 3—a great deal of influence. Standard deviations for the 8 state-sex groups on this variable range from .86 to 1.02. Aspiration groups are comprised of equal numbers of students from the 4 SES and the 2 race groups.

[+]State composites are used when differences among the educational aspiration groups in those states are similar.

[o]Not significant at .05 level of probability.

mid-high SES with limited aspirations tended most to perceive grades as a possible barrier to continued education. Apparently there are many low SES males in California who are not concerned about their grades and aspire to avail themselves of low cost public education provided by the junior colleges. Perhaps also males of mid-high SES, who probably can financially afford other colleges, but who are insecure about their grades, plan to take advantage of the open admissions policy in California junior colleges. The profile of high SES students shows a similar phenomenon, though it is less dramatic.

Surprisingly, variable 7, not getting much encouragement to go, is not related to students' educational aspirations (Chart 7-7). In fact, students generally do not perceive this as a barrier to continued education. The only exception is that males in California and Illinois with limited educational aspirations tend slightly more than other students to perceive lack of encouragement as a barrier, but the level is still relatively low, compared to other variables in this set. Yet previous research, as cited earlier, has shown that parental encouragement is highly related to college attendance and persistence. It may be that lack of encouragement creates an unperceived vulnerability for high school seniors, or perhaps high school seniors simply do not want to admit or recognize that the encouragement, or lack thereof, received from others will have any effect on the realization of their educational aspirations. In other SCOPE findings, student reports of parental aspirations for their education have been at least as high as those of the students themselves (Tillery, 1973).

For California males there is an interaction between SES and educational aspiration (Chart 7-8). This shows that students of mid-high SES with limited educational aspirations do perceive lack of encouragement as a potential barrier to continued education. These are the same students who cited grades as a potential barrier (Chart 7-6); perhaps with the insecurity shown about their grades, they recognize the importance of support from others to the realization of their educational aspirations. California males of low SES, who cited grades as being influential in a decision not to go to college, also indicate lack of encouragement as being influential. One wonders if lack of encouragement might not affect both students' grades, and therefore, their educational aspirations.

Variable 8, the influence of not being given the right advice on what courses to take, is related to educational aspiration in all state-sex groups except North Carolina males (Chart 7-9). Other SCOPE findings show that North Carolina students, across aspiration groups, find high school teachers and counselors more helpful than do their peers in the other states (Tillery, 1969). In the other state-sex groups, the distinction is mainly between college aspirants and noncollege aspirants. Noncollege aspirants simply do not perceive poor advice concerning courses as having influenced their decision.

Variable 9, the influence of believing that the important things in life are not learned in college, is not related to students' educational aspirations, except that North Carolina males with limited or no college aspirations perceive

(California Males)

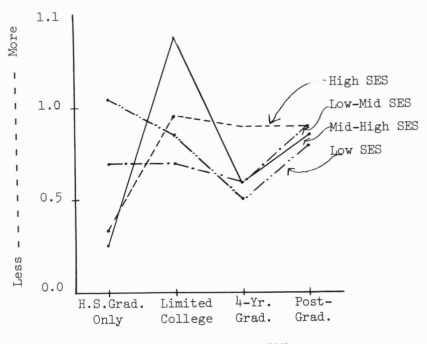

EDUCATIONAL ASPIRATION

Chart 7-8. Influence of Not Getting Much Encouragement To Go on Present or Potential Future Decision Not To Go To College: Interaction of Educational Aspiration and SES*

*Variable codes were: 0—no influence; 1—a little influence; 2—some influence; 3—a great deal of influence.

This graph shows the 4 SES groups separately for California Males; the ways in which educational aspiration groups differed depended upon the level of SES.

this as being somewhat more influential than do North Carolina males with four-year or postgraduate aspirations (not displayed).

Wanting to get married (variable 10) is also not related to students' educational aspirations except for California females (not displayed). Girls from this state with postgraduate aspirations perceive marital desires as having less potential influence on the realization of their aspirations than do other females;

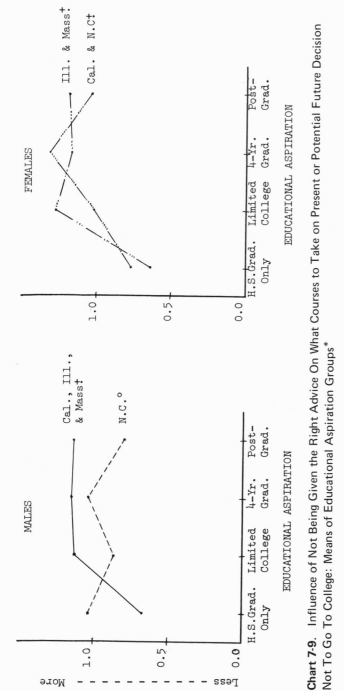

Chart 7-9. Influence of Not Being Given the Right Advice On What Courses to Take on Present or Potential Future Decision Not To Go To College: Means of Educational Aspiration Groups*

*Variable codes were: 0—no influence; 1—a little influence; 2—some influence; 3—a great deal of influence. Standard deviations for the 8 state-sex groups on this variable range from 1.01 to 1.13. Aspiration groups are comprised of equal numbers of students from the 4 SES and the 2 race groups.

+State composites are used when differences among the educational aspiration groups in those states are similar.

°Not significant at .05 level of probability.

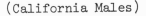

(California Males)

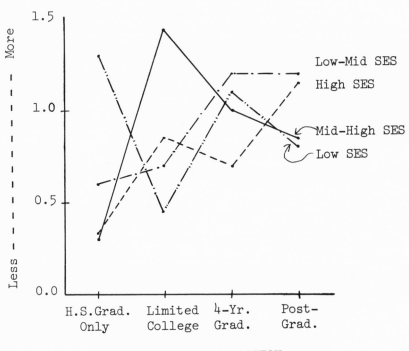

EDUCATIONAL ASPIRATION

Chart 7-10. Influence of Wanting To Get Married on Present or Potential Future Decision Not To Go To College: Interaction of Educational Aspiration and SES*

*Variable codes were: 0—no influence; 1—a little influence; 2—some influence; 3—a great deal of influence.
This graph shows the 4 SES groups separately for California Males; the ways in which educational aspiration groups differed depended upon the level of SES.

on the other hand, all other California females perceive marriage as a greater barrier than do other female groups. As a group, females scored higher on this variable than did males. This is consistent with other research.

For California males, there is a relationship between the influence of wanting to get married and educational aspirations, depending on the socioeconomic level of family. Again, the salient features of the interaction, shown in Chart 7-10, involve students of low and mid-high SES. The mid-high SES students with limited educational aspirations perceive wanting to get married as having potentially greater influence on a possible decision to discontinue their education. And students of low SES indicate a relatively small influence of wanting to get married on their decision against going to college.

The influence of wanting to make money as a barrier to college is inversely related to educational aspirations in all state-sex groups except Massachusetts females. This relationship is slightly more pronounced for females than for males. Apparently, one component in the decisions of high school seniors with less extensive educational aspirations is a desire to earn money relatively soon, rather than defer this satisfaction for a more lengthy period of schooling. The implications of Chart 7-11 are consistent with the other research regarding the relative willingness of groups with differing educational orientation to defer economic rewards.

THE DISCRIMINANT ANALYSES

This variable set yielded a moderately large degree of discrimination among educational aspiration groups. Chart 7-12 displays the separation obtained for Illinois males, the largest obtained with this variable set. In this diagram, educational aspiration groups 3 and 4 are shown to be essentially the same in terms of the variable set. The limited college group is partially separated by the second discriminant function (vertical axis), which is comprised mainly of the influence of academic factors (variables 4 and/or 5) and the influence of lack of encouragement (variable 7). Group 1 is fairly well separated from the other groups along discriminant function I. This function is weighted heavily with the influence of economic factors, not being admitted to the preferred college, and, with the opposite valence, the desire to make money. The economic factors are the strongest components of this dimension. Chart 7-13 depicts a lesser degree of discrimination and a more typical pattern of separation among the Massachusetts male educational aspiration groups. It is noteworthy that the four-year aspirant group is highest on the second discriminant function-academic factors and a lack of encouragement.

CONCLUSION

The results have shown that the perceived influence of economic factors is related to the educational aspirations of high school seniors. However, even though noncollege aspirants report a lack of the funds necessary for college attendance, it is the college bound aspirants, not the noncollege groups, who report that financial factors could act as a barrier to their education. Thus, while college

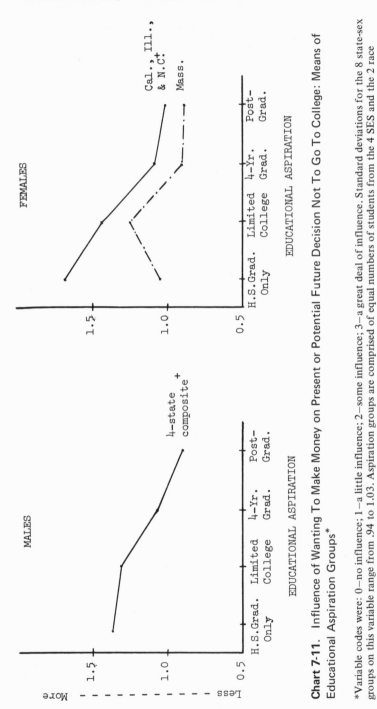

Chart 7-11. Influence of Wanting To Make Money on Present or Potential Future Decision Not To Go To College: Means of Educational Aspiration Groups*

*Variable codes were: 0–no influence; 1–a little influence; 2–some influence; 3–a great deal of influence. Standard deviations for the 8 state-sex groups on this variable range from .94 to 1.03. Aspiration groups are comprised of equal numbers of students from the 4 SES and the 2 race groups.

†State composites are used when differences among the educational aspiration groups in those states are similar.

(Illinois Males)

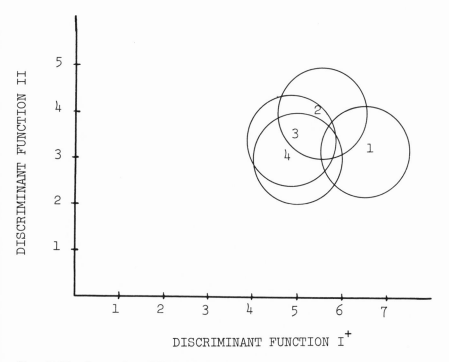

DISCRIMINANT FUNCTION I⁺

Chart 7-12. Separation of Educational Aspiration Groups on the Basis of Barriers to Continued Education*

*Educational aspiration groups are: 1—high school graduation only; 2—limited college; 3—graduation from a four-year college; 4—postgraduate attendance.

⁺Discriminant functions I and II summarize the ways in which the educational aspiration groups are distinguished on the basis of this variable set. The scales are in terms of standard deviation units with aspiration group 4 set at points (5, 3). The circles represent the estimated dispersion of approximately 50 percent of the students in each aspiration group.

aspirants perceive themselves as being potentially vulnerable to economic difficulties, this has not kept them from aspiring to continue education after high school graduation. The fact that noncollege aspirants do not perceive economic factors as having much influence on their noncollege orientation is consistent with the conclusions of other researchers, cited earlier, that the findings about the effect of financial factors on college going are difficult to interpret because they are influenced by other factors, such as motivation. The present findings

(Massachusetts Males)

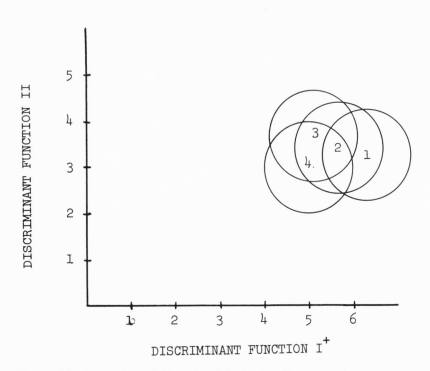

DISCRIMINANT FUNCTION II

DISCRIMINANT FUNCTION I$^+$

Chart 7-13. Separation of Educational Aspiration Groups on the Basis of Barriers to Continued Education*

*Educational aspiration groups are: 1—high school graduation only; 2—limited college; 3—graduation from a four-year college; 4—postgraduate attendance.

+Discriminant functions I and II summarize the ways in which the educational aspiration groups are distinguished on the basis of this variable set. The scales are in terms of standard deviation units with aspiration group 4 set at points (5, 3). The circles represent the estimated dispersion of approximately 50 percent of the students in each aspiration group.

lend some support to the notion that economic factors at the turn of this decade are not necessarily primary determinants of college-going behavior.

Academic factors (variables 4, 5, and 6) as potential barriers to college generally do not distinguish among aspiration groups. Noncollege aspirants found the possibility of not being admitted to the preferred college as having less influence on a noncollege decision, but this is probably simply reflective of few applications for admission to college on the part of noncollege aspirants. Otherwise, it was only for Illinois, Massachusetts, and North Carolina males that there was any relationship between academic factors and educational aspirations. The results lead to the conclusion that while academic attitudes and behaviors are in fact related to students' educational aspirations (Chapter 1) (which might be said to constitute a differential situational vulnerability), a psychological vulnerability due to academic factors does not in general have a strong relationship to students' educational aspirations. This is a surprising result. It can be noted that all groups tended to score moderately high on these variables. Yet it is surprising not to find a strong and consistent relationship between students' perception of the influence of academic factors on their decisions and their educational aspirations. Are students' self-assessments unrealistic, as many educators believe, or are there other factors which students perceive as being more influential in their decisions? It is also a possibility that the form of the question, which posed a hypothetical situation ("If in the future you decide that you don't want to go to college . . ."), does not yield very accurate self-assessments.

Similarly, it is surprising that the potential influence of lack of encouragement to go to college is not more generally related to students' educational aspirations. It is known that in the recent past, encouragement is highly related to college going. Several possible reasons for this lack of relationship were suggested. High school seniors generally may not recognize or admit the importance of this influence. On the other hand, the fact that most parents seem to want their children to attend college may, in fact, be perceived as encouragement.

Other factors which were related to students' educational aspirations included poor advice on courses, which was perceived as a potential barrier by students with college aspirations, and the desire to make money, which was negatively related to students' educational aspirations.

Several interactions involving California males point to an interesting phenomenon. It appears that California males of mid-high SES with limited college aspirations have a relatively pronounced psychological vulnerability with respect to thinking that their grades aren't good enough, not getting much encouragement, and wanting to get married. Students of high SES showed some of the same phenomena, to a lesser degree. It is difficult to interpret these findings, however, it may be that there are a number of two-year aspirants who, though they may be able economically to afford going to a four-year college, have performed poorly academically and therefore lowered their sights. These students may have a special need of continuing support and encouragement in the junior college setting in which they will matriculate almost exclusively.

On the other hand, male students of low SES in California with noncollege aspirations cite the same three factors—lack of encouragement, poor grades, and wanting to get married—as having been influential in their noncollege decisions. In contrast to the upper SES students, these students probably do not have the money to give themselves a second chance, so to speak, even at the relatively low cost public two-year college. They very likely cannot afford to forego an income, although the junior college setting does offer the possibility of part-time study for those who need to work. As with other students, it may be that lack of encouragement is related to the poor grades.

In sum, the factors cited by college aspirants as potential barriers are not the same as those cited by noncollege aspirants as having influenced their decisions. The main barriers to continued education perceived by students who aspire to continue are economic in nature, along with not being given the right advice on courses and not being admitted to the preferred college. Students not aspiring to continue say they wouldn't have the money, but do not cite economic factors as being influential in their decisions, although they do indicate a desire for making money as having some influence.

An important finding in this study may be that some factors which are known to be related to college attendance and persistence are not highly related to the educational aspirations of high school seniors. These include academic factors, lack of encouragement, and wanting to get married. Some of these are cited by all students as an influence or potential influence on a decision not to go to college, regardless of their educational aspirations.

Thus it can be suggested that, while these are elements which comprise situational vulnerabilities with respect to college-going outcomes, psychological vulnerability arising from academic factors, lack of encouragement, or wanting to get married is not, in general, highly related to the declarations students make about the education they seek after high school.

Chapter Eight

Decisions About Postsecondary Life

An important aspect in the development of young people is setting aspirations and making choices. The period of adolescence can be seen as a kind of telescoping towards the future, in which some avenues are eliminated from view and others are brought more closely into focus. Two components of this process have been described as the experiencing of crisis and the making of commitments (Erikson, 1963; Marcia, 1968). However, as the analogy of the telescope illustrates, commitments and choices tend to narrow the field.

REVIEW OF THE LITERATURE

Ginzberg's (1951) principle that the choice process is irreversible is often reiterated in the literature on career development and decision making (cf., Kroll et al., 1970; Super and Overstreet, 1960). There is evidence that premature decisions can limit the development of an adolescent, leading to a rigidity of approach to life (Kroll et al., 1970). Field (1964) noted this result in a group of subjects who selected specific goals early in life and made their decisions accordingly. On the other hand, failure to make decisions regarding the future would lead to what has been termed identity confusion (Erikson, 1963) or role diffusion (Marcia, 1968). There is a necessary duality, a tension between commitment and tentativeness (Kroll et al., 1970).

Schemas of vocational development describe a tentative adolescent stage. Ginzberg, the first to propose in this country that vocational choice be viewed as a developmental process, posited that the Tentative Choice stage, consisting of four substages, comprised the entire period of adolescence (Ginzberg et al., 1951). Super, in the Career Pattern Study, proposed an adaptation of Ginzberg's scheme in which later adolescence and early adulthood (about ages 15-24) is labeled the Exploration stage, the first substage of which is described as the Tentative substage (Super et al., 1957, pp. 40-41). Yet this development constitutes a movement towards realistic choices and, in Erikson's term, toward commitment. Thus, as put by Kroll, "Guidance practitioners . . . should help adolescents realize that while they should make decisions and set goals toward which they can move purposively, they should also be aware of the tentativeness of these decisions and open to change in the light of new information about themselves and society" (Kroll et al., 1970, p. 131).

In this chapter, among other things, the relationship between the year high school seniors say they decided whether or not to go to college and their educational aspirations will be reported. This relationship is important because school programs, college admission procedures, and the social order generally are structured such that students need to make some decisions about their future as early as junior high school in order to use their high school years to the fullest advantage. Thus students are pressured by the nature of the system into making early decisions. If they make such decisions before reaching stages in their development in which they actively seek and consider relevant information or without an awareness of the necessary tentativeness of such decisions, the result could be a kind of foreclosure.

Super and Overstreet (1960), in studying the vocational maturity of ninth grade boys (Career Pattern Study) in Middletown, New York, found that the specificity of planning was low. More than one-half of the ninth graders had done little about obtaining information on which to base high school plans and about one-third made no mention of appropriate high school plans in relation to their preferred occupations. The picture was similar regarding post-high school planning. This does not say that these students did not make choices; they had to make some choices in order to implement their high school programs. In addition, it was found that acceptance of responsibility for choice was fairly widespread in the group.

In the longitudinal Career Development Study, Gribbons and Lohnes found that of fifteen students who were in their fourth year of college, four years after high school, fourteen had been enrolled in a college preparatory curriculum in the twelfth grade, and thirteen had stated a preference for a college preparatory curriculum in the eighth grade. There were a number of students still in college but not yet in their fourth year who also had taken college preparatory curricula in high school. On the other hand, very few who had taken high school business curricula completed more than one year of post-high school education (Gribbons and Lohnes, 1969). These results would seem to suggest rather early planning on the part of the subjects. However, the authors concluded that the data support Ginzberg's theory that occupational choice is an irreversible process in that only one student not in the college preparatory curriculum completed four years of college. The reverse was not true—a number of students who had taken the college preparatory curriculum did not complete four years of college.

Trent and Medsker (1968) studied the relationship between college attendance and time of decision to attend college. They found that early decision making about college was highly related to subsequent entrance and persistence in college, with over a third of the four-year college persisters having made their decision before they left elementary school. While the same relationship held, women as a group made this decision earlier than men. The findings have been reaffirmed by a recent SCOPE study which also shows that the timing of decisions is also highly related to type of college attended (Tillery, 1973).

But Shill (1968) reported that three-fourths of the high school seniors he studied in rural Mississippi selected their educational levels in the eleventh and twelfth grades; those who said they made their decisions in the ninth or tenth grades generally aspired to relatively less formal education. The subjects in Shill's study are probably less representative of the general population than those in any of the other studies cited, but the contrasting results do suggest possible urban-rural differences.

Thus the results cited are suggestive, but not conclusive. The Career Pattern Study suggests that ninth graders are not particularly planful, while the Career Development Study indicates that at least college-persisters made decisions accordingly in junior high school. The results obtained by Trent and Medsker support this, but Shill's findings with rural Mississippi students do not. The present SCOPE investigation, using a more comprehensive sample and controlling for race, SES, state of residence, and sex, will provide additional knowledge concerning the relationship of time high school seniors decided about college to their educational aspirations. These results will be viewed in the context of the tension between commitment and tentativeness.

Another aspect of decision making concerns the reality of decisions. This could be assessed in terms of appropriateness of decision: is a decision appropriate considering one's abilities, interests, economic resources, etc. This always involves a measure of arbitrary judgment on the part of the assessor. Another facet of realism in decision making might be the degree to which several different decisions or expectations concerning the future seem consistent with each other. This also involves a measure of judgment.

THE VARIABLE SET

The variable set in this chapter includes students' reports of when they think they will enter military service, get married, and enter their "permanent" occupation. These three variables were considered to be of interest aside from the reality question. It is expected, however, they would vary with the length of time students think they will remain in school. This should be especially true when students think they will enter the occupation in which they want to settle down.

Finally, this variable set includes an item asking students about whether or not they think they actually will go to college.

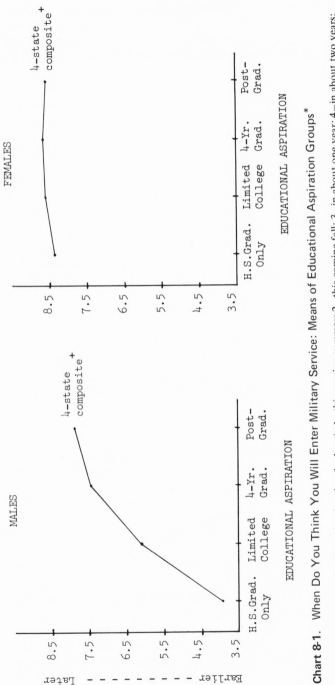

Chart 8-1. When Do You Think You Will Enter Military Service: Means of Educational Aspiration Groups*

*Variable codes were: 0–this spring (or already done); 1–this coming summer; 2–this coming fall; 3–in about one year; 4–in about two years; 5–in about three years; 6–in about four years; 7–in about five years; 8–more than five years from now; 9–probably never. Standard deviations for the 8 state-sex groups on this variable range from 1.52 to 2.39. Aspiration groups are comprised of equal numbers of students from the 4 SES and the 2 race groups.

+State composites are used when differences among the educational aspiration groups in those states are similar.

To summarize, this variable set consists of the following five variables:

1. When, if ever, do you think you will enter one of the military services for the first time?
2. When, if ever, do you think you will get married?
3. When, if ever, do you think you will get the job you want to settle down in?
4. Do you think you actually will go to college after high school?
5. When did you make your present decision to go or not to go to college?

A complete explication of these variables is in Appendix A.

THE MULTIVARIATE ANALYSES OF VARIANCE

The results of the analyses show that students with differing educational aspirations are different from each other on the basis of this variable set in each of the eight state-sex groups. For Illinois males, Massachusetts males, and Illinois females, this relationship is influenced by socioeconomic level of family (SES). For Massachusetts males and North Carolina females, the relationship depends on race. The statistics are summarized in Appendix B.

Variable 1, anticipated entry into the military, is directly related to educational aspirations for males, but not for females. The means are shown in Chart 8-1. Males not aspiring to go to college expect to enter the military considerably sooner than males aspiring to four or more years of college. Thus students aspiring to college are apparently planning to obtain military deferments to avoid this interruption of their studies. These results very likely would be different under changing Selective Service regulations.

Anticipated time of getting married is positively related to educational aspirations for both sexes (Chart 8-2). This relationship appears to be considerably stronger for females than for males, so that females with limited or with no college aspirations expect to get married considerably sooner than do males with similar educational aspirations. This is more true of students with less extensive educational aspirations. It suggests, perhaps, a greater domestic interest on the part of women. Women who are not aspiring to go to college probably traditionally have fewer options open to them in our society than men, and this result may be a reflection of the definition of woman's role as wife and mother in American society. The contemporary women's liberation movement may result in fewer women looking to marriage as their sole means of security and identity.

The anticipated time of entering one's ultimate occupation is also positively related to educational aspirations for both sexes, as shown in Chart 8-3. This relationship is influenced by SES for Illinois males and by race for Massachusetts males. These interactions are shown in Charts 8-4 and 8-5. It ap-

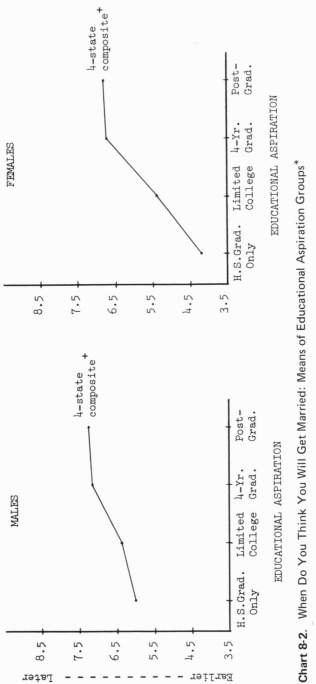

Chart 8-2. When Do You Think You Will Get Married: Means of Educational Aspiration Groups*

*Variable codes were: 0—this spring (or already done); 1—this coming summer; 2—this coming fall; 3—in about one year; 4—in about two years; 5—in about three years; 6—in about four years; 7—in about five years; 8—more than five years from now; 9—probably never. Standard deviations for the 8 state-sex groups on this variable range from 1.86 to 2.33. Aspiration groups are comprised of equal numbers of students from the 4 SES and the 2 race groups.

+State composites are used when differences among the educational aspiration groups in those states are similar.

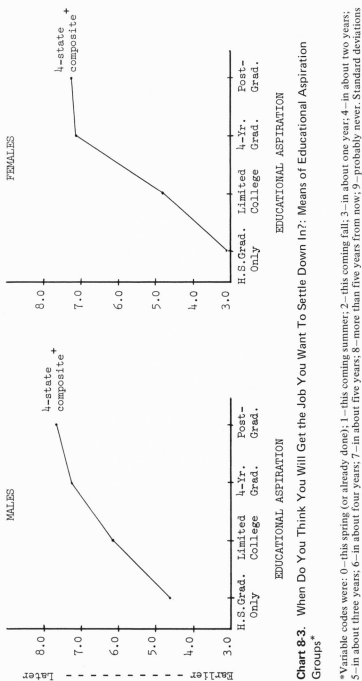

Chart 8-3. When Do You Think You Will Get the Job You Want To Settle Down In?: Means of Educational Aspiration Groups*

*Variable codes were: 0—this spring (or already done); 1—this coming summer; 2—this coming fall; 3—in about one year; 4—in about two years; 5—in about three years; 6—in about four years; 7—in about five years; 8—more than five years from now; 9—probably never. Standard deviations for the 8 state-sex groups on this variable range from 1.95 to 2.21. Aspiration groups are comprised of equal numbers of students from the 4 SES and the 2 race groups.

+State composites are used when differences among the educational aspiration groups in those states are similar.

(Illinois Males)

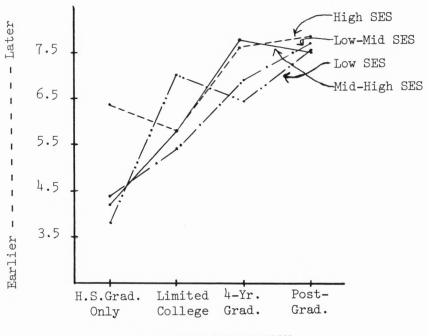

EDUCATIONAL ASPIRATION

Chart 8-4. When Do You Think You Will Get the Job You Want To Settle Down In: Interaction of Educational Aspiration and SES*

*Variable codes were: 0–this spring (or already done); 1–this coming summer; 2–this coming fall; 3–in about one year; 4–in about two years; 5–in about three years; 6–in about four years; 7–in about five years; 8–more than five years from now; 9–probably never.

This graph shows the four SES groups separately for Illinois Males; the ways in which educational aspiration groups differed depended upon the level of SES.

pears that among males who do not aspire to go to college, those in the second SES group (low-mid) expect to wait longer before settling down in an occupation than those in the other SES groups. It also appears that students of low SES with limited educational aspirations expect to wait somewhat longer than other students with limited educational aspirations. For students with baccalaureate

(Massachusetts Males)

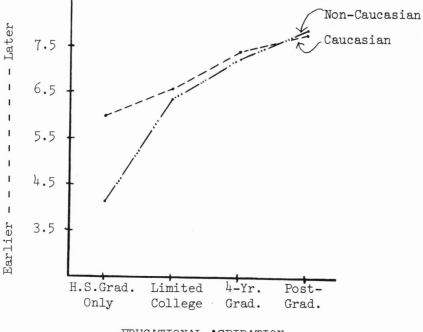

EDUCATIONAL ASPIRATION

Chart 8-5. When Do You Think You Will Get the Job You Want To
Settle Down In: Interaction of Educational Aspiration and Race*

*Variable codes were: 0–this spring (or already done); 1–this coming summer; 2–this
coming fall; 3–in about one year; 4–in about two years; 5–in about three years; 6–in
about four years; 7–in about five years; 8–more than five years from now; 9–probably
never.

This graph shows the two race groups separately for Massachusetts Males; the ways in which
educational aspiration groups differed depended upon race.

aspirations, the results are more in line with what might be expected—the lower
two SES groups expect to settle down in an occupation somewhat sooner than
do students in the two higher SES groups. Similar results were not obtained in
the other state-sex groups.

In Massachusetts (Chart 8-5) non-Caucasian males not aspiring to go

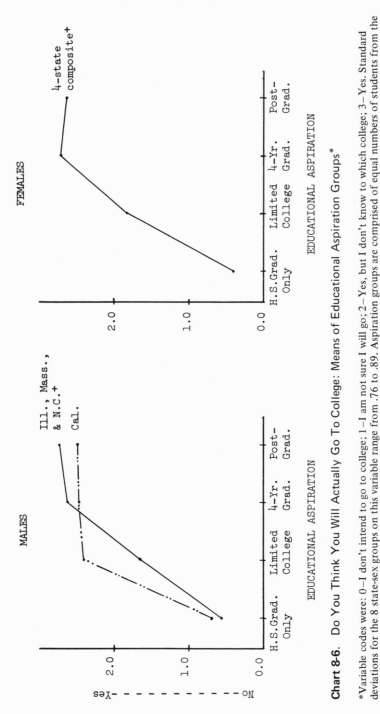

Chart 8-6. Do You Think You Will Actually Go To College: Means of Educational Aspiration Groups*

*Variable codes were: 0–I don't intend to go to college; 1–I am not sure I will go; 2–Yes, but I don't know to which college; 3–Yes. Standard deviations for the 8 state-sex groups on this variable range from .76 to .89. Aspiration groups are comprised of equal numbers of students from the 4 SES and the 2 race groups.

+State composites are used when differences among the educational aspiration groups in those states are similar.

(North Carolina Males)

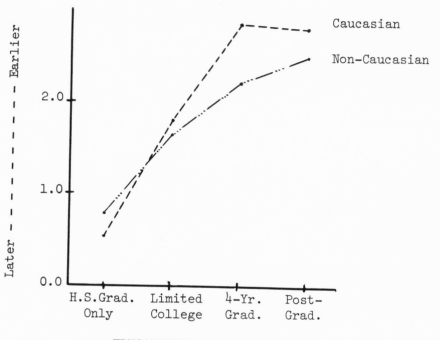

EDUCATIONAL ASPIRATION

Chart 8-7. Do You Think You Will Actually Go To College: Interaction of Educational Aspiration and Race*

*Variabe codes were: 0–I don't intend to go to college; 1–I am not sure I will go; 2–Yes, but I don't know to which college; 3–Yes.

This graph shows the 2 race groups separately for North Carolina Males; the ways in which educational aspiration groups differed depended upon race.

to college say they will get the job they want to settle down in sooner than do Caucasian males not aspiring to go to college. Again this was not apparent in the other state-sex groups.

The results on these three variables indicate a degree of consistency in the aspirations and expectations of students; on the whole, their expectations concerning when they will enter the military, get married, and settle down in a job are consistent with their educational aspirations.

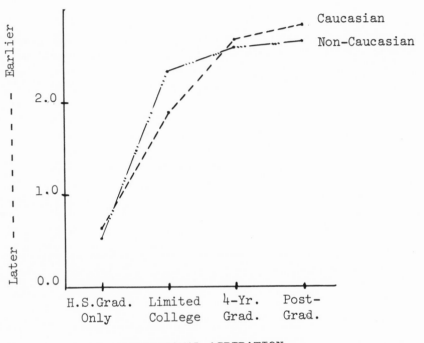

(Massachusetts Males)

EDUCATIONAL ASPIRATION

Chart 8-8. Do You Think You Will Actually Go To College: Interaction of Educational Aspiration and Race*

*Variable codes were: 0–I don't intend to go to college; 1–I am not sure I will go; 2–Yes, but I don't know to which college; 3–Yes.
This graph shows the 2 race groups separately for Massachusetts Males; the ways in which educational aspiration groups differed depended upon race.

Variable 4 (Chart 8-6) reflects some reality testing about college. It is not surprising to note that whether students said they really believe they will go to college is related significantly to their educational aspirations. California males are shown separately in Chart 8-6 because those students with limited college aspirations scored higher on this variable than did males with limited college aspirations in the other three states. This is probably related to a double phenomenon. In California, the community colleges attract many entering stu-

(Massachusetts Males)

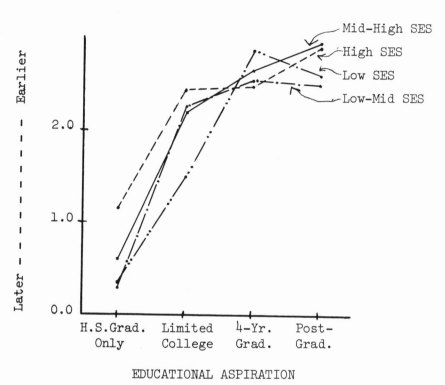

EDUCATIONAL ASPIRATION

Chart 8-9. Do You Think You Will Actually Go To College: Interaction of Educational Aspiration and SES*

*Variable codes were: 0–I don't intend to go to college; 1–I am not sure I will go; 2–Yes, but I don't know to which college; 3–Yes.

This graph shows the 4 SES groups separately for Massachusetts Males; the ways in which educational aspiration groups differed depended upon the level of SES.

dents who would attend senior colleges in the other three states. In addition, the local public community colleges in California provide more easily accessible higher education for students aspiring to some college who otherwise may not be able to actualize their aspirations.

There are some interesting interactions on this "reality" variable. For North Carolina males and Massachusetts males, the relationship of whether or not these groups said they actually would go to college after leaving high school to their educational aspirations depends somewhat on race. In North Carolina (Chart 8-7) non-Caucasian males aspiring to four or more years of college scored a little lower on this measure of expectation than did Caucasian males with the same aspirations. But in Massachusetts non-Caucasian males with limited college aspirations scored somewhat higher than did Caucasian males with limited college aspirations (Chart 8-8). No such interactions were present in the other state-sex groups, and in most cases the two race groups were almost identical on this variable.

Charts 8-9, 8-10, and 8-11 show interactions with SES for Massachusetts males, Massachusetts females, and Illinois females. The most salient feature seems to be slightly lower scores for low SES, and in the case of Massachusetts males, low and low-mid SES students, who aspire to graduate school than for other students aspiring to graduate school.

None of these interactions show large effects, and the overall relationship seen in Chart 8-4 is not modified.

Variable 5, (Chart 8-12) also has a positive relationship to educational aspirations. It is clear that the more extensive students' educational aspirations are, the earlier they decided whether or not to go to college, according to their reports as high school seniors. California males with limited college aspirations as a group made this decision earlier than males from other states with limited college aspirations. Again, this may be due to the community colleges which in that state attract more early deciders who in other states might opt for senior colleges and universities for first entry to college. It is also likely that the community college puts higher education more easily within the sights of students who may otherwise not be able to decide until later whether or not they can go to college at all.

THE DISCRIMINANT ANALYSES

This variable set, more than any other in this study, resulted in the greatest extent of discrimination among the educational aspiration groups. It is suspected that this is so because variable 4, the expectation of really going to college, is highly correlated with the educational aspiration factor itself.

The extent and pattern of discrimination is typified in Chart 8-13, a separation graph for North Carolina females. Educational aspiration groups three and four are almost identical in terms of this variable set. But groups one and two are well separated. In one state-sex group, California males, the pattern of discrimination was appreciably different. The extent of discrimination was also less. This is shown in Chart 8-14, in which one observes that students with limited college aspirations (group two) are much more like students aspiring to four or more years of college (groups three and four). Again, this is probably the influence of the junior college system. Noncollege aspirants are still well separated.

(Massachusetts Females)

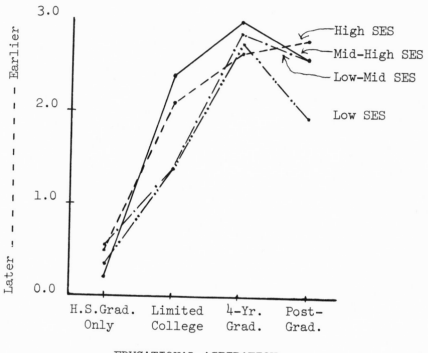

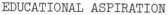

EDUCATIONAL ASPIRATION

Chart 8-10. Do You Think You Will Actually Go To College: Inter-action of Educational Aspiration and SES*

*Variable codes were: 0—I don't intend to go to college; 1—I am not sure I will go; 2—Yes, but I don't know to which college; 3—Yes.

This graph shows the 4 SES groups separately for Massachusetts Females; the ways in which educational aspiration groups differed depended upon the level of SES.

The contributions of individual variables to the discriminant func-tions were not consistent across the eight state-sex groups. However, variable 4 (will actually go to college?) was always the heaviest contributor to the first function, and variable 5 (when decide on college?) was in most cases a strong negatively-weighted component in the second function, often along with variable 4.

(Illinois Females)

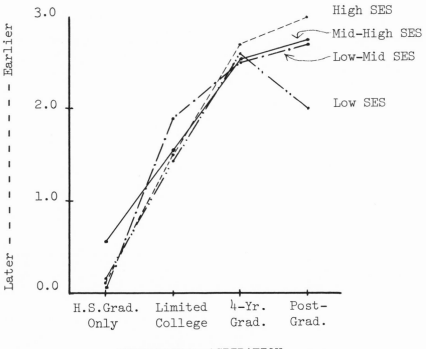

EDUCATIONAL ASPIRATION

Chart 8-11. Do You Think You Will Actually Go To College: Interaction of Educational Aspiration and SES*

*Variable codes were: 0–I don't intend to go to college; 1–I am not sure I will go; 2–Yes, but I don't know to which college; 3–Yes.

This graph shows the 4 SES groups separately for Illinois Females; the ways in which educational aspiration groups differed depended upon the level of SES.

CONCLUSION

These results buttress other observations which have been seen in this SCOPE study of twelfth graders. That is, there are a number of ways in which high school seniors who aspire to relatively little higher education can be seen differently on developmentally relevant variables than students with more extensive

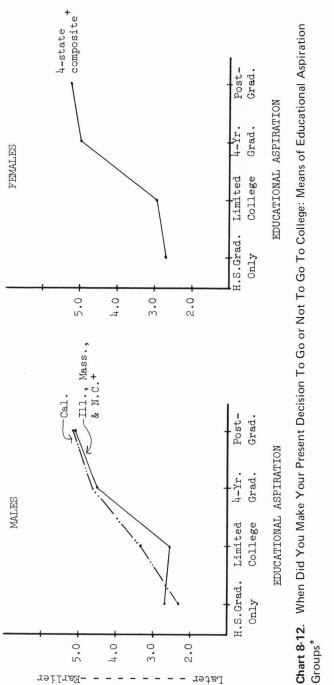

Chart 8-12. When Did You Make Your Present Decision To Go or Not To Go To College: Means of Educational Aspiration Groups*

*Variable codes were: 0–I haven't decided yet; 1–this semester; 2–earlier this year; 3–in the 11th grade; 4–in the 10th grade; 5–in the 9th grade; 6–in the 7th or 8th grade; 7–before the 7th grade. Standard deviations for the 8 state-sex groups on this variable range from 1.80 to 2.17. Aspiration groups are comprised of equal numbers of students from the 4 SES and the 2 race groups.

+State composites are used when differences among the educational aspiration groups in those states are similar.

(North Carolina Females)

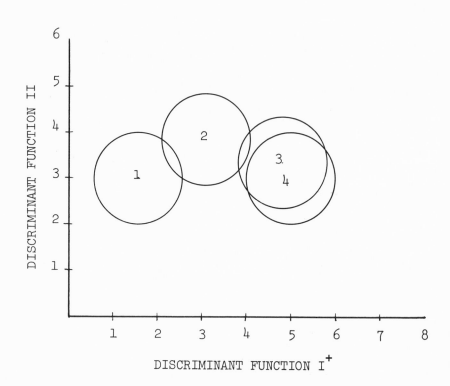

Chart 8-13. Separation of Educational Aspiration Groups on the Basis of the Decisions Variable Set*

*Educational aspiration groups are: 1—high school graduation only; 2—limited college; 3—graduation from a four-year college; 4—postgraduate attendance.
+Discriminant functions I and II summarize the ways in which the educational aspiration groups are distinguished on the basis of this varaible set. The scales are in terms of standard deviation units with aspiration group 4 set at points (5, 3). The circles represent the estimated dispersion of approximately 50 percent of the students in each aspiration group.

educational aspirations. It will be possible, therefore, to suggest ways in which students with less extensive educational aspirations have different needs than students with more extensive aspirations.

In the present variable set it has been observed that the earliness of students' decisions about whether or not they will go to college is positively related to their educational aspirations: students with no college or limited col-

(California Males)

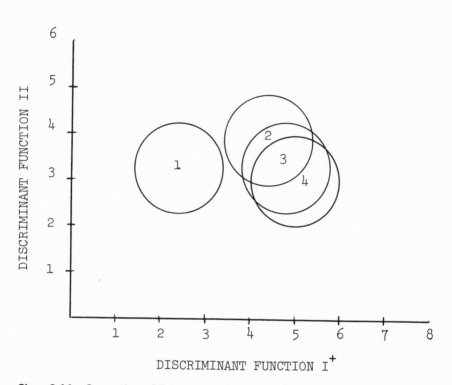

DISCRIMINANT FUNCTION I[+]

Chart 8-14. Separation of Educational Aspiration Groups on the Basis of the Decisions Variable Set*

*Educational aspiration groups are: 1—high school graduation only; 2—limited college; 3—graduation from a four-year college; 4—postgraduate attendance.

[+]Discriminant functions I and II summarize the ways in which the educational aspiration groups are distinguished on the basis of this variable set. The scales are in terms of standard deviation units with aspiration group 4 set at points (5,3). The circles represent the estimated dispersion of approximately 50 percent of the students in each aspiration group.

lege aspirations made this decision relatively late in high school, whereas students aspiring to four or more years of college made this decision in early high school or even before that.

In terms of tentativeness and commitment, this would suggest that students with limited or no college aspirations are considerably less likely to make commitments, but are plagued with indecision throughout high school and beyond. This, of course, leaves them vulnerable finally to decision by default—having to decide not to go to college because they have not made the appropriate plans. There need to be ways to help these students make at least tentative decisions about their post-high school plans earlier in their high school careers. The students aspiring to four or more years of college, who report that they decided about college relatively early, are in less difficulty unless their early decisions were made without an awareness of the need for tentativeness or with such strong commitment that it resulted in closing other alternatives that later would have been more desirable. It would seem unlikely that pursuit of a program leading toward college would foreclose non-college options; however, a strong commitment toward a particular college goal, which would include choice of field of study, might tend to be limiting with respect to alternative options. This danger is probably not too great in high school as long as the college preparatory program has breadth.

It has also been observed that there is a certain amount of reality in students' decision making, as measured by the consistency of several aspirations and expectations. The strongest points in support of this were the findings that the length of time before expected entry into "the occupation I want to settle down in" is positively related to students' educational aspirations, and that whether or not students think they will actually go to college after high school is directly related to their educational aspirations. In addition, the anticipated length of time before getting married and, for males, the length of time before expected entry into the military were positively related to how long they said they expected to stay in school.

Chapter Nine

Summary, Conclusions, and Interpretations

INTRODUCTION

The primary purpose of this study was to investigate the relationship of a variety of attributes and behaviors to the educational aspirations of high school seniors. The subjects were high school seniors of each sex and from each of the four SCOPE states, California, Illinois, Massachusetts, and North Carolina, comprising eight state-sex groups. Each state-sex group consisted of 320 cases, for a total N of 2560, drawn from SCOPE master files of 34,000 subjects. Eighty-eight measures of student characteristics, the dependent variables, were selected from data files based on the SCOPE 1969 twelfth-grade questionnaire. In final form, after recoding, all of the variables could be considered as at least ordinal scale measurements. Some of the variables resulted from prior scaling work.

The variables were classified according to a taxonomy of areas of interest, resulting in eight variable sets. This classification was somewhat arbitrary, but was utilized as a convenience. Each variable set was analyzed using multivariate analysis of variance (manova) and discriminant analysis. The factor, or independent variable, of primary interest was a four-level classification of students' educational aspirations, obtained when the subjects were high school seniors. This is not a pure aspiration variable, but is thought to be closer to aspirations than to expectations. Other independent variables were SES (four levels based on father's occupation) and race (two classifications: Cautain when the relationship of the dependent variables to educational aspirations is different for students of differing race of SES. Identical analyses (applying the same design) were conducted with each of the eight dependent variable sets. In addition, these analyses were done separately by state and sex. In other words, the analysis of each variable set was duplicated in each of the eight state-sex groups. This was done to provide comparisons among states and sexes.

The design provided a means of performing statistical tests and drawing inferences. However, subjective evaluation has also been involved in the reporting of results and the drawing of conclusions. Certain interests described in chapter introductions guided the interpretation of results. Some results which were statistically significant but not characterized by large differences among educational aspiration groups did not receive much attention. In other cases, small differences received special attention because they were replicated in most or all of the state-sex groups. Where state-sex groups differed the picture was often confusing or difficult to interpret. Since emphasis was placed on results which were duplicated across state-sex groups, the error (Type I) inherent in making a large number of statistical tests was reduced.

This final chapter consists of a summary of the most salient results which were common to all or most of the state-sex groups; an integration of some of the conclusions with implications for educators and for high school programs; and finally, a discussion of some state-sex differences which did seem to comprise meaningful patterns. It must be remembered throughout that all statements about differences among students with differing educational aspirations refer to group central tendencies, and should not be applied to specific individuals.

SUMMARY OF RESULTS

Academic Attitudes, Values, and Behaviors

The results provided evidence that students differing in their educational aspirations also differ in their attitudes toward education. The importance of getting good grades, the importance of learning in school, and the attractiveness of an academic college environment were all positively related to students' educational aspirations. The attractiveness of colleges which emphasize job preparation was highest for students with two-year educational aspirations.

Academic striving behaviors also were shown to be related to how long students want to stay in school. There was a positive relationship between the grades students aim for and the amount of time they spent studying and SCOPE's measure of educational goal projections of high school seniors. Also, the more extensive students' educational aspirations, the more likely students are to have a high evaluation of their ability to do college work. This appeared to be more the case for men than for women. Finally, ability and academic achievement, as measured by the Academic Aptitude Test and self-reported grades, are both positively related to educational aspirations as declared in late spring before graduation.

The discriminant analyses yielded two meaningful dimensions on which students with differing educational aspirations were separated. The first was interpreted to be an academic orientation. It had a positive linear relationship to educational aspirations; the more extensive the educational aspirations, the greater the academic orientation. The second dimension was considered to represent an orientation to nonacademic college environments, specifically attraction to colleges characterized by a high level of school spirits or by an occupational emphasis. Students with limited (two-year) educational aspirations were highest on this dimension, followed closely by students aspiring to obtain a baccalaureate degree. Students with no college or with graduate school aspirations were lowest on this dimension. It was concluded that students with limited educational aspirations (essentially junior college bound), and to a lesser degree those with four-year aspirations (who were also relatively high on the academic orientation dimension), are attracted to different kinds of colleges than students with aspirations for postgraduate degrees.

These results indicate that students of varying educational aspirations differ in their academic attitudes and behaviors in much the same way as do students who actually have achieved corresponding educational outcomes in the years beyond high school.

Personal Propensities and Values

It was shown that students with more extensive educational aspirations have greater degrees of intellectual orientation, as measured by several scales constructed from selected Omnibus Personality Inventory items, than do students with less extensive educational aspirations. This was largely a linear relationship. The results also provided evidence that high school seniors who want extensive education beyond high school tend to endorse work ethic ideals. Scores on importance of being a leader and a short work ethic scale were both positively related to educational aspirations.

For men, the evidence does not suggest any relationship between liberal versus conservative attitudes toward social issues and educational aspirations. In general, more women aspiring to extensive higher education tend to be more liberal on some issues than those with more limited aspirations. The more extensive their educational aspirations, the greater the likelihood that women will see protest movements in a favorable light; disagree that disrespect for law and order is a major problem; and have a tolerant attitude toward refusal to fight in Vietnam.

The dimensions abstracted in the discriminant analyses were interpreted as: (1) intellectual orientation and leadership values, and (2) autonomy and negative work ethic. The first of these was positively related to educational aspirations. On the second dimension, students with limited and four-year educational aspirations tended to be slightly higher than either students who declared themselves not to be college bound or at the other extreme who said they expected to earn a postgraduate degree.

In large part the findings again corresponded to results from other studies in which educational outcomes, rather than aspiration, was the criterion variable.

Information-gathering Behavior

The findings led to the conclusion that the extent of information gathering concerning college is positively related to level of students' educational aspirations. Information gathering about jobs does not appear to be so related. In fact, students with extensive educational aspirations appeared to have engaged in as much information gathering about jobs as did students with less extensive aspirations. However, the discriminant analytic results suggested that for some students, job information gathering acts as a kind of mediating variable: students whose scores on college information gathering are midway between the central tendencies of two aspiration groups will be more likely to be members of the groups with less extensive aspirations if they engaged in a relatively high extent of job information gathering. Conversely, they will be more likely to be members of the group with more extensive educational aspirations if they engaged in relatively little job information gathering.

The first function abstracted in the discriminant analyses was the only one which differentiated among the educational aspiration groups. It was interpreted as a bipolar job-college dimension.

These results were viewed in the context of vocational development, since information gathering is one of the major dimensions of vocational maturity.

Problems and Conflicts

Personal and interpersonal problems and conflicts comprised two separate variable sets. The results will be summarized together. The evidence given in connection with interpersonal problems and conflicts came from only five of the state-sex groups. Another variable set, helpfulness of others, is also included in this section.

The results suggested that there is some relationship between variables concerned with college choice and academic factors and students' educational aspirations. The extent of having problems with the choice of college, choice of major, and fitting college choice to abilities and interests was positively related to levels of educational aspirations. The degree of difficulty in choosing between college and a job was negatively related to educational aspiration level. Having problems in working out difficulties with parents about college choice was also positively related to how long students aspired to stay in school. Otherwise there were few relationships between interpersonal problems and conflicts about college and academic issues and educational aspirations.

The degree of problems and conflicts concerning jobs seems not to be related to how much education students seemed to be seeking after high school. In general, there is a relatively high level of such problems reported across aspiration groups, which corresponds to the results obtained with job information gathering. There is a slight tendency for agreement with parents concerning occupational choice to be positively related to how far seniors aspire to go in school.

The results did not indicate that the extent of problems associated with personal-social issues has relationship to educational goal differences. These issues included where one stands on politics, religion, what kind of person to be, and others. However, the extent of agreement with significant adults on such issues as the Vietnam war, law and order, student protest movements, and religion does appear to discriminate among aspiration groups. The results indicated that women tend to disagree more with their parents if they have extensive educational aspirations. There was some suggestion that men with limited college or baccalaureate goal objectives disagree more with significant adults than do men who may not be college bound or who indicate they may end up in graduate school.

The discriminant analyses of the personal problems and conflicts variable set yielded one meaningful dimension, characterized as a job versus college factor. For the interpersonal problems and conflicts variable set, the single discriminant function which differentiated among aspiration groups can be characterized by problems with parents about college choice but agreement with parents on occupational choice, and disagreement with parents on social issues.

These results were viewed in the context of the adolescent identity crisis. Conflicts and problems are an important part of development in adolescence, and the experiencing and resolution of crises is a necessary step in the movement toward ego identity. In this connection, one might wonder who students perceive as being most helpful to them with some of their problems and conflicts, and if the relative helpfulness of significant others is related to their educational aspirations.

The helpfulness of others variable set provided very little differentiation among aspiration groups. It was observed, however, that fathers and counselors tend to be perceived as being most helpful to boys; mothers and counselors to girls. It was further observed that teachers were perceived as being relatively unhelpful in dealing with the specific problems in question. There were a few indications that the relative helpfulness of counselors may be positively related to the level of educational aspirations. There were some problems with this variable set, and the observations advanced which were thought to be suggestive, rest on scant evidence. More rigorous studies are clearly needed in this area.

Barriers to Continued Education

While the results indicated that students aspiring to go to college are more likely to say that they will have enough money than are students not aspiring to go to college, it was also shown that those apparently college bound are more likely to perceive economic contingencies as potential obstacles to college going.

Academic factors, wanting to get married, and lack of encouragement, all factors known to be related to educational outcomes as perceived barriers to continued education, were not shown to be highly related to differential
educational aspirations. The lack of discriminating power for such variables
suggest that some seniors may not be aware of their own vulnerability to such
potential barriers to actually realizing their own goal projections for education
beyond high school.

The discriminant analyses abstracted two meaningful dimensions to
account for the obtained discrimination among groups on the basis of this variable set. The first of these was mostly an economic factor, which was positively
related to educational aspirations except that groups aspiring to the baccalaureate degrees and to postgraduate degrees had similar scores. The second dimension was comprised of the potential barriers resulting from academic factors and
from lack of encouragement. Students with limited college aspirations were
partially separated from the other three aspiration groups on this dimension.
Thus, while there are not large differences among educational aspiration groups
as to whether they perceived certain academic factors or lack of encouragement
as influences on a decision not to continue education, these variables do have
some value in discriminating students who only aspire to some college (less than
four years).

It was noted that the form of the items in this variable set may not
have yielded very sensitive measurements of vulnerability. Yet, the lack of
stronger differentiations among aspiration groups in terms of some variables
known to be related to actual educational outcomes after high school is suggestive. Further, more controlled research on this question would be warranted.

The results were consistent with those of other researchers who
maintain that the effects of economic factors on educational outcomes are difficult to interpret because of the influence of other factors and that family income per se is not necessarily a primary determinant of college going at this
time.

Decisions

The results showed a logical consistency in the timing of certain key
life decisions for young adults. The anticipated time of getting married, entering
one's "ultimate" occupation, and entering the military (for males) were positively related to the extent of education to which they aspired. Whether or not
students believe they will actually go to college (expectation) was highly related
to their declarations of aspirations.

The earliness of deciding whether or not to go to college was shown
to be positively related to how much higher education students aspired to. This
is consistent with research on educational outcomes. This result was viewed in
the context of a necessary tension between tentativeness and commitment in the
decision making of adolescents.

The discriminant analyses revealed a high degree of differentiation among aspiration groups on the basis of this variable set. The educational expectation variable was a consistent component of the first dimension. The earliness of making a decision about college was negatively associated with the second dimension in most of the eight state-sex analyses. The first dimension was positively related to educational aspirations, with educational aspiration groups 3 and 4 (B.A. or postgraduate degrees) being nearly identical. The second dimension differentiated educational aspiration group 2 (limited college) from the other three groups, confirming other SCOPE findings that a high percentage of junior college students were late deciders.

DIFFERENTIAL NEEDS OF STUDENTS

Several aspects of developmental theory have been used to understand the findings of this study. In addition, comparisons, where available, were made between previous findings with educational outcomes as the criterion and findings with educational aspirations as the criterion. An implicit assumption is that educational aspirations, and the ways in which attributes and behaviors of high school seniors are related to their educational aspirations, form precursors of later educational outcomes. Viewing the findings of this study from these perspectives should suggest the differing needs which students with varying visions of their futures have during the high school years.

The developmental themes included Erik Erikson's conceptualizations of ego identity development in adolescence (Chapter 6). Attention was also given to aspects of decision-making theory (Chapter 8), and to vocational development theory (Chapters 5 and 8). Two parameters basic to the development of ego identity in adolescence are crisis and commitment. Crisis implies a process of upheaval, doubt, questioning, and a reorganization of basic identifications and loyalties. Commitment refers to a decided orientation in some direction with respect to values, goals, occupation, and the like. Commitment may or may not occur as a result of crisis; if commitment occurs without the experience of crisis, it usually means the unquestioning appropriation of parental values and orientations. This of course represents bypassing a crucial part of the developmental process. Studies in vocational development and decision making suggest that there needs to be a tension between commitment and tentativeness in adolescent decision making. There is a sense in which certain decisions are, in effect, irreversible. A strong orientation in a given direction without an awareness of the necessary tentativeness, pending the acquisition of further information about oneself and about other available options, can lead to a premature restriction of alternatives. This can be seen as a truncation of development, in that it represents a kind of foreclosure. Information gathering and the extent of information about vocational alternatives have been identified as dimensions of vocational maturity in adolescence.

The choices, problems and conflicts, and perceived barriers to educational fulfillment which have been among the variables used in this study may, on the surface, appear to fall short of common-sense notions of crisis in life experiences. This may well be true for some late adolescents. But the actual termination of the school years is a propitious event in the life of most, if not all, persons in American society. Graduation from high school has been seen as a rite of passage to the adult world even if by the indirect route of higher education (Tillery, 1973). It is a time when all must decide or accept other's decisions; when relationships and life styles change, will it or not; and when self-assessment can scarcely be escaped. It is within this context that the concept of crisis in adolescent development has been of great interest in formulating the issues and findings of this study of educational aspirations. These several aspects of adolescent development are not antagonistic, but can be seen as being complementary. A number of the findings of the present study, viewed from this framework, combine to suggest the high school students grouped on the basis of their educational aspirations have different needs from a developmental standpoint. For example, women tend to agree less with significant adults on social issues as educational aspirations increase, and there was some evidence that men with limited or four-year educational aspirations disagree most with significant adults. The work of Erikson suggests that the experiencing of crisis may lead to more disagreement with significant adults since crisis is a period of questioning in which one arrives at his own personal stand on issues of importance. Students with more extensive educational aspirations are more concerned with problems related to college, and engage in more activities to gather information about college, than students with less extensive educational aspirations. This is not surprising, simply from a practical standpoint.

Concern with problems about work and information gathering about jobs are not as related to students' educational aspirations as are concerns about college-related problems. While all students, regardless of their educational aspirations, seem to have relatively high or moderately high scores on work-related variables in comparison to the corresponding college variables, concern with the world of work is certainly more pressing for students who do not see themselves as college bound. To be sure, the problems about work sampled in this study dealt mostly with immediate rather than long-range, post-high school activities. At the least, this apparent inconsistency suggests further study and observation to determine if noncollege-bound students have developmental needs, particularly about career choice and preparation, which are not being met in school.

The concern is further buttressed by other findings. Students with less extensive educational aspirations seem less psychologically vulnerable to some factors known to affect educational outcomes beyond high school; they do not, for example, report academic factors or lack of encouragement as potential obstacles to college going. This is seen in part as an information or an awareness dimension, although it must be recognized that these students responded from the vantage point of their lack of aspiration for higher education, whereas those aspiring to go to college were more likely to be attempting to anticipate factors which could potentially prevent the realization of their aspirations. However, students with less extensive educational aspirations made their decisions about whether or not to go to college relatively late in high school, as compared to their peers with extensive educational aspirations. In fact, high school seniors whose aspirations did not include senior college appear still (as groups) to be struggling with the choice of going to college versus getting a job. Thus the decision is apparently not yet settled for many high school seniors with limited or noncollege educational aspirations.

These findings combine to suggest the hypothesis that students with limited aspiration for higher education are, as a group, less certain in their decision making. They seem to be vulnerable to decisions by default, by their very lack of goal orientation and related preparation. They may not have experienced what Erikson has called crisis, or as high school seniors they may still be in a state of crisis regarding life goals. At any rate they seem to be lacking in a sense of direction. They are less autonomous than their college-aspiring peers, and lower in their endorsement of work ethic ideals.

Other research findings have suggested that a strong college orientation in high school does not seem to foreclose noncollege, post-high school options, whereas a strong noncollege orientation in high school definitely places a limit on college-going options. This may have as much to do with the kinds of persons who develop different goal orientations in high school as it does with the orientation of their schools and the range of school experiences available to them. At any rate, it would seem that encouraging a commitment in some direction, with a healthy regard for its tentative nature, would help prevent vulnerability to default in the key decisions about postsecondary life.

This means that high schools need to give more attention to the particular needs of students who are not strongly oriented to college going. This, like other studies, suggests that counselors are less helpful to noncollege-bound students than to students who are aspiring to higher education with the baccalaureate or higher degrees in mind. A stronger effort to meet the needs of these students would not mean persuading them to become like college-bound students. It would be, rather, an attempt to help them learn more about themselves and the options open to them so that they may be able to make some tentative commitments and engage in explorations of options earlier in high school.

As it is, findings of the present investigation indicate that many students who are not at all or only hesitantly college bound are "turned off" to the traditional high school setting, or to education in general. They do not place as much emphasis on the importance of achievement or of learning in school as do peers who have declared aspirations for extensive higher education. They also are lower in their intellectual orientation as measured by short scales composed of OPI items and they are not attracted to colleges with pronounced academic orientations. High school seniors with two-year educational aspirations seem to find colleges characterized primarily by attributes other than the academic emphasis to be attractive. Instead of trying to find ways to fit these students into the academic-intellectual mold, it would seem efficacious to find ways to fit the high school programs to their particular interests, talents, and life styles. If in the process some students become more excited about learning and decide to continue their educations, that would be well and good; but this would be a by-product of education for diversity.

In this connection, it is regrettable that the present study did not include a control for level of measured ability. This would have facilitated the identification of other interesting groups of students, such as students of high ability, and perhaps high intellectual orientation, who also for various reasons are turned off to education and do not aspire to continue their education beyond high school. A longitudinal case study of such groups is now in progress as one of the major SCOPE endeavors (Tillery and Omelich, 1973).

It is not the purpose of this study to design and delineate programs for meeting these needs in the high schools. However, some directions can be indicated. It would seem that an attack on a number of fronts could be useful. These could include such things as small discussion groups for students who are interested in exploring their own lives, interests, talents; more opportunities for personal and group counseling by counselors who are interested in the personal development and growth of individuals; information retrieval programs, perhaps modeled after the decision-making program developed in the Palo Alto schools (Clarke, Gelatt, and Levine, 1965) which makes relevant educational-vocational information more readily available and useable; games for the simulation of decision-making situations; more diversified curricula to meet diverse interests and abilities. These could include programs for occupational and educational experiences and exploration in the community, but in any case would involve the development of curricula which respond to the interests of, and make learning more fun and exciting for, high school students who do not have strong intellectual or college orientations.

STATE-SEX DIFFERENCES

A number of interesting state-sex differences were reported in the preceding chapters of this book. A few such differences, which seemed to form a pattern, will be summarized here.

North Carolina

A number of the findings of this study seem to suggest that students in North Carolina are more conventional in their outlook and perhaps in some ways more disadvantaged than their peers in the other three project states. They are somewhat more inclined to accept traditional middle class values in contrast to more liberal, critical orientations found among students in the more urban states. Furthermore, the high ratio of black to white students in the Southern state accounts for the evidence of relative educational disadvantage.

Men in North Carolina are more likely than those in the other states to state that good grades and learning are important, regardless of their educational goal projections. This is also true of women in North Carolina, who scored higher on these variables than other women. However, the results indicated that high school seniors in North Carolina score lower on measures of ability than students in the other states. It seems all too obvious to point out that traditional measures of academic ability are inappropriate for students from many poor and minority backgrounds. In addition, North Carolinians scored lower in autonomy, higher in work ethic ideals, and were generally more conservative in their stance on social issues than other students.

It was only for North Carolina students that the issue of where one stands on religion turned out to be a problem related to educational aspirations. Most students indicated that this is not a great problem. North Carolinians, particularly men with two-year or no college goal projections indicated the importance of this problem.

In contrast to other students, North Carolinians indicated a relatively high degree of agreement with significant adults on social issues (e.g., Vietnam, law and order, protest movements).

In contrast to the results in other state-sex groups, there was no relationship between certain of the college information-gathering activities—visiting campuses and talking with college personnel—and the educational aspirations of male seniors in North Carolina. This was because seniors with less extensive educational aspirations engaged in these activities as much as those with goal projections toward four or more years of post-high school education. To top it off, men in North Carolina also reported more activities in job information gathering than anyone else.

A more traditional conservative orientation, as compared to other students, seems to be apparent in the greater degree of work ethic endorsement, more positive attitudes toward school and learning, more conservative attitudes toward social issues and the greater agreement with adults on these same issues. There is some impression that many seniors have foreclosed in Marcia's sense of identity development and may not be experiencing the crises of late adolescence. On the other hand, the greater orientation to a work ethic, and the relatively high degree of information-gathering activities are, in association with the helpfulness of others, strengths in preparation for postsecondary life.

While the racial and SES proportions in the North Carolina subsamples were the same as those in the other state-sex groups, the composition of these groups may well be quite different. The four SES groups, being based on college productivity, may be generally of a somewhat lower income or occupational level than the corresponding four groups in the other states. The non-

Caucasians in North Carolina probably consist of more blacks and American Indians than, for example, California, in which the non-Caucasians included large numbers of Mexican-Americans and Orientals. These differences very likely influenced the results reported above.

California

Californians generally were slightly lower than other students in the SCOPE work ethic measures. But only males with senior college aspirations tended to have more conservative stances regarding protest movements and law and order than their peers. However, the morality of refusing to fight in Vietnam was negatively related to level of aspirations, thus the boys who were not bound for college had the most conservative attitudes on this war issue. These issues tended to be unrelated to the educational goal projections of men in the other three states. The tendency in other states for girls to agree with parents concerning occupational choice more so if they have high rather than low educational goals was not apparent for California girls.

Male high school seniors in California with two-year educational aspirations were more convinced that they would actually go to college than were two-year aspirants in the other states. The same group of students made their decision about whether or not to go to college earlier than comparable groups in the other states. The widespread availability of free comprehensive education at local community colleges would seem to be a factor in this California uniqueness.

In the discriminant analyses of the set of variables about key life decisions, male two-year aspirants in California were more like those aspiring to senior college degrees than were the two-year aspirants in Illinois, Massachusetts, and North Carolina. In a somewhat different way this difference seems related to the California community colleges namely, that they may serve more students who were eligible to enter senior colleges and who are likely to transfer after work in the community college. In addition, California community colleges provide easier access to college for students who in other states may find college going unthinkable.

Massachusetts

Males in Massachusetts, like those in Illinois, who aspire to limited higher education see the possibility of not being admitted to a preferred college as a more serious barrier to college attendance than do their peers in the other two states. This seems congruent with other SCOPE findings which show that students generally in Massachusetts and Illinois apply to more public and private institutions for first admission than do California and North Carolina students.

Fear of failing as a barrier to college attendance is characteristic of boys in Massachusetts who seem to be headed for graduate education. On the other hand, for Massachusetts girls, wanting to make money as a barrier to higher education is not inversely related to their level of aspiration as in the other states. It should also be noted that for these groups of girls in the Northeastern state, those who declared aspirations to earn baccalaureate degrees are most conservative on selected social issues, while the girls headed for graduate degrees are the most liberal.

Finally, among their peers Massachusetts males who apparently are not college bound are least likely to believe that by high school graduation they should know where they are headed.

Illinois

Illinois girls, like their California counterparts, are less likely than the other girls to have differing degrees of agreement with their parents on choice of occupation depending upon their levels of educational aspiration.

For Illinois boys, note has already been made of the fact that the two-year college group see academic factors as greater barriers to college than their peers elsewhere. This group, too, like their state peers who say they are headed to graduate study, see fear of failure as a possible barrier to college going.

CONCLUSION

Many of the results of this study, some of which were suggestive but not conclusive, should prove to be of heuristic value in providing questions for additional research. Focusing on such problems by the use of certain theoretical conceptualizations in viewing the results enhances the heuristic value, even though much of this effort was post hoc.

In closing, it seems appropriate to stress the fundamental importance to the improvement of education of qualities and qualifications of those who teach, who provide guidance and services, and who manage schools. Recognition and respect by all of these *significant others* is essential. Equally so is the willingness of school people to get close enough to students to serve as models for them. The possibilities of influencing developmental identifications during the school years will be dependent, in part, on such personal characteristics of these key adults as race and ethnic origins, age, sex, life styles, and interests. In many places there is still little congruence between the characteristics of students and those who serve them. In short, new attention needs to be given to personal growth and development of the remarkable range of human beings in our schools in contrast to the current emphasis on academic achievement.

Appendix A

Variable Sets and Lists

Outline of Variable Sets

5	Problems and Conflicts—Interpersonal A. College and Academic Variables B. Job and Career Variables C. Personal-Social Issue Variables	10
6	Helpfulness of Others	5
7	Barriers to Continued Education	11
8	Decisions	5

8 Separate
Variable Sets

88 Total
Variables

ATTITUDES TOWARD SCHOOL, ACADEMIC
BEHAVIOR, AND ACHIEVEMENT

Variable Set 1
Chapter 3

Variable
Number

Values and Attitudes Concerning Education

1 "Getting good grades."
   0. Not important
   1. Fairly important
   2. Very important
   3. One of the most important things in my life

2 "Importance of learning as much as possible in school."
   Scoring same as variable 1

3 "Believing that the important things in life are not learned in college."—This variable is based on a question which asks the student how influential such a belief was (or would be) on a decision not to go to college. Scoring was as follows:
   0. A great deal of influence
   1. Some influence

2. A little influence
3. No influence

Variables 4-9 are based on items subsumed under the question: "Look over the six types of colleges described below. If you had the opportunity, how much would you like to attend each of these types? (answer even if you are not now planning to go on to college.")

4 Attractiveness of academic (intellectual) type of college—"At College A there are many good students who try to get top grades. Professors expect them to study a lot, but often are willing to discuss such things as current world affairs and other serious topics outside of classes. Students enjoy going to concerts and lectures on campus."
  0. Not at all
  1. A little
  2. Quite a bit
  3. Very much

5 Attractiveness of friendly student activities type of college—"At College B there are many activities and students are encouraged to take part. The professors go out of their way to make sure that students understand the class work, and everyone is friendly on campus."
  Scoring same as variable 4.

6 Attractiveness of philosophically-oriented type of college—"At College C students are more interested in searching for the meaning of life and in examining their own values than in extracurricular activities, athletics, or traditional 'school spirit.' Many classes are small and informal and everyone has a chance to present his own ideas."
  Scoring same as variable 4.

7 Attractiveness of political-social activist type of college—"At College E there is a lot of interest in current social issues. Students as well as professors are often active in political and community affairs, both on-campus and off-campus."
  Scoring same as variable 4.

8 Attractiveness of career- or occupation-oriented college—"At College F students are preparing for a particular job or career. They are mostly interested in courses which train them for occupations they have chosen. Many of the students are working part time to pay for their education."
  Scoring same as variable 4.

9 Attractiveness of school spirit, low pressure type of college—"At College D

there is a lot of school spirit and most students go to athletic events. Most students do not study on Saturdays and feel free to go to movies during the week. Many of the girls at this school expect to be married as soon as they graduate."

Scoring same as variable 4.

Academic Striving

10 "What grades do you *try* to get?"
   0. Not passing (mostly D's and F's)
   1. Poor, but passing (mostly C's and D's)
   2. Average (mostly C's)
   3. Good (mostly B's)
   4. Excellent (mostly A's)

11 "About how many hours each week during the school year do you spend doing homework?"
   0. None
   1. 1-5 hours
   2. 6-10 hours
   3. 11-15 hours
   4. More than 15 hours

12 "Which of the following statements best describes your attitude toward school work in grade twelve?"
   0. I didn't care how well I did in any of my courses.
   1. I usually did only enough to get by in each course.
   2. I did the best I could in some courses; in others I did just enough to get by.
   3. I did the very best I could in all my courses.

Self-evaluation of Academic Ability

13 "In general, do you feel you can do college work?"
   0. I don't know
   1. I definitely do not have the ability
   2. I probably do not have the ability
   3. I probably have the ability
   4. I definitely have the ability

Measured Aptitude and Achievement

14 Verbal score on the Academic Aptitude Test.

15 Math score on the Academic Aptitude Test.

16 "How do you think you are rated by your teachers?"
      0. Not passing (mostly D's and F's)
      1. Poor, but passing (mostly C's and D's)
      2. Average (mostly C's)
      3. Good (mostly B's)
      4. Excellent (mostly A's)

PERSONAL PROPENSITIES AND VALUES

Variable Set 2

Chapter 4

Variable
Number

Intellectual Orientation

1 "Autonomy"—The SCOPE Autonomy Scale was comprised of the following fifteen OPI Au items which were summed to form a single scale. The scoring for each item, before summing, was: 0-true; 1-false.
      a. Nothing in life is worth being separated from your family.
      b. More than anything else, it is good hard work that makes life worth-while.
      c. It is a pretty cold-hearted person who does not feel love and gratitude to his parents.
      d. Only a fool would try to change our American way of life.
      e. It is never right to disobey the government.
      f. I am in favor of strict enforcement of laws no matter what.
      g. The most important qualities of a husband are determination and ambition.
      h. Every wage earner should be required to save a certain part of his salary each month so that he will be able to support himself and his family in later years.
      i. Young people sometimes get rebellious ideas, but as they grow up they ought to get over them and settle down.
      j. I have been taught to live by certain standards which I carefully follow.
      k. Every person ought to be proud of his own home town.
      l. Communism is the most hateful thing in the world today.
      m. The surest way to a peaceful world is to improve the way people behave.

    n. I dislike women who try to be different.
    o. People ought to be satisfied with what they have.

2 "Theoretical Orientation-Science"—The SCOPE TO-Science was based on the summation of the following three OPI-TO items:

    a. I like to read about science.
       0. False
       1. True

    b. The idea of doing research does not appeal to me.
       0. True
       1. False

    c. I would enjoy writing a paper on the possible long-term effects or results of a significant research discovery.
       0. False
       1. True

3 "Theoretical Orientation-Problem-Solving"—The following three OPI-TO items were summed to form a single scale:

    a. I prefer to have a problem explained to me rather than trying to figure it out myself.
       0. True
       1. False

    b. I want to know that something will really work before I am willing to take a chance on it.
       0. True
       1. False

    c. I prefer a long, rather complicated problem to several shorter ones.
       0. False
       1. True

4 "Thinking Introversion-Music"—The scale was based on the summation of the following three OPI-TI items:

    a. I leave the radio tuned to a symphony concert rather than to popular music.
       0. False
       1. True

b. I prefer popular music to classical music.
   0. True
   1. False

c. I have spent a lot of time listening to serious music.
   0. False
   1. True

5 "Thinking Introversion-Analysis"—The summation of the following six OPI-TI items formed the single scale:

   a. I would enjoy studying the causes of an important international event and writing a theme or report on it.
      0. False
      1. True

   b. I enjoy writing what I like or dislike about a book or story.
      0. False
      1. True

   c. I like to discuss the causes and possible solutions to political or international problems or such problems as racial integration.
      0. False
      1. True
   d. I like to read serious poetry.
      0. False
      1. True

   e. I enjoy reading about serious subjects.
      0. False
      1. True

   f. I prefer just to read a story rather than discuss what the author was thinking about when he wrote it.
      0. True
      1. False

Work Ethic and Identification With the Establishment

Variables 6, 7, and 8 were grouped under the overall question, "How important is each of these to you now?"

6 Being a leader.

    0. Not important
    1. Fairly important
    2. Very important
    3. One of the most important things in my life.

7 Being able to do at least one thing very well.
    Scoring same as variable 6.

8 Putting up a good fight when you compete with others.
    Scoring same as variable 6.

9 "By high school graduation people should know where they are headed in life and what they want to become."
    0. Strong disagreement
    1. Some disagreement
    2. Neutral
    3. Some agreement
    4. Strong agreement

10 When I am with friends "I expect the best of others."
    0. Never
    1. Sometimes
    2. Often
    3. A lot

11 When I am with friends "I like people who are hard workers."
    0. Never
    1. Sometimes
    2. Often
    3. A lot

12 "Work Ethic"—based on summation of the following three items. The scoring for each item, before summing, was: 0-false; 1-true.

    a. The most important qualities of a husband are determination and ambition.
    b. Every wage earner should be required to save a certain part of his salary each month so that he will be able to support himself and his family in later years.
    c. More than anything else, it is good hard work that makes life worthwhile.

Attitudes Toward Social Issues

13 "It's more important to work for the good of the community than for one's own self-interests."
   0. Strong disagreement
   1. Some disagreement
   2. Neutral
   3. Some agreement
   4. Strong agreement

14 "Student protest movements do more harm than good."
   Code same as variable 13.

15 "Attending religious meetings regularly is necessary to lead a good life."
   Code same as variable 13.

16 "It is morally wrong for a person to refuse to fight in Vietnam even if doing so violates his beliefs."
   Code same as variable 13.

17 "Disrespect for law and order is the major problem in our society today."
   Code same as variable 13.

INFORMATION-GATHERING BEHAVIOR

Variable Set 3
Chapter 5

Variable
Number

College

Variables 1-3 assess the extent of activities engaged in by students for gathering information about prospective colleges. Each of the original questionnaire items was subsumed under the question, "In getting information about the college you would especially like to go to, how did you react to the following things?" The original response choices for each of the items were:

   a. I haven't done this
   b. It triggered a decision

    c. It encouraged me to go ahead
    d. I opened up new ideas
    e. It was sort of useful
    f. It didn't teach me much
    g. It left me really mixed up
    h. It left me angry
    i. It killed my interest

The choices were dichotomized to yield an indication of whether or not the particular information gathering activity was undertaken by the student: choice *a*, indicating the student had not undertaken the activity, was assigned a score of zero; any of choices *b* through *i*, indicating the student had undertaken (though not necessarily profited by) the activity, was assigned a score of one. It is important to note that these variables assess the extent of information-gathering activity but not the amount of information gained.

1 Talking with high school personnel—This variable consists of the sum of the following two items, each having been recoded as described above. Thus, if a student had engaged in neither activity, he should have a score of 0 on variable one; if he had done either activity, he would have a score of 1; and if he had done both, he would have a score of two.

    a. Talking with my counselor
    b. Talking with my teacher(s)

2 Talking with college personnel—This variable consists of a sum of the following four items, each having been dichotomously scored as described above. Thus, the resulting scores on variable 2 could range from 0 to 4.

    a. Talking with people who went to the college
    b. Talking with admissions people from this college
    c. Talking with financial aid counselor at this college
    d. Talking with people from athletic department at this college

3 Visiting colleges—This variable was formed by summing the following two items, each with the previous described dichotomous scoring.

    a. Visiting this campus on my own
    b. Taking school tours to one or more colleges

Career

Variables 4-6 ascertain the extent to which certain activities were engaged in by students in gathering information about prospective employment. Each of the original questionnaire items was subsumed under the question, "In looking into future jobs, how did you react to the following things?" Response choices as well as scoring were the same as described above for variables 1-3.

4 Talking with high school personnel—This variable was formed by summing the following two items, each having dichotomous scoring described above.

    a. Talking with my counselor
    b. Talking with teacher(s)

5 Personally exploring job possibilities—This variable consists of a summation of the following four items, each dichotomously scored as described above.

    a. Visiting a place where I might work
    b. Talking to people who might employ me
    c. Talking with people who do kinds of work that interest me
    d. Watching people do kinds of work that interest me

6 Learning from mass media—This variable is the sum of the following two items, each dichotomously scored.

    a. Reading about job opportunities
    b. Learning about job(s) on TV or radio

PROBLEMS AND CONFLICTS—PERSONAL

Variable Set 4
Chapter 6

Variable
Number

College and Academic Variables

1 "Is deciding what your college major will be a problem for you now?"
    0. Not at all
    1. A little
    2. Quite a bit
    3. Very much

2 Discrepancy between actual (as reported by the student) and aspired high

school grades—This variable represents the difference between the following two items. If this difference was negative (actual grades higher than aspired grades) a score of zero was assigned.

 a. "On the basis of this year's grades, how do you think you are rated by your teachers?"
   0. Excellent (mostly A's)
   1. Good (mostly B's)
   2. Average (mostly C's)
   3. Poor, but passing (mostly C's and D's)
   4. Not passing (mostly D's and F's)

 b. "What grades do you *try* to get?"
   Scoring same as (a).

3 "Is deciding what kind of a student to be a problem for you now?"
   0. Not at all
   1. Somewhat
   2. Quite a bit
   3. Very much

4 "Has finding out what kinds of colleges suit your abilities and interests been a problem for you?"
   0. Not at all
   1. Somewhat
   2. Quite a bit
   3. Very much

5 "Has deciding what to do if rejected by your first choice college been a problem for you?"
   Scoring same as variable 4.

6 Immediacy of problem—"When will it be (has it been) *most* difficult for you to choose between going to college to (a) develop a philosophy of life or (b) prepare for a job?"
   0. Never a problem
   1. Earlier in my life OR probably in the future
   2. Right now

7 Immediacy of problem—"When will it be (has it been) *most* difficult for you to choose between (a) applying for a job which is now available or (b) going to school to prepare for a better job?"
   Scoring same as variable 6.

Job and Career Variables

8 Agreement between aspired and expected occupations—This variable utilized the following three items:

    a. The occupation most like what I really want to be
    b. The occupation most like my second choice
    c. The occupation most like what I think I'll really be

The response choices for each item were a list of 80 occupations taken from the Project Talent Interest Inventory. The scoring of these three items to constitute variable 8 was as follows:

    0. Neither the 1st choice nor the 2nd choice agrees with the anticipated occupation.
    1. The second choice agrees with the anticipated occupation.
    2. The first choice agrees with the anticipated occupation.

9 "Has deciding what to do if you don't get the job you want been a problem for you?"

    0. Not at all
    1. Somewhat
    2. Quite a bit
    3. Very much

10 "Has learning how your interests fit with different jobs been a problem for you?"

    Scoring same as variable 9.

11 "Has finding out about job requirements been a problem for you?"

    Scoring same as variable 9.

12 "Has finding out where to train for the job you want been a problem for you?"

    Scoring same as variable 9.

Personal-Social Issue Variables

13 "Is where you stand on politics a problem for you now?"

    0. Not at all
    1. A little
    2. Quite a bit
    3. Very much

14 "Is where you stand on religion a problem for you now?"
Scoring same as variable 13.

15 "Is deciding what kind of a person to be a problem for you now?"
Scoring same as variable 13.

16 Immediacy of problem—"When will it be (has it been) *most* difficult for you
to choose between (a) trying to control what happens to you or (b) taking
things as they come?"
0. Never a problem
1. Earlier in my life OR probably in the future
2. Right now

17 Immediacy of problem—"When will it be (has it been) *most* difficult for you
to choose between (a) doing something you know you're good at or (b) trying something you've never done before?"
Scoring same as variable 16.

18 Immediacy of problem—"When will it be (has it been) *most* difficult to
choose between (a) keeping problems to yourself or (b) talking to others
who might help you?"
Scoring same as variable 16.

PROBLEMS AND CONFLICTS—INTERPERSONAL

Variable Set 5
Chapter 6

Variable
Number

College Choice Variables

1 "Has working out difficulties with your parents about which college to
attend been a problem for you?"
0. Not at all
1. Somewhat
2. Quite a bit
3. Very much

2 Immediacy of problem—"When will it be (has it been) *most* difficult for you
to decide between (a) choosing a college major you like or (b) choosing one
your parents want for you?"

0. Never a problem
1. Earlier in my life OR probably in the future
2. Right now

Variables 3 and 4 are based on several items which were subsumed under the following question: "Suppose you were in college and you had to choose a major. Answer the following questions about such a major field of study even if you might not go to college." Response categories were provided by the following list of 21 general college majors:

a. Undecided or I don't know
b. Business
c. English, speech
d. Social sciences such as history, psychology, anthropology, economics
e. Agriculture, forestry
f. Biological sciences
g. Physical sciences
h. Mathematics
i. Vocational, trade, and industrial arts
j. Languages, fine arts, philosophy
k. Military
l. Elementary education
m. Engineering, architecture
n. General education (Liberal arts)
o. Theology, religion
p. Music, drama, graphic arts
q. Medical technology, nursing
r. Pre-professions such as medicine, dentistry, pharmacy
s. Pre-law
t. Physical education
u. Other

3 Agreement with parents on choice of college major—To assess the extent of agreement this variable utilized the following three items (see above explanation):

a. My first choice (of college major)
b. The major my mother would want me to choose
c. The major my father would want me to choose

Scoring of these three items to constitute variable 3 was as follows:
0. Student's hypothetical first choice of major does not agree with either parent's choice (as reported by student)

1. Student's choice agrees with the choice of one parent only
2. Student's choice agrees with the choice of both parents

4 Agreement with counselor and best-liked teacher on choice of college major—To assess the extent of agreement this variable utilized the following three items (see above explanation):

   a. My first choice (of college major)
   b. The major my counselor would recommend
   c. The major my best-liked teacher would recommend

Scoring of these three items to constitute variable 4 was as follows:

   0. Student's hypothetical first choice of major does not agree with the recommendation (as reported by the student) of either his counselor or his best-liked teacher
   1. Student's choice agrees with the recommendation of either his counselor or his best-liked teacher
   2. Student's choice agrees with the recommendation of both his counselor and his best-liked teacher

Occupation Variable

5 Agreement with parents on aspired career—To asses the extent of agreement this variable utilized the following three items:

   a. The occupation most like what I really want to be
   b. The occupation most like what my mother (female guardian) wants me to be
   c. The occupation most like what my father (male guardian) wants me to be

The response choices for each item were the same list of occupations described in variable 8 of the preceding section. Scoring of these items was as follows:

   0. Student's hypothetical choice of occupation does not agree with either parent's choice (as reported by student)
   1. Student's choice agrees with the choice of one parent only
   2. Student's choice agrees with the choice of both parents

Personal-Social Issue Variables

Variables 6-10 assess generalized agreement with significant others on the following size statements concerning personal-social issues:

a. By high school graduation people should know where they are headed in life and what they want to become
b. Student protest movements do more harm than good
c. It is more important to work for the good of the community than for ones' own self-interests
d. Attending religious meetings regularly is necessary to lead a good life
e. It is morally wrong for a person to refuse to fight in Vietnam even if doing so violates his beliefs
f. Disrespect for law and order is the major problem in our society today

Each of variables 6 to 10 utilize responses to the following questions: "Do you agree with each statement? Do you *think* your parents, teachers, and friends would agree with the statements? Give your opinion even if you are not sure." The response choices were:

a. Strong disagreement
b. Some disagreement
c. Neutral
d. Some agreement
e. Strong agreement

Each of variables 6 to 10 was formed by first taking the absolute difference, for each of the six issues, between the student's own agreement and the agreement of a significant other (as reported by the student) with each of the six items. Each absolute difference was then subtracted from a constant (4) so that a high score (4) represents congruence between one's own attitude and one's perception of the other's attitude toward a particular item while a low score (0) represents lack of congruence. These scores for each of the size issues were then summed to yield a scale of absolute disagreement (0) to absolute agreement (24) with a significant other on attitudes toward the social issues.

6 Agreement with mother on attitudes toward the above six issues.
   A scale of agreement, derived as described above

7 Agreement with father on attitudes toward the above six issues.
   A scale of agreement, derived as described above

8 Agreement with best-liked teacher on attitudes toward the above six issues.
   A scale of agreement, derived as described above

9 Agreement with best-liked girl on attitudes toward the above six issues.
   A scale of agreement, derived as described above

10 Agreement with best-liked boy on attitudes toward the above six issues.
A scale of agreement, derived as described above

HELPFULNESS OF OTHERS

Variable Set 6

Chapter 6

Variable
Number

Variables 1-5 assess the relative overall helpfulness of significant others with
the following 14 selected potential problems:

a. Making sure that my school work is right for what I want to do after
graduation
b. Finding out about my interests and what I do best
c. Learning how my interests fit with different jobs
d. Finding out requirements for job I want
e. Finding out where to train for job I want
f. Finding out whatkinds of colleges suit my abilities and interests
g. Working out differences with parents about which college to attend
h. Finding out about admission requirements to college
i. Finding out about tuition and living costs at different colleges
j. Finding out about financial aid for college
k. Deciding what to do if I don't get job I want
l. Deciding what to do if first choice college rejects me
m. Deciding what to do if more than one accepts me
n. Deciding job to accept if more than one is offered to me

For each of the above problems the student indicated "which one of the
following people was most helpful":

a. Best-liked teacher
b. Counselor
c. Mother (female guardian)
d. Father (male guardian)
e. Brothers or sisters
f. Friends of the same age
g. A college official

1 Helpfulness of best-liked teacher with the above 14 problems. The frequency

of "teacher" responses yielded a scale of least helpfulness (0) to most help-fulness (14) with the problems listed above.

2 Helpfulness of counselor with the above 14 problems.
  A scale of helpfulness based on the frequency of "counselor" responses, derived as described above

3 Helpfulness of mother with the above 14 problems.
  A scale of helpfulness based on the frequency of "mother" responses, derived as described above.

4 Helpfulness of father with the above 14 problems.
  A scale of helpfulness based on the frequency of "father" responses, derived as described above

5 Helpfulness of peers with the above 14 problems.
  A scale of helpfulness based on the frequency of "friends same age" responses, derived as described above

BARRIERS TO CONTINUED EDUCATION

Variable Set 7
Chapter 7

Variable
Number

1 "If you wanted to attend college next year, would you have the money to do so?"
  0. I would have the money
  1. I'm not sure I'd have the money
  2. I wouldn't have the money

Variables 2-11 are based on items subsumed under the question: "If in the future you decide you don't want to go to college or are unable to go, how much influence do you think the following would have on such a decision? If you have already decided not to go, how much influence did the following have on your decision?"

2 "Parents (or guardians) not having enough money"
  0. A great deal of influence
  1. Some influence

    2. A little

    3. No influence

3 "Not being able to earn enough money to go"
   Scoring same as variable 2.

4 "Thinking that my grades aren't good enough"
   Scoring same as variable 2.

5 "Being afraid I might not make it"
   Scoring same as variable 2.

6 "Not being admitted to the college I wanted to attend"
   Scoring same as variable 2.

7 "Not getting much encouragement to go"
   Scoring same as variable 2.

8 "Not being given the right advice on what courses to take"
   Scoring same as variable 2.

9 "Believing that the important things in life aren't learned in college"
   Scoring same as variable 2.

10 "Wanting to get married"
   Scoring same as variable 2.

11 "Wanting to make money"
   Scoring same as variable 2.

DECISIONS

Variable Set 8

Chapter 8

Variable
Number

Variables 1-3 were based on the question, "When, if ever, do you think you will do the following things *for the first time*?"

1 "Enter one of the military services."
    0. This spring (or already done)

1. This coming summer
2. This coming fall
3. In about one year
4. In about two years
5. In about three years
6. In about four years
8. More than five years from now
9. Probably never

2 "Get married."
   Scoring same as variable 1.

3 "Get the job you want to settle down in."
   Scoring same as variable 1.

4 "Do you think you actually will go to college after high school?"
   0. I don't intend to go to college
   1. I am not sure I will go
   2. Yes, but I don't know to which college
   3. Yes, to college like best; or
      Yes, to college liked second best; or
      Yes, but to some other college.

5 "When did you make your present decision to go or not to go to college?"
   0. I haven't decided yet
   1. This semester
   2. Earlier this year
   3. In the 11th grade
   4. In the 10th grade
   5. In the 9th grade
   6. In the 7th or 8th grade
   7. Before the 7th grade

Appendix B

The Analyses

Each of the tables following in this appendix presents a summary of the multivariate analytic results obtained in each of the eight state-sex groups from the analyses of one variable set. A general description of the strategy used in applying multivariate analysis of variance and discriminant analysis was provided in Chapter 2. Technical details can be found in Bock (1966), Cooley and Lohnes (1971), and Morrison (1967). It is necessary to provide some comments here about the measure of association.

Multivariate analysis of variance (MANOVA) can be seen as an extension of univariate analysis of variance (ANOVA), and in fact the univariate F-tests obtained in the MANOVA for any given variable are exactly the same as would be obtained were that variable used in an ANOVA of the same design with the same independent variables. However, there is much that is not understood about multivariate analyses. One of the major problems is the derivation of a measure of association.

Ideally, a measure of association should be an unbiased representation of the percentage of variance in the dependent variables which is accounted for or can be associated with a given effect (or independent variable). Thus, it is an index similar to a coefficient of determination or the multiple R^2 in regression analysis, and can be thought of as the percentage of redudction in the variance of the dependent variables obtained by knowing the given independent variable. Such coefficients have been presented by Hays (1963) and Marascuilo (1971) for use in ANOVA. No adequate coefficient has been developed for use in MANOVA (Bavry, 1972).

The index of association presented in the following tables is biased. This index is Roy's criterion, obtained in the discriminant analysis. The discriminant analyses were obtained only for the three main effects. The number of independent dimensions oriented in a discriminant analysis is always equal to one less than the number of groups comprising the independent variable. There is a Roy's criterion statistic associated with each function.

Appendix B-1.   Set 1 Academic Attitudes and Behaviors
Summary Tables of Multivariate Analyses of Variance (By State and Sex)

State Sex	Source of Variation	F	$df_{1,2}$	Decision α≤.05	Univariate p≤.05 for Sig. Multivariate Effect*	Index of Association FnI	FnII	FnIII
CA MALES	ED ASP	4.21	48,792	SIG.	1,2,4,5,6,8-16	.42	.09	.04
	SES	1.32	48,792	N.S.				
	RACE	2.51	16,266	SIG.	10-14	.13		
	RACE X SES	.67	48,792	N.S.				
	RACE X ED ASP	1.09	48,792	N.S.				
	SES X ED ASP	1.07	144,2118	N.S.				
	RACE X SES X ED ASP	.86	144,2118	N.S.				
IL MALES	ED ASP	6.45	48,816	SIG.	1,2,4-15	.54	.11	.08
	SES	.99	48,816	N.S.				
	RACE	3.57	16,274	SIG.	10-14	.17		
	RACE X SES	.96	48,816	N.S.				
	RACE X ED ASP	1.13	48,816	N.S.				
	SES X ED ASP	.89	144,2181	N.S.				
	RACE X SES X ED ASP	.82	144,2181	N.S.				
MA MALES	ED ASP	6.28	48,816	SIG.	1,2,4,5,6,8-16	.52	.14	.06
	SES	1.23	48,816	N.S.				
	RACE	1.71	16,274	SIG.	10,11	.09		
	RACE X SES	.93	48,816	N.S.				
	RACE X ED ASP	.89	48,816	N.S.				
	SES X ED ASP	1.15	144,2181	N.S.				
	RACE X SES X ED ASP	1.17	144,2181	N.S.				
NC MALES	ED ASP	4.94	48,810	SIG.	2,3,4,5,8-15	.45	.09	.07
	SES	1.25	48,810	N.S.				
	RACE	6.61	16,272	SIG.	1,2,3,8-12,14	.28		
	RACE X SES	.67	48,810	N.S.				
	RACE X ED ASP	1.09	48,810	N.S.				
	SES X ED ASP	.86	144,2165	N.S.				
	RACE X SES X ED ASP	.98	144,2165	N.S.				

Sample	Effect	F	df	SIG.	Significant items			
CA FEMALES	ED ASP	5.04	48,789	SIG.	1,2,4-15	.45	.11	.08
	SES	1.41	48,789	SIG.	1,2,10,11,15,16	.14	.07	.02
	RACE	3.62	16,265	SIG.	10,11,12,14	.18		
	RACE X SES	1.07	48,789	N.S.				
	RACE X ED ASP	1.00	144,2110	N.S.				
	SES X ED ASP	1.04	144,2110	N.S.				
	RACE X SES X ED ASP	.95		N.S.				
IL FEMALES	ED ASP	3.83	48,810	SIG.	1-15	.39	.09	.03
	SES	.96	48,810	N.S.				
	RACE	4.55	16,272	SIG.		.21		
	RACE X SES	1.22	48,810	N.S.				
	RACE X ED ASP	1.09	144,2165	N.S.				
	SES X ED ASP	1.11	144,2165	N.S.				
	RACE X SES X ED ASP	1.31		SIG.	1,6,11,12,14			
MA FEMALES	ED ASP	4.05	48,792	SIG.	1,2,4,5,7-16	.36	.13	.06
	SES	2.05	48,792	SIG.	1,4,9,10,14	.18	.11	.03
	RACE	1.58	16,266	N.S.				
	RACE X SES	.82	48,792	N.S.				
	RACE X ED ASP	.84	48,792	N.S.				
	SES X ED ASP	1.15	144,2118	N.S.				
	RACE X SES X ED ASP	.97	144,2118	N.S.				
NC FEMALES	ED ASP	4.90	48,792	SIG.	2,4,5,6,7,9-15	.46	.09	.07
	SES	1.57	48,792	SIG.	2,7,9,10,11	.15	.08	.03
	RACE	9.49	16,266	SIG.	1,2,7,9,10-14	.36		
	RACE X SES	.77	48,792	N.S.				
	RACE X ED ASP	1.15	48,792	N.S.				
	SES X ED ASP	1.17	144,2118	N.S.				
	RACE X SES X ED ASP	.82	144,2118	N.S.				

Appendix B-2. Set 2 Personal Propensities and Values
Summary Tables of Multivariate Analyses of Variance (By State and Sex)

State Sex	Source of Variation	F	$df_{1,2}$	Decision $\alpha \leqslant .05$	Univariate $p \leqslant .05$ for Sig. Multivariate Effect*	Index of Association FnI	FnII	FnIII
CA MALES	ED ASP	2.80	51,790	SIG.	1,5,7,8,12-15,17	.22	.14	.09
	SES	1.63	51,790	SIG.	6,14,15	.16	.07	.06
	RACE	1.19	17,265	N.S.				
	RACE X SES	1.14	51,790	N.S.				
	RACE X ED ASP	1.11	51,790	N.S.				
	SES X ED ASP	1.28	153,2139	SIG.	3,			
	RACE X SES X ED ASP	1.17	153,2139	N.S.				
IL MALES	ED ASP	3.38	51,814	SIG.	1,5,7,9,11,13-15,17	.35	.08	.06
	SES	1.34	51,814	N.S.				
	RACE	1.89	17,273	SIG.	7,12,13	.11		
	RACE X SES	.94	51,814	N.S.				
	RACE X ED ASP	1.27	51,814	N.S.				
	SES X ED ASP	1.08	153,2203	N.S.				
	RACE X SES X ED ASP	.97	153,2203	N.S.				
MA MALES	ED ASP	3.45	51,814	SIG.	1-4,6,9,13-15,17	.35	.09	.06
	SES	.90	51,814	N.S.				
	RACE	.87	17,273	N.S.		.05		
	RACE X SES	.97	51,814	N.S.				
	RACE X ED ASP	1.16	51,814	N.S.				
	SES X ED ASP	.98	153,2203	N.S.				
	RACE X SES X ED ASP	.97	153,2203	N.S.				
NC MALES	ED ASP	2.10	51,808	SIG.	1,6,13-15,17	.23	.08	.03
	SES	.99	51,808	N.S.				
	RACE	3.56	17,271	SIG.	1,4,7,8,13,17	.18		
	RACE X SES	1.04	51,808	N.S.				
	RACE X ED ASP	1.26	51,808	N.S.				
	SES X ED ASP	1.12	153,2187	N.S.				
	RACE X SES X ED ASP	.98	153,2187	N.S.				

CA FEMALES	ED ASP	2.50	51,787	SIG.	1,8,12-15,17	.29	.06	.04
	SES	1.19	51,787	N.S.	5,7,13	.10		
	RACE	1.81	17,264	SIG.				
	RACE X SES	1.24	51,787	N.S.				
	RACE X ED ASP	.89	51,787	N.S.				
	SES X ED ASP	1.19	153,2131	N.S.				
	RACE X SES X ED ASP	1.08	153,2131	N.S.				
IL FEMALES	ED ASP	2.72	51,808	SIG.	1,4,7,8,9,12-17	.31	.06	.04
	SES	1.15	51,808	N.S.	5,7,13	.12		
	RACE	2.21	17,271	SIG.				
	RACE X SES	.76	51,808	N.S.				
	RACE X ED ASP	.80	51,808	N.S.				
	SES X ED ASP	.89	153,2187	N.S.				
	RACE X SES X ED ASP	.87	153,2187	N.S.				
MA FEMALES	ED ASP	3.86	51,790	SIG.	1,5-7,11,13-17	.35	.17	.05
	SES	1.61	51,790	SIG.	4,6,13,16	.18	.06	.04
	RACE	.66	17,265	N.S.				
	RACE X SES	1.04	51,790	N.S.				
	RACE X ED ASP	.70	51,790	N.S.				
	SES X ED ASP	.85	153,2139	N.S.				
	RACE X SES X ED ASP	1.05	153,2139	N.S.				
NC FEMALES	ED ASP	3.16	51,790	SIG.	1,4,7,8,10,12-15,17	.34	.08	.06
	SES	1.09	51,790	N.S.	7,8,13	.12		
	RACE	2.03	17,265	SIG.				
	RACE X SES	.59	51,790	N.S.				
	RACE X ED ASP	.72	51,790	N.S.				
	SES X ED ASP	.94	153,2139	N.S.				
	RACE X SES X ED ASP	1.07	153,2139	N.S.				

*The variable numbers designate variables as listed in Appendix I.

Appendix B-3.   Set 3 Information-Gathering Behaviors
Summary Tables of Multivariate Analyses of Variance (By State and Sex)

State Sex	Source of Variation	F	$df_{1,2}$	Decision α≤.05	Univariate p≤.05 for Sig. Multivariate Effect*	Index of Association FnI	FnII	FnIII
CA MALES	ED ASP	3.23	18,781	SIG.	1	.15	.03	.0046
	SES	.48	18,781	N.S.				
	RACE	.68	6,276	N.S.				
	RACE X SES	.70	18,781	N.S.				
	RACE X ED ASP	.63	54,1412	N.S.				
	SES X ED ASP	.49	54,1412	N.S.				
	RACE X SES X ED ASP	.92	54,1412	N.S.				
IL MALES	ED ASP	4.98	18,804	SIG.	1,2,3,6	.21	.06	.01
	SES	.56	18,804	N.S.				
	RACE	1.80	6,284	N.S.				
	RACE X SES	.51	18,804	N.S.				
	RACE X ED ASP	.88	18,804	N.S.				
	SES X ED ASP	.78	54,1453	N.S.				
	RACE X SES X ED ASP	.77	54,1453	N.S.				
MA MALES	ED ASP	4.31	18,804	SIG.	1,2,3	.21	.02	.01
	SES	.79	18,804	N.S.				
	RACE	1.84	6,284	N.S.				
	RACE X SES	1.02	18,804	N.S.				
	RACE X ED ASP	1.12	18,804	N.S.				
	SES X ED ASP	.94	54,1453	N.S.				
	RACE X SES X ED ASP	.62	54,1453	N.S.				
NC MALES	ED ASP	2.35	18,798	SIG.	1	.12	.02	.01
	SES	.87	18,798	N.S.				
	RACE	3.96	6,282	SIG.	2,4,6	.08		
	RACE X SES	.77	18,798	N.S.				
	RACE X ED ASP	.82	18,798	N.S.				
	SES X ED ASP	.97	54,1443	N.S.				
	RACE X SES X ED ASP	1.34	54,1443	N.S.				

Group	Variable	F	df	SIG.	Variables			
CA FEMALES	ED ASP	6.04	18,778	SIG.	1,2,3	.29	.02	.01
	SES	1.30	18,778	N.S.				
	RACE	1.59	6,275	N.S.				
	RACE X SES	1.12	18,778	N.S.				
	RACE X ED ASP	1.01	18,778	N.S.				
	SES X ED ASP	1.14	54,1407	N.S.				
	RACE X SES X ED ASP	.71	54,1407	N.S.				
IL FEMALES	ED ASP	9.07	18,798	SIG.	1,2,3,6	.38	.05	.003
	SES	1.69	18,798	SIG.	6	.07	.03	.01
	RACE	.45	6,282	N.S.				
	RACE X SES	.98	18,798	N.S.				
	RACE X ED ASP	1.30	18,798	N.S.				
	SES X ED ASP	.99	54,1443	N.S.				
	RACE X SES X ED ASP	.90	54,1443	N.S.				
MA FEMALES	ED ASP	7.22	18,781	SIG.	1,2,3	.31	.04	.02
	SES	1.26	18,781	N.S.				
	RACE	.88	6,276	N.S.				
	RACE X SES	1.23	18,781	N.S.				
	RACE X ED ASP	2.03	18,781	SIG.	1,2,4			
	SES X ED ASP	.79	54,1412	N.S.				
	RACE X SES X ED ASP	.85	54,1412	N.S.				
NC FEMALES	ED ASP	6.09	18,781	SIG.	1-4	.28	.03	.02
	SES	1.38	18,781	N.S.				
	RACE	1.49	6,276	N.S.				
	RACE X SES	1.04	18,781	N.S.				
	RACE X ED ASP	1.39	18,781	N.S.				
	SES X ED ASP	1.17	54,1412	N.S.				
	RACE X SES X ED ASP	1.24	54,1412	N.S.				

*The variable numbers designate variables as listed in Appendix I.

Appendix B-4. Set 4 Problems and Conflicts—Personal
Summary Tables of Multivariate Analyses of Variance (By State and Sex)

State Sex	Source of Variation	F	df,1,2	Decision α≤.05	Univariate p≤.05 for Sig. Multivariate Effect*	Index of Association FnI	FnII	FnIII
CA MALES	ED ASP	2.22	54,787	SIG.	3,6,8,16	.23	.09	.07
	SES	1.19	54,787	N.S.				
	RACE	.73	18,264	N.S.				
	RACE X SES	.95	54,787	N.S.				
	RACE X ED ASP	.85	54,787	N.S.				
	SES X ED ASP	1.02	162,2155	N.S.				
	RACE X SES X ED ASP	1.05	162,2155	N.S.				
IL MALES	ED ASP	3.09	54,811	SIG.	2,3,4,6-8,10-12	.25	.15	.09
	SES	.93	54,811	N.S.				
	RACE	1.62	18,272	N.S.				
	RACE X SES	1.02	54,811	N.S.				
	RACE X ED ASP	1.21	54,811	N.S.				
	SES X ED ASP	.83	162,2220	N.S.				
	RACE X SES X ED ASP	1.07	162,2220	N.S.				
MA MALES	ED ASP	3.31	54,811	SIG.	2,3,6,7	.34	.13	.05
	SES	1.25	54,811	N.S.				
	RACE	1.63	18,272	N.S.				
	RACE X SES	.92	54,811	N.S.				
	RACE X ED ASP	.99	54,811	N.S.				
	SES X ED ASP	.91	162,2220	N.S.				
	RACE X SES X ED ASP	1.05	162,2220	N.S.				
NC MALES	ED ASP	3.44	54,805	SIG.	3,6,7,9-12,14,15	.36	.12	.05
	SES	1.12	54,805	N.S.				
	RACE	3.80	18,270	SIG.	1-7,9-13	.20		
	RACE X SES	.76	54,805	N.S.				
	RACE X ED ASP	1.14	54,805	N.S.				
	SES X ED ASP	.97	162,2204	N.S.				
	RACE X SES X ED ASP	1.10	162,2204	N.S.				

CA FEMALES	ED ASP	3.69	54,784	SIG.	1-3,5-7,13,17	.38	.10	.08
	SES	1.49	54,784	SIG.	2,12	.14	.07	.06
	RACE	2.11	18,263	SIG.	2-7,9,12,14,15	.13		
	RACE X SES	.64	54,784	N.S.				
	RACE X ED ASP	.83	54,784	N.S.				
	SES X ED ASP	1.09	162,2147	N.S.				
	RACE X SES X ED ASP	.77	162,2147	N.S.				
IL FEMALES	ED ASP	3.67	54,805	SIG.	2,3,5-7,12,13	.40	.10	.03
	SES	1.39	54,805	SIG.	10,11,13	.16	.06	.03
	RACE	2.26	18,270	SIG.	2,3,6,12	.13		
	RACE X SES	1.20	54,805	N.S.				
	RACE X ED ASP	.98	54,805	N.S.				
	SES X ED ASP	1.05	162,2204	N.S.				
	RACE X SES X ED ASP	1.08	162,2204	N.S.				
MA FEMALES	ED ASP	3.22	54,787	SIG.	2,3,6,7,8,10-13,17	.36	.09	.06
	SES	1.83	54,787	SIG.	6,7,15,17	.18	.09	.05
	RACE	2.18	18,264	SIG.	4,6,12,17	.13		
	RACE X SES	1.05	54,787	N.S.				
	RACE X ED ASP	.85	54,787	N.S.				
	SES X ED ASP	1.17	162,2155	N.S.				
	RACE X SES X ED ASP	.89	162,2155	N.S.				
NC FEMALES	ED ASP	3.62	54,787	SIG.	2,3,4,6,7,10,12,15,16	.40	.11	.04
	SES	1.02	54,787	N.S.	1,2,4-6,12	.20		
	RACE	3.72	18,264	SIG.				
	RACE X SES	1.01	54,787	N.S.				
	RACE X ED ASP	1.44	54,787	SIG.	6,18			
	SES X ED ASP	1.27	162,2155	SIG.	2,3			
	RACE X SES X ED ASP	1.01	54,787	N.S.				

*The variable numbers designate variables as listed in Appendix I.

Appendix B-5. Set 5 Problems and Conflicts—Interpersonal Summary Tables of Multivariate Analyses of Variance (By State and Sex)

State Sex	Source Variation	F	$df_{1,2}$	Decision $\alpha \leqslant .05$	Univariate $p \leqslant .05$ for Sig. Multivariate Effect*	FnI	Index of Association FnII	FnIII
CA MALES	ED ASP	1.41	30,799	N.S.				
	SES	1.04	30,799	N.S.				
	RACE	1.57	10,272	N.S.				
	RACE X SES	.58	30,799	N.S.				
	RACE X ED ASP	1.21	30,799	N.S.				
	SES X ED ASP	1.00	90,1855	N.S.				
	RACE X SES X ED ASP	1.02	90,1855	N.S.				
IL MALES	ED ASP	2.13	30,823	SIG.	1,5,6,8,9	.13	.06	.03
	SES	1.09	30,823	N.S.				
	RACE	1.72	10,280	N.S.				
	RACE X SES	1.10	30,823	N.S.				
	RACE X ED ASP	1.04	30,823	N.S.				
	SES X ED ASP	.92	90,1909	N.S.				
	RACE X SES X ED ASP	.96	90,1909	N.S.				
MA MALES	ED ASP	2.21	30,823	SIG.	1,5,9,10	.17	.03	.02
	SES	1.13	30,823	N.S.				
	RACE	2.04	10,280	SIG.	2,9	.07		
	RACE X SES	1.00	30,823	N.S.				
	RACE X ED ASP	1.41	30,823	N.S.				
	SES X ED ASP	1.05	90,1909	N.S.				
	RACE X SES X ED ASP	1.04	90,1909	N.S.				
NC MALES	ED ASP	1.20	30,817	N.S.				
	SES	1.19	30,817	N.S.				
	RACE	3.75	10,278	SIG.	1,2,4,5	.12		
	RACE X SES	.91	30,817	N.S.				
	RACE X ED ASP	1.08	30,817	N.S.				
	SES X ED ASP	.69	90,1896	N.S.				
	RACE X SES X ED ASP	.86	90,1896	N.S.				

				SIG.				
CA FEMALES	ED ASP	1.71	30,796	SIG.	1,6,7	.11	.05	.01
	SES	.96	30,796	N.S.		.08		
	RACE	2.28	10,271	SIG.	1,2,5			
	RACE X SES	1.77	30,796	SIG.	1,8			
	RACE X ED ASP	.67	90,1848	N.S.	None			
	SES X ED ASP	1.28	90,1848	SIG.				
	RACE X SES X ED ASP	.80	90,1848	N.S.				
IL FEMALES	ED ASP	1.75	30,817	SIG.	1,6,7	.13	.03	.01
	SES	.83	30,817	N.S.				
	RACE	1.12	10,278	N.S.				
	RACE X SES	.93	30,817	N.S.				
	RACE X ED ASP	1.47	30,817	N.S.				
	SES X ED ASP	.96	90,1896	N.S.				
	RACE X SES X ED ASP	.92	90,1896	N.S.				
MA FEMALES	ED ASP	2.89	30,799	SIG.	1-7	.18	.06	.04
	SES	.89	30,799	N.S.				
	RACE	1.13	10,272	N.S.				
	RACE X SES	.99	30,799	N.S.				
	RACE X ED ASP	.88	30,799	N.S.				
	SES X ED ASP	1.08	90,1855	N.S.				
	RACE X SES X ED ASP	.74	90,1855	N.S.				
NC FEMALES	ED ASP	1.42	30,799	N.S.				
	SES	1.23	30,799	N.S.				
	RACE	2.76	10,272	SIG.	1,2	.09		
	RACE X SES	1.15	30,799	N.S.				
	RACE X ED ASP	1.26	30,799	N.S.				
	SES X ED ASP	1.27	90,1855	SIG.	1			
	RACE X SES X ED ASP	.80	90,1855	N.S.				

*The variable numbers designate variables as listed in Appendix I.

Appendix B-6. Set 6 Helpfulness of Others

Summary Tables of Multivariate Analyses of Variance (By State and Sex)

State Sex	Source of Variation	F	$df_{1,2}$	Decision $\alpha \leqslant .05$	Univariate $p \leqslant .05$ for Sig. Multivariate Effect*	FnI	FnII	FnIII
							Index of Association	
CA MALES	ED ASP	1.21	15,765	N.S.				
	SES	.81	15,765	N.S.				
	RACE	2.05	5,277	N.S.				
	RACE X SES	.82	15,765	N.S.				
	RACE X ED ASP	.45	15,765	N.S.				
	SES X ED ASP	.81	45,1242	N.S.				
	RACE X SES X ED ASP	.57	45,1242	N.S.				
IL MALES	ED ASP	1.76	15,787	SIG.	1	.06	.02	.01
	SES	1.31	15,787	N.S.				
	RACE	1.04	5,285	N.S.				
	RACE X SES	7.15	15,787	N.S.				
	RACE X ED ASP	1.50	15,787	N.S.				
	SES X ED ASP	1.10	45,1278	N.S.				
	RACE X SES X ED ASP	1.33	45,1278	N.S.				
MA MALES	ED ASP	1.06	15,787	SIG.	2	.07	.02	.01
	SES	.56	15,787	N.S.				
	RACE	.57	5,285	N.S.				
	RACE X SES	.81	15,787	N.S.				
	RACE X ED ASP	.87	15,787	N.S.				
	SES X ED ASP	1.23	45,1278	N.S.				
	RACE X SES X ED ASP	.72	45,1278	N.S.				
NC MALES	ED ASP	1.73	15,782	SIG.	2	.07	.02	.0026
	SES	1.33	15,782	N.S.				
	RACE	.71	5,283	N.S.				
	RACE X SES	.81	15,782	N.S.				
	RACE X ED ASP	1.11	15,782	N.S.				
	SES X ED ASP	1.30	45,1269	N.S.				
	RACE X SES X ED ASP	1.23	45,1269	N.S.				

CA FEMALES	ED ASP	1.29	15,762	N.S.				
	SES	.78	15,762	N.S.				
	RACE	1.58	5,276	N.S.				
	RACE X SES	.99	15,762	N.S.				
	RACE X ED ASP	.51	15,762	N.S.				
	SES X ED ASP	1.00	45,1238	N.S.				
	RACE X SES X ED ASP	.94	45,1238	N.S.				
IL FEMALES	ED ASP	2.25	15,782	SIG.	3,4	.06	.05	.01
	SES	1.85	15,782	SIG.	1	.07	.02	.00
	RACE	.28	5,283	N.S.				
	RACE X SES	.99	15,782	N.S.				
	RACE X ED ASP	1.73	15,782	SIG.	1,2			
	SES X ED ASP	.77	45,1269	N.S.				
	RACE X SES X ED ASP	.77	45,1269	N.S.				
MA FEMALES	ED ASP	1.47	15,765	N.S.				
	SES	1.76	15,765	SIG.		.05	.03	.01
	RACE	.40	5,277	N.S.				
	RACE X SES	.33	15,765	N.S.				
	RACE X ED ASP	.74	15,765	N.S.				
	SES X ED ASP	1.03	45,1242	N.S.				
	RACE X SES X ED ASP	.71	45,1242	N.S.				
NC FEMALES	ED ASP	2.53	15,765	SIG.	1,5	.09	.02	.02
	SES	2.32	15,765	SIG.	2,4	.10	.01	.01
	RACE	1.29	5,277	N.S.				
	RACE X SES	1.29	15,765	N.S.				
	RACE X ED ASP	1.35	15,765	N.S.				
	SES X ED ASP	.80	45,1242	N.S.				
	RACE X SES X ED ASP	.80	45,1242	N.S.				

*The variable numbers designate variables as listed in Appendix I.

Appendix B-7. Set 7 Barriers to Continued Education
Summary Tables of Multivariate Analyses of Variance (By State and Sex)

State Sex	Source of Variation	F	$df_{1,2}$	Decision α≤.05	Univariate p≤.05 for Sig. Multivariate Effect*	FnI	Index of Association FnII	FnIII
CA MALES	ED ASP	3.74	33,799	SIG.	1,2,4,5,7,10,11	.28	.05	.04
	SES	.86	33,799	N.S.				
	RACE	1.45	11,271	N.S.				
	RACE X SES	1.05	33,799	N.S.				
	RACE X ED ASP	.87	33,799	N.S.				
	SES X ED ASP	1.33	99,1923	SIG.	3,5,6			
	RACE X SES X ED ASP	1.01	99,1923	N.S.				
IL MALES	ED ASP	5.31	33,823	SIG.	1,2,4-8,10,11	.31	.14	.04
	SES	1.10	33,823	N.S.				
	RACE	1.55	11,279	N.S.				
	RACE X SES	1.13	33,823	N.S.				
	RACE X ED ASP	1.16	33,823	N.S.				
	SES X ED ASP	.84	99,1979	N.S.				
	RACE X SES X ED ASP	.89	99,1979	N.S.				
MA MALES	ED ASP	3.30	33,823	SIG.	1,2,4,7,8,10,11	.23	.06	.05
	SES	1.34	33,823	N.S.				
	RACE	1.08	11,279	N.S.				
	RACE X SES	1.00	33,823	N.S.				
	RACE X ED ASP	1.08	33,823	N.S.				
	SES X ED ASP	1.05	99,1979	N.S.				
	RACE X SES X ED ASP	.80	99,1979	N.S.				
NC MALES	ED ASP	2.78	33,817	SIG.	1,6-9,11	.20	.07	.03
	SES	1.41	33,817	N.S.				
	RACE	1.23	11,277	N.S.				
	RACE X SES	.96	33,817	N.S.				
	RACE X ED ASP	.91	33,817	N.S.				
	SES X ED ASP	.81	99,1965	N.S.				
	RACE X SES X ED ASP	.96	99,1965	N.S.				

		F	df	SIG.	Variables			
CA FEMALES	ED ASP	4.71	33,796	SIG.	1-4,7,10,11	.34	.08	.03
	SES	1.22	33,796	N.S.		.10		
	RACE	2.80	11,270	SIG.	3,5,8,11			
	RACE X SES	.83	33,796	N.S.				
	RACE X ED ASP	1.06	33,796	N.S.				
	SES X ED ASP	.99	99,1915	N.S.				
	RACE X SES X ED ASP	.96	99,1915	N.S.				
IL FEMALES	ED ASP	4.04	33,817	SIG.	1,2,4,7,9-11	.29	.08	.02
	SES	1.34	33,817	N.S.				
	RACE	1.81	11,277	N.S.				
	RACE X SES	.95	33,817	N.S.				
	RACE X ED ASP	1.12	33,817	N.S.				
	SES X ED ASP	1.21	99,1965	N.S.				
	RACE X SES X ED ASP	.92	99,1965	N.S.				
MA FEMALES	ED ASP	3.28	33,799	SIG.	1,2,4,10,11	.27	.05	.02
	SES	1.34	38,799	N.S.				
	RACE	.41	11,271	N.S.				
	RACE X SES	.62	33,799	N.S.				
	RACE X ED ASP	.86	33,799	N.S.				
	SES X ED ASP	1.02	99,1923	N.S.				
	RACE X SES X ED ASP	1.12	99,1923	N.S.				
NC FEMALES	ED ASP	4.04	33,799	SIG.	1,2,4,7,10,11 11	.32	.04	.02
	SES	1.50	33,799	SIG.		.09	.07	.01
	RACE	3.85	11,271	SIG.	3,7,8,10,11	.14		
	RACE X SES	.76	33,799	N.S.				
	RACE X ED ASP	1.22	33,799	N.S.				
	SES X ED ASP	1.24	99,1923	N.S.				
	RACE X SES X ED ASP	.96	99,1923	N.S.				

*The variable numbers designate variables as listed in Appendix I.

Appendix B-8. Set 8 Decisions About Postsecondary Life Summary Tables of Multivariate Analyses of Variance (By State and Sex)

State Sex	Source of Variation	F	df,1,2	Decision α≤.05	Univariate p≤.05 for Sig. Multivariate Effect*	Index of Association		
						FnI	FnII	FnIII
CA MALES	ED ASP	18.81	15,765	SIG.	1-5	.53	.10	.0015
	SES	1.16	15,765	N.S.				
	RACE	1.56	5,277	N.S.				
	RACE X SES	.52	15,765	N.S.				
	RACE X ED ASP	1.31	15,765	N.S.				
	SES X ED ASP	1.14	45,1242	N.S.				
	RACE X SES X ED ASP	1.46	45,1242	SIG.	1,5			
IL MALES	ED ASP	28.18	15,787	SIG.	1-5	.67	.08	.003
	SES	1.59	15,787	N.S.				
	RACE	1.24	5,285	N.S.				
	RACE X SES	.79	15,787	N.S.				
	RACE X ED ASP	.64	15,787	N.S.				
	SES X ED ASP	1.45	45,1278	SIG.	2			
	RACE X SES X ED ASP	.77	45,1278	N.S.				
MA MALES	ED ASP	29.28	15,787	SIG.	1-5	.65	.16	.01
	SES	1.52	15,787	N.S.				
	RACE	2.04	5,285	N.S.				
	RACE X SES	.88	15,787	N.S.				
	RACE X ED ASP	2.14	15,787	SIG.	2,5			
	SES X ED ASP	1.40	45,1278	SIG.	5			
	RACE X SES X ED ASP	.89	45,1278	N.S.				
NC MALES	ED ASP	25.71	15,782	SIG.	1-5	.63	.10	.0005
	SES	1.08	15,782	N.S.		.05		
	RACE	2.79	5,283	SIG.	4,5			
	RACE X SES	1.23	15,782	N.S.				
	RACE X ED ASP	1.37	15,782	N.S.				
	SES X ED ASP	.95	45,1269	N.S.				
	RACE X SES X ED ASP	1.38	45,1269	N.S.				

CA FEMALES							
ED ASP	29.40	15,762	SIG.	2-5	.67	.11	.02
SES	1.67	15,762	N.S.				
RACE	.63	5,276	N.S.				
RACE X SES	1.15	15,762	N.S.				
RACE X ED ASP	.29	15,762	N.S.				
SES X ED ASP	1.18	45,1238	N.S.	5			
RACE X SES X ED ASP	1.47	45,1238	SIG.				
IL FEMALES							
ED ASP	34.24	15,782	SIG.	2-5	.71	.15	.0008
SES	1.29	15,782	N.S.				
RACE	6.08	5,283	SIG.	4,5	.10		
RACE X SES	.69	15,782	N.S.				
RACE X ED ASP	1.37	15,782	N.S.				
SES X ED ASP	1.39	45,1269	SIG.	5			
RACE X SES X ED ASP	.93	45,1269	N.S.				
MA FEMALES							
ED ASP	25.25	15,765	SIG.	2-5	.65	.05	.01
SES	1.57	15,765	N.S.				
RACE	1.20	5,277	N.S.				
RACE X SES	.67	15,765	N.S.				
RACE X ED ASP	.99	15,765	N.S.				
SES X ED ASP	1.13	45,1242	N.S.	4,5			
RACE X SES X ED ASP	1.50	45,1242	SIG.				
NC FEMALES							
ED ASP	30.62	15,765	SIG.	2-5	.69	.12	.01
SES	.44	15,765	N.S.		.0860		
RACE	5.22	5,277	SIG.	2,3,4			
RACE X SES	1.12	15,765	N.S.	None			
RACE X ED ASP	1.86	15,765	SIG.				
SES X ED ASP	.89	45,1242	N.S.				
RACE X SES X ED ASP	1.11	45,1242	N.S.				

*The variable numbers designate variables as listed in Appendix I.

It has been shown empirically by the junior author of this book that if, in a one-way MANOVA, discriminant function scores are computed for each subject on any discriminant function, and these scores are used as the dependent variable in an ANOVA with the same independent variable, the obtained omega squared statistic (Hays, 1963) as an index of association will be the same as the Roy's criterion originally obtained in the discriminant analysis. Since the discriminant functions obtained for any given independent variable are uncorrelated, these statistics are additive across discriminant functions, and their sum represents the total percentage of the variance of the dependent variables which is associated with the independent variable. This interpretation of Roy's criterion as omega squared does not apply, however, in an analysis with more than one independent variable. Furthermore, Hays' measure of association, the omega squared, is a biased estimate (Marascuilo, 1971).

Because of these considerations, the index of association shown in the accompanying tables, which is Roy's criterion, should be viewed only in a relative sense. It can be seen that these estimates are uncommonly large. If they were to be interpreted in an absolute sense, the indication would be that in some cases more than 75 percent of the variance of a set of dependent variables can be accounted for by educational aspirations. It is thought, however, that this statistic is useful for comparative purposes, giving some idea of the relative amounts of variance among sets of dependent variables which are accounted for by educational aspirations.

It can be seen that, for the educational aspiration effect, most of the discrimination among aspiration groups is represented in the first or first and second discriminant functions. There is a direct correspondence between the relative magnitudes of these measures of association and the appearance of the separation graphs which were presented in preceding chapters, since both are based on the discriminant analyses. Where the indices of association are larger, the corresponding separation graph shows a greater degree of separation among aspiration groups.

In the tables which follow, no significant univariate effects or indices of association are entered where the multivariate F was not statistically significant; a nonsignificant multivariate F does not provide evidence that the several aspiration groups differ from each other on the basis of the dependent variable set. This is in accordance with the decision strategy outlined in Chapter 2.

Statement About the Scope Project

School to College: Opportunities for Postsecondary Education is a longitudinal study of students sponsored by the Center for Research and Development in Higher Education and by the College Entrance Examination Board. CEEB has been the primary source of financial support for SCOPE and has also provided technical assistance through its regional and New York offices, its educational advisory committees, and its publication division. The CRDHE at the University of California, Berkeley has directed and conducted the project as part of its continuing research and development focus on students in higher education. Together these sponsoring organizations conceived SCOPE as a means of "discovering the decision-making patterns among high school students—the ways in which they acquire information about colleges and vocations; the nature and relative importance of parental, school, and general community influences on their decisions; and when various stages in the decision-making process occur" (Tillery et al., 1966b).

The project, at a time of great demand on American schools, received the active and sustained cooperation of teachers and administrators in schools, colleges, and educational systems. No one, of course, contributed more than the students who are the subjects of this and other reports.

Although SCOPE, as such, terminated in early 1972, a SCOPE Information Center is being maintained in Berkeley so that the staff of CRDHE and CEEB, as well as other researchers can continue to use the massive data base for continuing research.

THE SAMPLES

The four project states were chosen because they represented some of the regional differences in education in the United States. They have differing commitments to public and private education, diverse systems of postsecondary education, and certain demographic characteristics. Some of these factors are discussed in Chapter 1 as are brief resumés of their plans for higher education. In brief, the original samples drawn from the four states (California, Illinois, Massachusetts, and North Carolina) were to be representative of the state populations of public and private school students. The basic sampling unit, because of administrative advantages and economic use of resources, was the individual school.

Determining the Sample Sizes

In determining sample sizes, it was necessary to know the type and number of interrelationships that must be analyzed in the final stages of the project. For example, at the close of the SCOPE project it may be desirable to determine whether there are meaningful differences between men and women who have differing academic abilities and economic resources for education, and who have chosen diverse fields of study in several types of colleges. The *number* of students from the initial samples needed for final data collection is determined by the number of interrelationships to be analyzed and the desired power of statistical tests for supporting or rejecting hypothesized differences among groups of students. Through the use of appropriate theoretical models, it was determined that 3954 students should be available for the final data collection in each of the four states. With this terminal number of students in mind it was possible, then, to take into consideration the differing dropout rates and college-going rates in the four states, as described in the next paragraph, in order to adopt appropriate initial sample sizes.

Since the major aspect of SCOPE is to study selected ninth and twelfth grade students as they move through school into their second semester of college attendance, as well as to follow up students who drop out of school or who go to work instead of to college, the initial sample sizes were determined by taking into consideration persistence rates of students through each period of schooling, college-going rates in the four states, and finally, a general persistence rate during the first year of college. Calculations based upon the overall retention rates, from grade nine or from grade twelve through the college freshman year, resulted in the following initial sample sizes: California, 8,204 grade nine, 7,757 grade twelve students; Illinois, 14,338 grade nine, 10,881 grade twelve students; Massachusetts, 11,673 grade nine, 9,793 grade twelve students; and North Carolina, 21,846 grade nine, 12,555 grade twelve students.

Selection of Counties and Schools

Once the required initial sample sizes were calculated, the next steps were to determine how, and from where, the students were to be drawn for the samples. Because of the limited nature of the consistent and relevant information about students and schools in the project states, and in order to keep the survey areas from being unnecessarily scattered geographically, a multi-stage, stratified, proportional random-sampling procedure was used.

The counties in each of the states were statistically grouped into similar clusters on the basis of several common characteristics. Several of the characteristics, as indicated in the 1960 census data and recent school data, were: median family income, percent white collar workers, white and nonwhite racial composition, mobility of the population, rate of school attendance of school age children, school size, and ratio of students who go to college to high school graduates. Counties were then randomly selected from within each cluster of counties in each of the four states in the study. School districts, and then schools, were randomly selected from within the selected counties so that there would be samples of grade nine and grade twelve students large enough to meet the requirements for the initial sample sizes.

In most SCOPE schools a few students were away when the testing was done and some students, though few in number, chose not to participate.

Actual Samples of the Four States

The initial sample sizes (given above) calculated for each of the four states were the estimated numers of students required to carry out the long-term analyses that are a major part of the SCOPE project. Because individual schools were chosen as the units of sampling, it was only possible to approximate samples of desired size. When a school became part of the project, all grade nine or grade twelve students were considered to be part of the original sample. As a result, the actual numbers of students tested in each state were: California, 9,836 in grade nine and 7,567 in grade twelve; Illinois, 13,223 in grade nine and 8,600 in grade twelve; Massachusetts, 7,501 in grade nine and 6,335 in grade twelve; and North Carolina, 15,552 in grade nine and 11,377 in grade twelve. The estimated enrollments of the schools in the samples indicate that, of the students in both ninth and twelfth grades, about 10 percent did not participate in California, Massachusetts, and North Carolina, and about 7 percent did not participate in Illinois. Any bias that may exist because of this apparent loss is expected to be minimal.

A more serious source of bias may be the loss of a metropolitan school district in each of three states, California, Illinois, and Massachusetts. Although the three districts chose not to participate, adjacent alternative schools in California and Illinois volunteered and became part of the SCOPE project. It would appear that proper representation of these two areas has thus been re-established. In Massachusetts, the large metropolitan area which chose not to participate was not replaced by other volunteer schools. Therefore, the state's public school systems are underrepresented with regard to some of the characteristics of metropolitan areas—high density populations, large minority groups, and major depressed areas. Its nonpublic school systems are well represented, however, even in the large metropolitan areas.

In spite of the losses outlined above, there should be considerable confidence in believing that SCOPE data—because of the size of the samples and the range of types of schools sampled—reflect the attitudes, abilities, and interests of a rather remarkable cross-section of youth in public and private schools of the SCOPE states. Specifically, the numbers of schools participating in the SCOPE project in its initial phase in each state are: California, 32 public and 12 nonpublic; Illinois, 46 public and 18 nonpublic; Massachusetts, 28 public and 21 nonpublic; and North Carolina, 138 public and four nonpublic.

After the first data collection in the original schools (Spring 1966) students in the ninth grade samples (the subjects of this report) were followed annually until one year after high school graduation. The 1966 grade twelve students were followed to determine if they went to college.

RETENTION RATES 1966-1969

In proposing the overall design for the SCOPE project, projections were made of retention rates from grade nine to grade twelve based on differential dropout rates for the four states. These estimates were: California .86, Illinois .69, Massachusetts .76, and North Carolina .63. These ratios did not take into consideration failure to locate students who moved from their original schools, illness or death at time of follow-up, or refusal to cooperate with the project. The numbers of students actually tested for each state over the four years of high school were:

	Grade 9	Grade 10	Grade 11	Grade 12
California	9,836	8,237	7,449	5,166
Illinois	13,223	11,468	10,875	9,241
Massachusetts	7,501	6,624	6,324	5,419
North Carolina	15,522	12,335	11,185	9,601
TOTAL	46,082	38,664	35,833	29,427

The greatest loss was in California between grades eleven and twelve. Shortly before the senior data collection in that state the governor signed legislation requiring written consent before the testing of minors. Although heroic efforts were made to obtain such written consent at the zero hour, only 69 percent of those tested in grade eleven were able to continue with the project. Had more time been available, it is likely that more parents would have given consent as indicated by selective telephone calls to nonrespondents. In summary, the loss over the school years has resulted from actual dropping out of school, inability to locate transient subjects, refusal to participate, illness and death, and restrictive state legislation. The number of students remaining well exceeds the number of subjects required for the most complex analyses. The representativeness of the persisting subjects remains in question. The fact that demographic characteristics look normative and that there is no evidence for special biases for non-withdrawal-from-school losses suggest that at each grade level the subjects are reasonably representative of peer students in that state.

PUBLICATION SCHEDULE

Shortly after collecting data in 1966, 1967, and 1968, state, composite, and local school profiles were prepared for wide distribution to school and college personnel. Subsequently the following publications or manuscripts have been prepared in addition to this one:

Tillery, D. "Will the Real Guidance Counselor Please Stand Up," *College Board Review*, New York, Winter, 1970.
Sherman, B. *Role Explorations in the Decision-Making Processes of Adolescents*. Berkeley, Center for Research and Development in Higher Education, 1971 (unpublished manuscript).
Tillery, D. *Distribution and Differentiation of Youth: A Study of Differential Outcomes of High School Graduates*. Cambridge: Ballinger Publishing Company, 1973.

Several major studies have also been based in part on SCOPE data and cooperation. They are:

Medsker, L., and Tillery, D. *Breaking the Access Barriers: A Profile of Two-Year Colleges*. McGraw-Hill, New York: Carnegie Commission on Higher Education, 1971.
Cross, K.P. *The Junior College Student: A Research Description*. Princeton, New Jersey: Educational Testing Service, 1968.
Cross, K.P. *Beyond the Open Door*. San Francisco: Jossey-Bass, 1971.
Anderson, C.A.; Bowman, M.; and Tinto, V. *Where Colleges Are and Who Attends: Effects of Accessibility on College Attendance*. New York: Carnegie Commission on Higher Education, McGraw-Hill, 1972.

A number of studies are now underway or in design stages. Among them are:

Tillery, D. and Omelich, C. *Students in Need*, in preparation for 1973 publication.
Dagenais, F. *Changes in Attitudes and Values of Adolescents from Ten Different Cultural Groups During the High School Years*. Paper presented at the 1973 Convention of the American Educational Research Association in New Orleans
Kildegaard, T. *Constancy of Educational Aspirations During the High School Years*. In preparation.
Kiser, J. *Educational Outcomes of Black High School Students in Charlotte, North Carolina*. In preparation.

Bibliography

Adams, J.F. "Adolescent Personal Problems as a Function of Age and Sex." *The Journal of Genetic Psychology* 104 (1964): 207-214.

Bailey, B.H. *Characteristics of High School Seniors as Related to Subsequent College Attendance.* (U.S. Office of Education, Cooperative Research Project 2152) Morganstown, West Virginia: West Virginia State, Division of Education, 1966.

Bavry, J.L. "The Measure of Association in Multivariate Analysis of Variance." Unpublished paper, School of Education, University of California, Berkeley, 1972.

Beezer, R.H., and Hjelm, H.F. *Factors Related to College Attendance.* (Cooperative Research Monograph No. 8) Washington, D.C.: U.S. Office of Education, 1961.

Birmingham, J. *Our Time is Now. Notes From the High School Underground.* New York: Bantam Books, 1970.

Bock, R.D. "Contribution of Multivariate Statistical Methods to Educational Research," in R.B. Cattell (ed.), *Handbook of Multivariate Experimental Psychology.* Chicago: Rand McNally, 1966.

Brookover, W.B.; Erickson, E.L.; and Joiner, L.M. "Educational Aspirations and Educational Plans in Relation to Academic Achievement and SES." *The School Review* 75 (1967): 392-400.

Clarke, R.; Gelatt, H.B.; and Levine, L. "Decision-Making Paradigm to Local Guidance Research." *Personnel and Guidance Journal* 44, 1 (September 1965): 40-51.

Coleman, J.S.; Campbell, E.Q.; Hobson, C.J.; McPartland, J.; Mood, A.M.; Weinfeld, F.D.; and York, R.L. *Equality of Educational Opportunity.* Washington, D.C.: U.S. Office of Education, 1966.

College Entrance Examination Board. *A Study of Educational and Occupational Aspirations of Virginia's 1966-67 High School Seniors.* New York: The Board, 1969.

Cooley, W.W., and Lohnes, P.R. *Multivariate Data Analysis.* New York: John Wiley, 1971.

Crites, J.O. "Measurement of Vocational Maturity in Adolescence: 1. Attitude Test of the Vocational Development Inventory." *Psychological Monographs* 79, 2 (1965).

Cross, K. Patricia. *Beyond the Open Door: New Students to Higher Education.* San Francisco: Jossey-Bass, 1971.

Dagenais, F., and Marascuilo, L.A. "Student Demonstrations in a Multi-Racial High School: A Case of Berkeley." Unpublished paper, University of California, Berkeley, 1971.

Darley, J.G. *Promise and Performance: A Study of Ability and Achievement in Higher Education.* Berkeley: Center for the Study of Higher Education, 1962.

Erikson, E.H. *Childhood and Society.* (2d ed.) New York: W.W. Norton, 1963.

_____. *Identity and the Life Cycle.* New York: International Universities Press, 1959.

_____. "The Problem of Ego Identity." *The Journal of the American Psychoanalytic Association* 4 (1956): 56-121.

_____. "Youth: Fidelity and Diversity." *Daedalus* 91 (1962): 5-27.

Field, F.L. "An Investigation of Decision-Making in an Educational-Vocational Context with Implications for Guidance." Doctoral dissertation, Graduate School of Education, Harvard University, 1964.

Flanagan, J.C.; Davis, F.B.; Dailey, J.T.; Shaycroft, M.F.; Orr, D.B.; Goldberg, I.; and Heyman, C.A. *The American High School Student.* (Final report to the U.S. Office of Education, Cooperative Research Project No. 635). Pittsburgh: Project Talent Office, University of Pittsburgh, 1964.

Froomkin, J. *Aspirations, Enrollments, and Resources.* Washington, D.C.: U.S. Department of Health, Education and Welfare, 1969.

Ginzberg, E.; Ginsberg, S.W.; Axelrod, S.; and Herma, J.L. *Occupational Choice: An Approach to a General Theory.* New York: Columbia University Press, 1951.

Gorton, R.A. "Militant Student Activism in the High Schools: Analysis and Recommendations." *Phi Delta Kappan* 51, 10 (June 1970): 545-49.

Gough, H.B., and Heilbrun, A.B., Jr. *Manual for the Adjective Check List.* Palo Alto, California: Consulting Psychologists Press, 1965.

Gribbons, W.D., and Lohnes, P.R. *Career Development From Age 13 to Age 25.* Washington, D.C.: Government Printing Office, 1969.

Hays, W.L. *Statistics for Psychologists.* New York: Holt, Rinehart, and Winston, 1963.

Heist, P., and Yonge, G. *Omnibus Personality Inventory Manual.* New York: Psychological Corporation, 1968.

Himmelweit, H.J.; Halsey, A.H.; and Oppenheim, A.N. "The Views of Adolescents on Some Aspects of Social Class Structure." *British Journal of Sociology* 3 (1952): 148-72.

Holloway, R.G., and Berreman, J.V. "The Educational and Occupational Aspirations and Plans of Negro and White Male Elementary Students." *Pacific Sociological Review* 2 (1959): 56-60.

Jung, C., and Wright, W.W. "Why Capable High School Students Do Not Continue Their Schooling." *Bulletin of the School of Education, Indiana University* 35, 1 (1959): 1-78.

Kandel, Denise B., and Lesser, G.S. "Parental and Peer Influences on Educational Plans of Adolescents." *American Sociological Review* 34, 2 (1969): 213-22.

Knoell, D.M. *People Who Need College.* Washington, D.C.: American Association of Junior Colleges, 1970.

Kroll, A.M.; Dinklage, L.B.; Lee, J.; Morley, E.D.; and Wilson, E.W. *Career Development: Growth and Crisis.* New York: John Wiley, 1970.

Kuvlesky, W.P. "Differences in the Occupational and Educational Projections of American High School Students and Dropout Age Peers." Paper for the Southwest Sociological Association, March 1970. (ERIC ED 039 989)

Lavin, D.E. *The Prediction of Academic Performance: A Theoretical Analysis and Review of Research.* New York: Russell Sage Foundation, 1965.

Lever, M.F., and Kuvlesky, W.P. "Socio-Economic Status and Occupational Status Projections of Southern Youth, By Race and Sex." Paper presented at the Rural Sociological Meeting, San Francisco, August 1970.

Liberale, M., and Seligson, T. (eds.) *The High School Revolutionaries.* New York: Random House, 1970.

Maddison, P., and Studdiford, W.B. *The Relationship of the Omnibus Personality Inventory to Academic Achievement of Princeton Freshmen.* Princeton, N.J.: The Counseling Service, Princeton University, 1963.

Marascuilo, L.A. *Statistical Methods for Behavioral Science Research.* San Francisco: McGraw-Hill, 1971.

Marcia, J.E. "The Case History of a Construct: Ego Identity Status, pp. 325-32 in W.E. Vinake (ed.), *Readings in General Psychology.* New York: American Book Company, 1968.

_____. "Development and Validation of Ego-Identity Status." *Journal of Personality and Social Psychology* 3, 5 (1966): 551-58.

_____. "Ego Identity Status: Relationship to Change in Self Esteem, 'General Maladjustment,' and Authoritarianism." *Journal of Personality* 35, 1 (1967): 118-33.

McClelland, D.C. et al. *The Achievement Motive.* New York: Appleton-Century-Crofts, 1953.

Medsker, L.L., and Trent, J. *The Influence of Different Types of Public Higher Institutions on College Attendance From Varying Socioeconomic and Ability Levels.* U.S. Office of Education Cooperative Research Project No. 438. Berkeley: Center for Research and Development in Higher Education, 1965.

Morrison, D.F. *Multivariate Statistical Methods.* San Francisco: McGraw-Hill, 1967.

Omnibus Personality Inventory. Research Manual. Berkeley: Center for the Study of Higher Education, 1962.

Parsons, T. "H.M. Robertson on Max Weber and His School." *Journal of Political Economy* 43 (1953): 688-96.

President's Commission on Campus Unrest. *Campus Unrest.* Washington, D.C.: Government Printing Office, 1970.

Rehberg, R.A. "Adolescent Career Aspirations and Expectations: Evaluation of Two Contrary Stratification Hypotheses." *Pacific Sociological Review* 10 (1967): 81-90.

Rice, M.C., and Mason, P.L. *Residence and Migration of College Students.* Wasington, D.C.: U.S. Department of Health, Education and Welfare, 1965.

Rosen, B.C. "Race, Ethnicity, and the Achievement Syndrome." *American Sociological Review* 24 (1959): 47-60.

SCOPE Project. Unpublished Working Papers. Berkeley, 1971.

Sherman, B. *Role Exploration in the Decision-Making Process of Adolesents.* Berkeley, Center for Research and Development in Higher Education, 1971 (Unpublished manuscript).

Shill, J.F. *Educational Aspirations, Expectations, and Abilities of Rural Male High School Seniors in Mississippi.* Report 24, Education Series 4. Washington, D.C.: U.S. Office of Education, May 1968.

Slocum, W.L. *Educational Aspirations and Expectations of Students in Rural Washington High Schools.* Washington, D.C.: U.S. Office of Education, January 1968. Report # BULL-990.

State University of New York. *A Longitudinal Study of the Barriers Affecting the Pursuit of Higher Education by New York State High School Seniors, Phase I.* Albany, N.Y.: State University of New York, 1969.

Stephenson, R.M. "Realism of Vocational Choice." *Personnel And Guidance Journal* 35 (1957): 482-88.

Strodtbeck, F.L. "Family Interaction, Values, and Achievement," in D.C. McClelland (ed.) *Talent and Society, New Perspectives in the Identification of Talent.* New York: Van Nostrand, 1958.

Super, D.E., et al. *Career Development: Self-Concept Theory.* College Entrance Examination Board Research Monograph, No. 4. New York: College Etrance Examination Board, 1963.

Super, D.E.; Crites, J.O.; Hummel, R.C.; Moser, Helen P.; Overstreet, Phoebe L.; and Warnath, C.F. *Vocational Development: A Framework For Research.* New York: Bureau of Publications, Teachers College, Columbia University, 1957.

Super, D.E., and Overstreet, Phoebe L. *The Vocational Maturity of Ninth-Grade Boys.* New York: Bureau of Publications, Teachers College, Columbia University, 1960.

Tillery, D. *Distribution and Differentiation of Youth: A Study of Differential Outcomes of High School Graduates.* Cambridge: Ballinger Publishing Company, 1973.

_____ . "Will the Real Guidance Counselor Please Stand Up?" *College Board Review* 74 Winter 1969-70, 17-23.

_____ . Differential Characteristics of Entering Freshmen at the

University of California and Their Peers at California Junior Colleges." Doctoral dissertation, University of California, Berkeley, 1964.

Tillery, D. and Omelich, C. *Students in Need.* In preparation for 1973 publication.

Tillery, D.; Donovan D.; and Sherman, Barbara. "Helpfulness of Parents, School Personnel, and Peers to Students With Different Educational Aspirations." Paper read at the American Psychological Association Convention, San Francisco, August 30, 1968.

_____. *SCOPE Grade Ten Profile, 1967.* (California, Illinois, Massachusetts, North Carolina) New York: College Entrance Examination Board, and The Center for Research and Development in Higher Education, 1967.

_____. *SCOPE Four-State Profiles, Grade Twelve, 1966.* (California, Illinois, Massachusetts, North Carolina) New York: College Entrance Examination Board and The Center for Research and Development in Higher Education, 1966a.

_____. *SCOPE State Profile Grade Nine, 1966.* (California, Illinois, Massachusetts, North Carolina) New York: College Entrance Examination Board, and The Center for Research and Development in Higher Education, 1966b.

Trent, J.W., and Medsker, L.L. *Beyond High School.* Berkeley: Center for Research and Development in Higher Education, 1967.

_____. *Beyond High School: A Psycho-Sociological Study of 10,000 High School Graduates.* San Francisco: Jossey-Bass, 1968.

Trow, M. "The Meaning of Impact," pp. 25-33 in *Proceedings of the 1966 Invitational Conference on Testing Problems.* Princeton, N.J.: Educational Testing Service, 1967.

Weber, M. *The Protestant Ethic and The Spirit of Capitalism.* New York: Charles Scribner, 1930.

Weiss, R.F. "Aspirations and Expectation: A Dimensional Analysis." *Journal of Social Psychology* 53 (1961): 249-54.

Whittaker, D., and Watts, W.A. "Personality Characteristics of a Nonconformist Youth Subculture: A Study of the Berkeley Non-Student." *Journal of Social Issues* 25, 2 (1969): 65-89.

Willingham, W.W. *Free-Access Higher Education.* New York: College Entrance Examination Board, 1970.

Wright, Wendell W. and Jung, Christian W. *Why Capable High School Students Do Not Continue Their Schooling.* Bulletin of the School of Education, Indiana University. Vol. 1, No. 1. Bloomington, Indiana, January 1959.

Index

About the Authors

Dale Tillery received his Ph.D. in psychology and education from the University of California, Berkeley. He is currently professor of higher education at Berkeley and senior researcher at its Center for Research and Development in Higher Education. In recent years Professor Tillery has developed and directed experimental programs at the University of California for the preparation of college teachers and administrative leaders.

Professor Tillery has been a Fullbright Professor in Athens, Greece, and has performed educational development work in Africa and South America. His recent publications include two books for the Carnegie Commission Series on higher education: *The Open Door Colleges* (primary author) and *Breaking the Access Barriers* (co-author). He is also the author of *Distribution and Differentiation of Youth: A study of Transition from School to College*, Ballinger Publishing Company, 1973.

Theodore C. Kildegaard is a Ph.D. candidate in Counseling Psychology at the University of California at Berkeley. He is an Associate Evaluator in the Career Education Program at the Far Western Laboratory for Education Research and Development. His past experience includes the position of Postgraduate Research Psychologist at the Center for Research and Development in Higher Education at the University of California, Berkeley; and instructor in the Department of Student Personnel at San Jose College.